Persistent Poverty

*The American Dream
Turned Nightmare*

Persistent Poverty
The American Dream Turned Nightmare

Richard H. Ropers, Ph.D.

Southern Utah University
Cedar City, Utah

Foreword by
Wayne K. Hinton, Ph.D.

 **INSIGHT BOOKS**

Plenum Press • New York and London

Library of Congress Cataloging-in-Publication Data

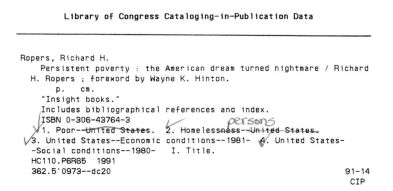

Ropers, Richard H.
    Persistent poverty : the American dream turned nightmare / Richard
  H. Ropers ; foreword by Wayne K. Hinton.
        p.   cm.
      "Insight books."
      Includes bibliographical references and index.
      ISBN 0-306-43764-3   persons
      1. Poor--United States. 2. Homelessness--United States.
  3. United States--Economic conditions--1981- 4. United States-
  -Social conditions--1980-   I. Title.
  HC110.P6R65   1991
  362.5'0973--dc20   91-14
                                                                  CIP

ISBN 0-306-43764-3

© 1991 Plenum Press, New York
A Division of Plenum Publishing Corporation
233 Spring Street, New York, N.Y. 10013

An Insight Book

Printed in the United States of America

For all the
dispossessed working people

Foreword

Poverty is not new to America. Despite predictions of its erad-
ication, and the implementation in the 1960s of a well-intended
but less than total "War on Poverty," the problem looms larger in
the last decade of the twentieth century than it has at any time
since the Great Depression of the 1930s.

Richard Ropers' earlier studies on the homeless helped to
open our eyes to the extent and sociological implications of
homelessness. This study on poverty complements his earlier
work by focusing on the broader problem of poverty, and by
offering us startling information regarding the extent, causes,
and consequences of being poor in America.

In Washington, D.C., politicians are aware that numbers
provide a powerful tool, one they often use. Statistical documentation tends to lend credibility to an argument, and politicians use it frequently to reinforce their positions on issues. The
statistics concerning the number of American citizens living below the poverty line have been poorly defined and variously
calculated, and this manipulation has enabled politicians and
federal agencies to successfully obscure the actual extent of the
problem. Consequently, the public remains unaware of the se-
riousness of the situation. Ropers skillfully leads us through the

maze of numbers and political rhetoric to help us find a more clear definition of poverty. He gives us an understanding of what constitutes poverty, what it means to be poor, and how extensive poverty actually is in this country.

Perhaps as important as the questions surrounding the extent and definitions of poverty are the questions about the causes of poverty and the means to eradicate it. Ropers does not generally see the causes as individual failings; rather, he focuses on the institutional causes. Many impoverished people draw regular paychecks, but their compensation cannot pull them above the poverty level. In fact, over 40 percent of those who live in poverty are gainfully employed. Certainly, many of the poor are unemployed, but a large portion of this population cannot work because they are aged, ill, or children. Usually beyond the control of individuals, general economic and political circumstances can create victims of poverty.

The U.S. economy has experienced both rising unemployment and declining wages. Replacement of the industrial belt by the rust belt has led to a corporate drain of many formerly high-paying industrial jobs which now are located in cheap foreign labor markets. Some industrial blue-collar workers have had to settle for low-paying service jobs in place of their former, high-paying skilled positions. Additionally, in recent years, virtually all social programs serving the poor have been cut back. It is ironic that while growing numbers of people are experiencing a need for a social safety net, food stamp programs and other welfare supports are being significantly reduced, thereby shredding the safety net for the poorest Americans.

In the face of an out-of-control national debt and sluggish economic growth, Ropers is not sanguine about finding immediate and easy solutions to the problem and burden of being poor in America. In the long run, it appears that answers are to be found in a major reevaluation of national priorities concerning the treatment of the nation's poor. Although solutions may be difficult and long term, Ropers makes significant contributions by enhancing our understanding of the causes and extent of the problem of *Persistent Poverty*. With such an understanding, it is possible to begin restructuring our national priorities in order to find some solutions.

WAYNE K. HINTON

Chair, Department of Behavioral
and Social Sciences
Southern Utah University
Cedar City, Utah

Acknowledgments

This book is an attempt to introduce and explain one of the root social problems and contradictions of American society to mainstream America. Less formal than the usual academic standard, this book has been written in what, I hope, is a more popular style. The book reflects a lifetime of personal and professional involvement with the issue of poverty.

The writing, editing, and production of this book would not have been possible without the participation, concern, and dedication of Mary Jane Nelsen. My children Ryan and Libby Ropers provided a certain type of personal motivation for the completion of this work; I want them to live in a better world. Friends like Carl Cluff and Wes Gibbs provided me with friendship and companionship on many hikes through the wilderness of southern Utah and helped me to occasionally get my mind off the content of this book.

The Department of Behavioral and Social Sciences, Southern Utah University, provided me with the facilities and freedom to write. Certain members of the department helped me deal with troubling personal issues, especially Dr. McRay Cloward. My department Chair, Wayne K. Hinton, strongly encouraged and supported my work on the book. Also, the staff patiently tolerated my changing moods throughout the year as I juggled my teaching responsibilities with the writing of the book.

My colleagues, Dr. Mark Winter and Dr. Oakley Gordon, provided helpful input. The Southern Utah University library staff was also very helpful and tolerant, especially Linda Ahlstrom and Tom Challis.

One of my students, Steven Burch, served as a congressional intern in Washington, D.C., and supplied me with invaluable congressional research documents and reports. Another of my students, David Eller, provided me with insightful discussions on a number of topics, as well as the photographs contained in the book.

My telephone conversations with Los Angeles Legal Aid attorney and president of The National Coalition for the Homeless, Gary Blasi, with whom I directly worked in the past, kept me posted on current developments in Los Angeles. Paul Tepper of Shelter Partnership, an advocacy organization for the poor and the homeless in Los Angeles, also gave me essential updates.

The staff of Plenum Press, and especially Norma Fox, executive editor, and Frank Darmstadt, her assistant, and Herman Makler, production editor, are thanked for their trust that I still had much more to say about the tragedy of American poverty than what was included in my first book, *The Invisible Homeless*, which they helped make a reality.

RICHARD H. ROPERS

Contents

Foreword by Wayne K. Hinton   vii
Acknowledgments   xi
Prologue by Dave Schmaltz   1

Introduction   9

1 • What Is Poverty?   23
That Was Then, This Is Now   23
The Meaning of Poverty   25
Ranking Each Other   27
Do We Have Any Class?   28
Moving On Up . . .   34
The Measure of Poverty   35
Number Games   37

2 • Who Are the Poor?   43
It's Not in the Stars   43
The Children   44
The Women   46

The Elderly   47
Minorities   48
Native Americans   49
The Working Poor   51
The Rural Poor   52

3 • A Tale of Two Countries   55
The Concentration of Income   57
The Concentration of Wealth   59
What About Welfare for the Rich?   62
Possible Consequences of the Concentration
    of Wealth   64

4 • Those at the Very Bottom: The New
    Homeless   69
How Many Millions?   71
Can the U.S. Census Count of the Homeless
    Be Valid?   72
Social Science Hoax   77
Homelessness: The American Nightmare   80
The McKinney Act   82
The HUD Scandal   83
Does Rent Control Cause Homelessness?   84
Free Enterprise Zones?   88
Institutionalizing Homelessness   89
Discussion   90

5 • Welfare: Not Even Treating the
    Symptoms   93
What Is Welfare?   96
Who Are Welfare Recipients?   99
Welfare: Perpetuating or Alleviating Poverty?   100

Los Angeles: A Case Study in the Failure
    of Public Welfare   101
Conclusion   111

6 • Blaming the Victim   115
Social Darwinism   116
Reductionism   117
Genetic Stupidity and Poverty   118
Craniology   119
Characterology   120
IQ Tests: Old Wine in New Bottles   121
From Inferior People to Unheavenly Cities   127
The Culture of Poverty   130
The Negro Family   132
Functional Inequality   144
Bad Personalities, Bad Brains, Bad Genes,
    and Bad Luck   146

7 • Blaming the System   155
Sweatshop America   155
Capital versus Community   159
The Truly Disadvantaged   161
Poverty and Inequality as Inherent
    in the System   162
Not in Their IQs   167
What Is Intelligence?   168
Functional Poverty   169
Conclusion   170

**8 • The Production of Poverty: What Produces
    Persistent Poverty?   173**
The Changing Global Economy   174
Deindustrialization   174

Unemployment/Underemployment   176
The Low-Income Housing Crisis   178
Inadequate Social Welfare   179
Big Government Corruption and Fraud   180
Increased Family Instability   181
The Polarization of the Stratification System   181
Racism and Sexism   182
The City of Los Angeles: A Case Study
    in the Production of Poverty and Related
    Social Problems   184
Summary   187

 9 • **The Politics of Poverty: Life, Liberty, and the
    Pursuit of Happiness   189**
Bush's Budget Proposals: Kinder and Gentler Talk,
    but the Same Old Reagan Action   193
Politics of Housing   196
Two Political Approaches to Understanding
    Poverty   197
Political Poverty Paradigm One   198
Political Poverty Paradigm Two   200

10 • **Justice?   205**
Invisible Inequality   209
New Choices?   210

Postscript by Robert G. Newby   215

References   225

Index   241

Prologue

We are at a critical point in American history, says Richard Ropers in *Persistent Poverty*. Signs show that the quality of life and standard of living is deteriorating for many Americans. As the number of poor and homeless reaches all-time highs and continues to rise at alarming rates, more and more of the poor are former members of the middle class. Ropers makes it clear that we are all tied to the same structural conditions that produce poverty and homelessness, and dealing effectively with this crisis will benefit everyone—not just the poor.

Public response has not matched the gravity of the situation, though public awareness has increased, as evidenced by the "Hands Across America" project, the annual "Comic Relief" telethon, and other private citizen-initiated programs geared to raising money and collecting articles of clothing.

"Public consciousness lags behind social reality," explains Ropers. What is the reality? Even though the Reagan Administration proclaimed an "economic recovery" in the 1980s, now, in the 1990s, more people are working, and working harder, just to keep up with the cost of living, especially increased housing costs. There are more full-time workers living in poverty, and more two-parent working families. Yet the poverty rate remains unchanged.

As Ropers points out, of all new jobs created in the 1980s, 75 percent were low-paying jobs—not the kind on which to build a career or a future, or that will enable people to climb out of poverty. Further, since 1975, there has been a 52 percent increase in the number of full-time workers living in poverty. And for every individual who entered the middle class in the 1980s, two joined the poor.

Yet, our political leaders, insulated from the accelerating numbers and sheer deprivation of shelterless souls who line the streets, sleep under bridges and alleyways, and pass their days in parks and shanty towns, claim that the nation is in an "economic recovery."

This is the battle that Ropers and other social scientists are engaged in—the struggle over whose view of social reality is most accurate. Lacking the same amount of free access to the media as those in political power have, the task of social investigators is made especially difficult. With more Americans—as many as half—receiving their news through television, increasingly those in power can dictate what version of reality will prevail. When President Reagan, in an interview with David Brinkley, expressed his belief that most people were homeless, "you might say, by choice," many understood this statement as "true and factual." Reagan's statement derives from an outdated, nineteenth-century theory—Social Darwinism.

Ropers' thorough investigation of factors contributing to poverty reveals that theories of Social Darwinism, genetic inferiority, and other psychological explanations of poverty are specious, and he convincingly shows the reader that the primary determinants of poverty and homelessness have structural-precipitant origins (e.g., lack of affordable housing, low-paying jobs, deindustrialization, intermittent employment). Instead of shaping facts to fit an idea of "economic recovery," which was the tendency in the federal government during the 1980s, Ropers presents us with a social reality based on facts. He provides us with authoritative facts and findings and a much-needed counterview of poverty, its causes, and possible solutions.

As Ropers points out, Social Darwinism is alive and well. It assumes that the poor will always be with us. It is "natural" for some to be poor. It is their choice and their responsibility. Anyone in America can get ahead if only they try hard enough. I believe that the belief that the homeless are lazy, not willing to work, and, therefore, undeserving of any serious governmental help prepared the way for the recent Department of Housing and Urban Development (HUD) scandal. If the poor will always be with us, then HUD programs are useless and misguided, so why not make a fast buck and pay off some political debts?

Too often poverty is politicized. It is not unusual then that HUD officials under Reagan played down the number of homeless while claiming an "economic recovery," and even saw fit to plunder the public coffers for themselves—the more deserving—instead of managing programs that were designed to benefit the poor.

At a time when low-income housing is of the greatest need, a HUD official was quoted as saying, "We're getting out of the housing business." The facts bear this out. Ropers cites in his work that HUD allocations for public housing have continued to drop throughout the 1980s and into the 1990s—and the remaining allocations exist only because of programs legislated during the 1970s.

The influence peddling (also known as "consulting fees" that ran upward of $9 billion intended for public housing for the poor) that characterized the HUD scandal underlines how pervasive the "blaming the victim" attitude was. Furthermore, not only was public money misappropriated for private gain but housing programs were set back by at least a decade as well. The costs of catching up could multiply many times over and, perhaps, make a difficult problem impossible.

Further, conservative ideology seeks to punish those who

have failed the Social Darwinist test. For instance, on their face workfare programs may seem an equitable arrangement between the welfare recipient and society, where the recipient works for all or part of his or her income allotment. However, as Ropers illustrates, the work is usually low-paying, unskilled, and not of the kind that can be used to better oneself, to advance a career, or to climb out of poverty. That workfare, food stamps, and other forms of social assistance are usually less than adequate to bring recipients even up to a poverty-level existence reflects an older disciplinary agenda that attempts to punish the poor for their perceived slothfulness.

It may be hard to believe, but someone who is poor and unemployed may expend as much energy on an everyday basis and experience just as much stress in trying to get ahead (possibly more because of money problems) as some young executive who is climbing the corporate ladder. Larry, 26, a homeless votech student whom I interviewed, expressed anger at people who view street people as lazy: "People wonder why 'these guys' don't do anything about their lives. 'These guys' use all of their energy simply to exist, and they don't have anything left over to better themselves." And, Ozzie, 38, a homeless carpet layer, wondered why more money wasn't spent to help people climb out of poverty: "One thing, if they can spend millions of dollars on prisons, why can't they spend as much on people in shelters that are hustling, trying to stay out of criminal activity?"

I have found, as have other ethnographic researchers, that the homeless fear that the government will put them in "detention centers" where they will be out-of-sight and out-of-mind, where they won't bother the public; thus, the problem will be "solved." Said Ron, 30, a homeless house painter:

> There's times I feel like a refugee in this f— country: "You can't sit here; move along, buddy!" It seems to me it's getting worse. I think if Reagan had his way he'd have set up reeducation camps for the homeless in the desert in Arizona somewhere. And then after that

maybe we'd have concentration camps. I really feel that, because the American public isn't sympathetic at all to people on the streets. To them street people are just trash—get them out of here! They don't care that the guy's suffering out there on the streets, freezing and starving, dirty. They have no feeling. They turn their noses up to that suffering.

Ropers reminds us that in the past America has chosen to punish the already punished, to punish rather than help those considered undesirable, undeserving, inferior, or dangerous, for example, by placing Native Americans on "reservations," and interning Japanese-Americans in "relocation centers" during World War II. History suggests that politicization of poverty is merely the latest form of a long-term and deeply ingrained psychological conflict in American culture—whether to punish or to help. We can see this conflict today in other areas of debate, notably in our quarrels over crime, drugs, and abortion.

It is important that the public perception of who the poor and homeless are catches up to reality, because there are warning signs that time is running out. With a soaring number of billionaires and the stock market at an all-time high, the administration may be encouraged to believe in its "economic recovery." But accompanying this increase in billionaires has been a disparity of wealth equal to that preceding the stock market crash of 1929, when the upper 1 percent of the population owned 36 percent of the country's wealth. The crash occurred when the stock market was healthy (as now) and ushered in the Great Depression. As the 1990s begin, the top 5 percent of the population in America owns 60 percent of the country's assets, which should be taken as a possible warning signal of economic danger. Further, as Ropers points out, the disparity today is even greater than that between the "richest of kings and poorest of peasants and slaves of the past."

Despite intervening years of social programs designed to alleviate the suffering of the poor, such as the New Deal and

Great Society programs of the Roosevelt and Johnson years, more people now live in poverty than during the War on Poverty of the late 1960s.

The severity and extensiveness of poverty in today's America finds its closest parallel in the Great Depression of the 1930s. Tens of millions of people now live in poverty, and millions more are homeless. Hundreds of thousands of even middle-class people are but one or two missed paychecks from being homeless. Seeking help, people wait outside overflowing homeless shelters, employment centers, and soup kitchens in lines that stretch around a city block. Shanty towns are springing up in American cities, modern-day "Reaganvilles"—reminiscent of the "Hoovervilles" of the 1930s. These are warning signs, danger signals that things are getting worse, not better.

What will we do with the growing army of homeless who wander the streets? Various cities have tried sweeping the problem under the rug, giving the homeless one-way tickets out of town. In other communities, officials order that locks be put on dumpsters or that dumpster food be purposely contaminated with chlorine. Extra police are hired to patrol shopping malls and downtown areas to sweep the streets free of unsightly people. Walls are built along freeways to screen people who live in cardboard shelters and shantytowns from public view and especially from the eyes of tourists.

Such "solutions" treat symptoms while doing nothing to cure the disease. They are as effective as putting make-up over a spot of cancer, or applying an ice bag to relieve the pain of a brain tumor. Our nation shows many symptoms—stress diseases, racism, ethnic scapegoating, drug and alcohol abuse, child abuse, and so on. One sign of increased tension between rich and poor is the concurrent rise in both the crime rate and the prison population. The instinct of a threatened class is to increase controls—more police, harsher penalties, bigger prisons, exactly the trend we see today. We get nowhere by blaming crime on the "criminal mentality." The name-calling may provide psychological satisfaction and rationalizations, but it also inflames emotions, perverts and diverts action, and cannot help but make matters worse. Name-calling and scapegoating is the habit of groups like the skinheads. We do not want it to be the habit of the nation, because such a habit can only sabotage our future.

We may be sabotaging our future in other ways. Reduced and nonexistent health care for the poor is especially ominous. The number of low birth-weight babies has become an especially serious trend. With limited access to, knowledge of, or ability to pay for health care, poor and homeless women are three times as likely to have low birth-weight babies. Low birth-weight has been associated with stunted cognitive and physical development. Thirty-one million Americans do not have basic health care insurance, and 30 percent of America's children have never seen a dentist. One out of four children now lives in poverty, and if the trend continues, by the end of the 1990s the number will reach one in three—many of them low birth-weight babies. The obvious inference to be drawn is that the developmental deficits of today's infants will result in social costs in the future, and if there is a large statistical increase in developmental deficits now, there may be a geometric increase in social costs in the future—to say nothing of the increase in human misery and social disequilibrium.

Regrettably, today, depending on federal leadership to correct public misconceptions of poverty and homelessness may mean waiting for a day that never comes. When one considers the barrage of ill-considered statements advanced by the Reagan Administration—that ketchup is a vegetable, that trees contribute to air pollution, and that the poor are poor by choice—statements demonstrably false and harmful in their consequences (in this case the children, the trees, and the poor), one can see how important the struggle to define reality is, and how easily myth, bias, political ideology, and self-interest can prevail over fact.

However, the recent twentieth anniversary of Earth Day in 1990 provides hope that public misconceptions can be corrected and that public officials can be persuaded to act. In 1970 "environmentalism" had hardly entered the language. Anyone associated with the environmental movement, by and large, was seen as a wild-eyed fanatic. Today, saving the environment is a major domestic and international priority to many, many people. Depletion of the rain forests, elimination of plant and animal species, global warming, acid rain, and the effects of overpopulation are generally recognized as real problems that must be confronted.

The public was misled about poverty and homelessness during the 1980s, and public programs were pursued which intensified a serious problem of manageable size into one of forbidding proportions. Other programs designed to alleviate poverty and homelessness were underfunded, sabotaged, and plundered for private or political gain.

Ropers brings us up to date, and provides objective observers with a wealth of information and perspectives with which to construct an understanding of present reality. He wants us to understand the gravity of the situation: poverty and homelessness are not situations we can afford to ignore, or dismiss as a minor problem, or blame on the poor themselves because of their perceived laziness. It's important that public perception of who the poor are catches up to reality. Delays can only aggravate an already extraordinarily unhealthy situation. Ropers is making his contribution. Now it is up to us to make ours.

DAVE SCHMALTZ

Department of Sociology
University of Colorado
Boulder, Colorado

Introduction

"The only thing that is permanent is change," said the ancient Greek philosopher Heraclitus. His words remain an appropriate maxim for the 1990s, which have ushered in unprecedented and tumultuous economic, social, and political transformations in nations around the world. From the Middle East to Panama and Nicaragua, into South Africa, and on up through Eastern Europe, including Germany and the Soviet Union, the winds of change continue to blow. The force of these disruptions has rendered entire libraries of social science books obsolete. On a superficial level, many of these world changes appear to confirm the ideals and practices of U.S. society. But the reforms and "democratization" occurring within the Soviet Union and other countries may be attributed more to the internal historical dynamics and problems of these countries than to any perceived imitation of the "laissez-faire" ideology and policies of the United States. Although many view the changes elsewhere as a celebration of American "free enterprise" ideology, after the fireworks have faded, the dark side of American reality will continue to expand as at least 32 million poor and maybe another 40 million near-poor citizens live what can only be described as an American nightmare.

Despite all the political slogans and rhetoric regarding equality of opportunity, equal protection, and equal access to allegedly unlimited opportunities, poverty persists. While in the 1980s, a supposedly limited economic recovery and a political policy of "trickle-down prosperity" were occurring, the American economic and social systems became sharply divided and polarized. Mass media reports express this polarization by featuring increasing numbers of stories about the homeless, which contrasted with features about flamboyant billionaires such as Donald Trump, who *Time* magazine called "a man who has come to embody the acquisitive 80s" (*Time*, January 16, 1989:4). As the United States begins the last decade of the twentieth century, American poverty not only persists but the number of poor Americans continues to grow.

At the same time that millions of Americans enjoy the bounty of the nation's resources and prosperity, increasing millions of other citizens endure lives of deprivation and misery. In the nation's capital, Washington, D.C., poverty among black residents, who comprise the majority of the capital's population, has resulted in an infant mortality rate of 21 deaths per 1000 live births (Lacyo, 1989)—a rate that matches Third World levels. In some cases, American poverty has become so absolute that more than a few citizens own literally nothing but the clothes on their backs and have nowhere to live but in the streets and alleys of the U.S. cities. More soup kitchens, food pantries, and emergency shelters for the poor exist today than at any time since the Great Depression of the 1930s. While these stopgap measures express a certain compassion, they also reflect a trend toward "institutionalizing" poverty. It is as if poverty is becoming an acceptable feature of our society. Poverty is viewed by many as an almost inevitable manifestation of the natural order of things.

C. Wright Mills, in his classic work *The Sociological Imagination* (1959), distinguished between "personal troubles" and "public issues." Personal troubles refer to aspects of an individual's inner life, character, self, and immediate relations with others, while public issues refer to those matters which transcend the individual and his immediate environment. The realm of public issues includes institutional, social structural, and historical conditions, causes, and processes (Mills, 1959:8).

Poverty in the United States is one condition where the distinction between troubles and issues is often confused, if not ignored. Much attention has been focused on the numerous personal troubles that afflict the poor, while larger societal conditions, causes, and processes of poverty—the public issues—have often been dismissed or ignored.

In the tradition of Mills, this book will attempt to distinguish between the personal and public aspects of poverty, and indicate how the two may interact. By taking a sociological perspective, this view will try to promote an understanding that individuals with personal troubles still live within institutional and social contexts. These contexts not only envelop but also precede their personal lives. The relation between personal troubles and social forces is one characterized by constant reciprocal interaction. This book takes the position that the condition and fate of the poor are inseparable from the dynamics of the society in which they live.

Contrary to prevailing stereotypes (which often suggest that the poor are predominantly unmotivated, undisciplined, undeserving able-bodied men and women), more than one-half of the poverty population consists of children and the elderly. The official poverty line is drawn at $12,675 for a family of four. According to Census Bureau figures, 32.5 million Americans live below the poverty line. This figure includes 6,163,000 families with children, and reflects an increase of 8 million more people living in poverty than did in 1978. Children total approximately 40 percent of the entire poverty population, while the elderly, those 65 or older, constitute another 11 percent of the poor.

By the time this book is published, the various numbers and percentages of different groups that are living in poverty and near poverty will undoubtedly have changed somewhat. Nevertheless, the numbers presented in this book represent the most recent data available at the time of its writing, and it is extremely unlikely that the basic trends described herein will have changed.

Minority groups continue to be disproportionately represented among the poor. Although the national poverty rate is 13.5 percent, with the rate for whites at 10.5 percent, the poverty rate for blacks is 33.1 percent. Another large group that does not fit the stereotype is the working poor. Although the official unemployment rate dropped significantly during the late 1980s, 58 percent of the 8 million new jobs created between 1979 and 1984 are "low wage" jobs, which the Senate Budget Committee has defined as those jobs that pay $11,611 or less for a family of four.

Not only has poverty persisted and grown, but the very nature and structure of American society is being altered by the increasing economic and social distance separating those at the top from those at the bottom of the stratification system. In 1987, the bottom 20 percent of the population received only 3.8 percent of the nation's aggregate family income. In 1967, this figure was 5.5 percent. In 1967, those in the top 20 percent of the population received 40.4 percent, while in 1987, this same group received 46 percent of the income.

The Consequences of Poverty

Poverty is not a problem that can be isolated and examined outside the scope of society's basic structure. Many individual and social problems are, to some degree, influenced by poverty, if not directly caused by it. A person's location in the socioeconomic stratification system can shape the "life chances" of that individual as well as those of entire social groups. Life chances refer to "probabilities of benefitting or suffering from the opportunities or disadvantages offered by society" (Robertson, 1989:167). A vast amount of research literature has provided documentation regarding the way in which poverty contributes to individual and social pathology. The individual who lives in or near poverty is at risk of suffering numerous social, psychological, and medical problems.

It has been established that higher incidence rates of psychiatric morbidity are linked to lower-class lifestyles. More than any other group, poor people stand a greater probability of being afflicted by psychiatric problems ranging from the most extreme forms of mental illness, like schizophrenia and various personality disorders, to more common conditions such as depression, anxiety, and low self-esteem. Certain health conditions and problems also appear to be disproportionately distributed among the lower classes. Although drug and alcohol abuse occur in all strata of society, specific drug and alcohol problems are associated with life at the bottom.

Economic insecurity can influence various forms of family instability, including domestic violence, separation, and divorce. It has often been demonstrated that crime, especially street crime and youth gangs, is linked to low socioeconomic status. Scarce economic resources coupled with keen competition produce types of social disorganization, including racial and ethnic conflict, urban blight, and homelessness.

Blaming the Victim or Blaming the System

How is the persistence of poverty and its many consequences explained? There is, of course, no lack of explanations. This book presents a unique comparison of selected social science explanations regarding poverty. Not only have many of these explanations helped form the basis for public stereotypes regarding the poor but they also reflect political and ideological biases. Following the lead of previous authors (Ryan, 1971), these various explanations of poverty have been organized into two major categories: (1) "blaming the victim" explanations, and (2) "blaming the system" explanations.

Blaming the Victim

William Ryan in his book, *Blaming the Victim*, was one of the first to suggest that a category of theories exist which attempts to account for various social problems by focusing on the characteristics, attributes, and behaviors of those individuals who suffer from specific social problems. A blaming the victim perspective, for example, would base its explanation of the disadvantaged position of blacks in American society primarily from a study of how blacks, as individuals and as a group, differ from whites. Once the "differences" are uncovered, they would then be offered as reasons for the situation of blacks in this society.

Numerous blaming the victim explanations have been developed to interpret many different types of social problems; this is especially true regarding the issue of poverty. This book will offer summaries of representative types of blaming the victim theories. These types will include a broad range of blaming the victim theories, with an exposition as to how they account for social stratification, inequality, and poverty. Some of these theories are components of major theoretical orientations within social science disciplines, such as anthropology, sociology, psychology, political science, and urban studies. In some cases, they comprise a significant portion of the theoretical foundation for conservative political ideologies and rhetoric.

The selection of blaming the victim theories covered in the book ranges from fully developed sociological theories to biological arguments. Davis and Moore's functionalist theory of social stratification, which maintains that inequality is a universal, eternal, and desirable feature of all societies, is examined, along with Oscar Lewis' theory of the Culture of Poverty, which posits that, for some of the poor, their behaviors, attitudes, and beliefs (i.e., their "culture") essentially perpetuate their poverty. Daniel Patrick Moynihan's ideas on the presumed pathology of black families and individuals as the cause of their disadvantaged position is presented, and Edward Banfield's explanation of urban problems as represented in his book *The Unheavenly City,* which blames an underclass of blacks for creating the majority of the nations social problems, is reviewed. Various attempts to account for poverty and racial inequality in terms of inherent intelligence and biological differences between races (as expressed in the works of Richard Herrnstein, Arthur Jensen, and William Shockley) are included. The Nobel prize-winning Shockley has gone so far as to actually create a sperm bank to be utilized in the production of a "master race." This, he believes, will put an end to poverty and the problems created by black people. The interpretations of Charles Murray concerning the role of welfare in the perpetuation of poverty, along with new psychiatric theories that argue that some forms of poverty result from genetic defects and mental illnesses, are also presented. Finally, because politics and political leaders influence the public's image of the poor, it is appropriate to review the official Reagan and Bush administrations' positions regarding the poor. These positions are, unfortunately, related to blaming the victim explanations because both Reagan and Bush have perceived poverty as a lifestyle which the poor freely chose to live.

Blaming the System

Following an overview of the leading blaming the victim explanations of poverty, this book provides the reader with an introduction and review of selected and prominent theories that shift the emphasis away from the characteristics of those who are poor onto various external social factors and forces that are believed to contribute to or cause poverty. Categorized under the rubric the "system," these social factors and forces include the structures of social and economic systems; specific institutions and/or institutional regulations and demands; political programs and policies; various cultural, ideological, and educational beliefs; and long-established patterns of social interaction such as racism, sexism, and ageism, which deny certain groups equal access to social and economic opportunities and resources.

Regardless of the political orientation of subsequent social theorists, Karl Marx is considered to be one of the intellectual forerunners of all blaming the system theories. Generally recognized as a significant contribution to social science, Marx's understanding of how the organization of social systems shape and influence social stratification, and how such systems influence the attitudes and behaviors of people within different social strata, transcends politics. A brief review of Marx's theory of "surplus value" is presented as an example of a comprehensive blaming the system explanation of poverty and inequality. Although Marx's theory of poverty appears to serve as a model (and perhaps an inspiration) to some contemporary blaming the system theories, the emphasis in this section will be to review more recent blaming the system theories developed by prominent social scientists.

In *The Deindustrialization of America* (1982), Bluestone and Harrison argue that growing poverty, the increasing polarization of the stratification system, and the disruption of community life across the nation have resulted from a conscious policy of "disinvestment" in American industry. Essentially, the motivation behind this process of deindustrialization through disinvestment is increased profits that are accrued by moving industries to countries where workers are employed for a fraction of the wages paid to U.S. workers. As a consequence of the deindustrialization of American industry, American workers have lost good-paying blue-collar jobs and job benefits. Many of these workers have been forced to settle for much lower paying jobs which offer little or no security. Furthermore, some of these displaced workers who cannot find even low-paying jobs eventually join the ranks of the poor and sometimes the homeless.

Sociologist William J. Wilson further emphasizes the role of deindustrialization as a major factor in the production of poverty and near poverty in *The Truly Disadvantaged* (1987). Wilson demonstrates that the creation of a poor black underclass during the 1980s was the result not of black pathology but of the specific impact upon working-class blacks of both deindustrialization and population movements.

Samuel Bowles and Herbert Gintis have empirically demonstrated that neither high IQ scores nor high levels of education are key determinants of an individual's ultimate social standing. Rather, as presented in their study, "IQ and the United States Class Structure" (1974), an individual's social class origin is the best predictor of that individual's ultimate social standing.

Herbert Gans stood the functionalist theory of social stratification on its head. In *More Equality* (1974), Gans contends that social inequality is not functional for societies in general. Instead, he finds that when particular societies are examined, inequality functions best for those at the top of the stratification system. The "powers that be" perpetuate stratification in order to protect their privileged positions.

Frances Fox Piven and Richard Cloward believe that it has never really been government generosity which brought aid and relief to the poor. Only when the poor themselves have united and organized have they been able to wrestle concessions away from the establishment. That the poor have occasionally succeeded presents a powerful argument against the view that they are hopelessly defective and pathological individuals.

The Production of Poverty

As with any complex social phenomenon, the causes of poverty are multiple and interdependent. Nonetheless, it is possible to analytically and conceptually identify and distinguish leading factors that contribute to the production of poverty. Being poor may be a personal problem, but poverty is a public issue. When poverty has become a social condition affecting tens of millions of people, it is necessary to identify the social forces that produced it. This book offers a model of the social production of poverty and examines the leading factors which appear to be perpetuating poverty in the United States. Many of these factors were introduced in the blaming the victim and blaming the system theories described above. An attempt has been made to integrate explanations which facilitate an understanding of American poverty as it exists in the 1990s into a comprehensive model that will account for both the individual and social aspects of the reality of poverty.

The Politics of Poverty

This book examines several programs, policies, and strategies for managing or ending poverty. They are organized into a conceptual framework that places them into models based on the distinction between blaming the victim and blaming the system approaches. This framework places programs, policies, and strategies into either "Poverty Paradigm One" or "Poverty Paradigm Two." Paradigm One flows out of assumptions from blaming the victim theories, and Paradigm Two out of assumptions from blaming the system theories. Prior to examining current programs, policies, and strategies, the major assumptions of each poverty paradigm are presented relative to the following dimensions: theoretical orientation, conceptualizations of American society, intervention strategy, and political orientation.

There are, of course, many other nations plagued by persistent poverty of even greater scope and magnitude than the problems that face the United States. This book is not a condemnation of U.S. society. Rather, it attempts to offer positive ideas for the improvement of life throughout the mainstream of a changing American society.

Although the focus is national, the conditions and problems

of the poor who live in the city of Los Angeles will be used as a localized case study in various segments throughout the book. Los Angeles is not only one of America's largest cities, it is also one in which the contradictions of wealth and poverty are most blatant. Another consideration in the choice of Los Angeles was my first-hand experience with the poor and homeless of that city.

As a postdoctoral scholar in the School of Public Health, UCLA, I spent three years researching the issue of poverty and homelessness in Los Angeles, and have published several journal articles and a previous book, *The Invisible Homeless: A New Urban Ecology* (1988), on these topics. This book, however, is not merely the result of academic ivy tower speculation, or of aloof intellectual titillation. While serving as an expert witness and research consultant for the Legal Aid Foundation of Los Angeles in several lawsuits and as a research consultant for the Single Room Occupancy Housing Corporation, City of Los Angeles, I experienced many opportunities to become "street smart" by going directly into the city's poor neighborhoods, meeting hundreds of poor people, and becoming directly involved in their struggles for more decent lives. Also, as an intern at DiDi Hirsch Community Mental Health Center, Los Angeles, and as a member of the Unemployed Council in Santa Monica, I gained first-hand experience with the problems and concerns of the unemployed. In addition, for fifteen months, during 1986 and 1987, I was the live-in manager of a shelter for the poor and the homeless in Cedar City, Utah. I was appointed by Governor Bangeter of Utah to the Governor's Homeless Coordinating Committee, and was a research consultant to Salt Lake City Mayor Palmer DePaulis' Task Force on the Homeless.

The canons of social science served as guidelines for researching this book. Previous empirical surveys, various forms of participant observation, and the use of government documents as well as journalistic accounts provided the "data" for the book. By no means, however, does the book pretend to be nonpartisan. One of the defining characteristics of our nation is its citizens; therefore, to care about and to love America means to care about and love her people. At a time when so many other nations are correcting their shortcomings, it is time for Americans to reexamine the unfulfilled promises of our own country. When so many of the country's most vulnerable citizens (children, women, and elderly) suffer tremendously, it is morally wrong to pretend to be "scientifically objective." To paraphrase a great nineteenth-century social scientist, "Philosophers only interpret the world in various ways; the point [of science] however is to change it."

In the introduction to *The State of Black America 1990* (1990), John E. Jacob, president of the National Urban League, aptly reminds us that despite reforms in other countries, the United States still has its own problems to clean up:

> During the heady days of the winter revolts against Eastern Europe's totalitarian regimes, a newspaper cartoon appeared that provides a stunningly accurate commentary on the current state of urban and Black America. The cartoon showed Uncle Sam looking over the Berlin Wall through binoculars. He says, "Gee, isn't it fascinating to watch the way communism is disintegrating." Behind him, on the U.S. side, is an urban landscape of mugging victims, hypodermic needles strewn on the ground, drug addicts, guns, potholed roads, and crumbling houses. That cartoon punctured the smugness that attended so many comments about the revolution in the East. While it is important to celebrate the spread of freedom, it is also important to be aware of the impediments to freedom here at home. (1990:1).

Over 250 years ago, Jonathan Swift penned a scathing satire that offered a solution to the problem of poverty in Ireland. In *A Modest Proposal*, Swift suggested selling the infant children of the poor as food for the rich. Shocking as the proposition may be, it illustrates the indifferent attitude most of society holds toward the plight of the poor. Swift recognized the outrageous nature of his essay; yet it appropriately addressed the outrageous nature of a life lived in poverty.

Some persons of a desponding spirit are in great concern about that vast number of poor people who are aged, diseased, or maimed, and I have been desired to employ my thoughts what course may be taken to ease the nation of so grievous an encumbrance. But I am not in the least pain upon that matter, because it is very well known that they are every day dying and rotting by cold and famine, and filth and vermin, as fast as can be reasonably expected. And as to the younger laborers, they are now in almost as hopeful a condition. They cannot get work, and consequently pine away for want of nourishment to a degree that if at any time they are accidentally hired to common labor, they have not strength to perform it; and thus the country and themselves are happily delivered from the evils to come. . . .

I desire those politicians who dislike my overture, and may perhaps be so bold to attempt an answer, that they will first ask the parents of those mortals whether they would not at this day think it a great happiness to have been sold for food at a year old in the manner I prescribe, and thereby have avoided such a perpetual sense of misfortunes as they have since gone through by the oppression of landlords, the impossibility of paying rent without money or trade, the want of common sustenance, with neither house nor clothes to cover them from the inclemencies of the weather, and the most inevitable prospect of entailing the like or greater miseries upon their breed forever.

This book contends that it will not take 250 years to overcome the enormous problems that have contributed to a situation which has forced millions of our citizens to live miserably impoverished lives, not the least of which is a lack of compassion. We are a country of optimists and innovators. This optimism and innovation can be focused toward a solution to the problem of poverty, and, it is hoped, render the title of this book obsolete.

1

What Is Poverty?

That Was Then, This Is Now

A little over fifty years ago, President Franklin D. Roosevelt told America:

> I see a great nation, upon a great continent, blessed with a great wealth of natural resources. . . . But here is the challenge to our democracy: In this nation I see tens of millions of its citizens—a substantial part of its whole population—who at this very moment are denied the greater part of what the very lowest standards of today call the necessities of life. . . . I see millions denied education, recreation, and the opportunity to better their lot and the lot of their children. I see millions lacking the means to buy the products of farm and factory and by their poverty denying work and productiveness to many other millions. I see one-third of a nation ill-housed, ill-clad, ill-nourished (Second Inaugural Address, January 20, 1937).

Until recently, most of us believed that as the United States approached the twenty-first century those words of Roosevelt could never ring true again; yet they continue to haunt us. Perhaps his words seem exaggerated when applied to the United

States in the 1990s because, for at least four decades, many Americans grew accustomed to relative prosperity, and social scientists wrote volumes regarding the virtual disappearance of poverty as a major social problem. Also, during the latter part of the 1980s, politicians assured us that economic recovery was the order of the day. For those at the top of the stratification system, that was certainly true. But for those at the bottom, the only thing that trickled down was increased misery. Meanwhile, we are once again confronted with increased American poverty, which, in many cases, is so desperate that it mimics the despair and deprivation of the Great Depression. After decades of social welfare programs, a war on poverty, and periods of economic boom and recovery, one-third of the nation's population lives near or in poverty. The National Association of Children's Hospitals predicts that by the end of the century one-third of all American children will live in poverty (AP, Washington, 1989). To some, that may seem like progress. But since the late 1970s the number of Americans facing tough economic times has been steadily expanding.

John Kenneth Galbraith, the well-known liberal economist, wrote in his much acclaimed book *The Affluent Society* (1958) that the affluence of American society had made widespread poverty a thing of the past, and only "pockets of poverty" remained in the 1950s. Through the 1960s and 1970s and into the early 1980s, many social scientists continued to predict the demise of the worst enclaves of American poverty (Bogue, 1963; Bahr, 1973; Lee, 1980; Miller, 1982). Contrary to all of our hopes and beliefs, however, as we enter the last decade of the twentieth century, we are assaulted by the contradiction of deprivation and misery being tolerated in a land of wealth. The poor appear to exist everywhere. No city or town, urban or rural, is immune to poverty. Daily, the mass media bombard our sensitivities with images of the dispossessed and, the most recent and cruel version of poverty, homelessness.

The Meaning of Poverty

Beyond the various technical definitions and conceptions of what constitutes poverty lies the reality of poverty and how it shapes the lives of millions of Americans. We cannot understand poverty if we don't know what it means to be poor. Poverty betrays the American Dream. To the unemployed and displaced steelworker poverty is a humiliating insult to self-esteem. Literally millions of blue-collar workers are losing their livelihoods, their homes, and their families as disinvestment transforms the American industrial landscape into a rust belt. A mother abandoned by a husband may experience her instant fall to poverty not only as broken wedding vows and forsaken promises but also as an exile to loneliness, isolation, and constant deprivation for herself and her children. How do we measure the hidden injuries, which may last a lifetime, to the many children growing up in emergency shelters for the homeless? Or what about the young black veteran, who, after serving his country and believing that legal and social barriers to the good life had been removed, finds himself unable to find a secure and decent paying job? For him, poverty means frustration, hostility, and anger. What is the meaning of a lifetime of hard work to a retired couple when a major medical problem wipes out their entire life savings? Only the home they worked 30 years to pay for stands between them and the world of the dispossessed. For the once proud but now militarily defeated Native Americans, poverty means powerlessness and the threat of extinction of their culture. Epidemics of suicide and alcoholism plague many Native American "reservations," where the unemployment and poverty rates often reach over 50 percent.

Poverty narrows and closes life chances. The victims of poverty experience a kind of arteriosclerosis of opportunity. Being poor not only means economic insecurity, it also wreaks havoc on one's mental and physical health. Emotional instability, anxiety, depression, frustration, and anger are often the byproducts of a life of uncertainty. Poverty creates greater susceptibility to practically all medical problems, along with limited access to health care. Not surprisingly, the poor have lower life expectancies than the rest of the population. The poor take nothing for granted. As poverty claims more victims, family ties are often severed, domestic violence runs rampant, and delinquency and crime increase. If you are poor, you will likely live in substandard housing, if it is available. If you are lucky enough to find employment, you will probably work at a financially inadequate, unfulfilling, and often dangerous or hazardous job. Poverty often means hunger; your stomach may be stuffed with bread and potatoes, but you will still suffer from malnutrition. The Harvard School of Public Health and the Physician Task Force on Hunger in America have defined hunger as being "chronically short of the nutrients necessary for growth and good health" (Brown, 1987, p. 37). Although nutritional ignorance is certainly a factor, it is simply the lack of enough money to purchase the proper balance of food that lies at the root of hunger. Picture small children, mere skeletons except for their bloated stomachs: no, not African children, but American children. It is currently estimated that 20 million of our citizens suffer from hunger! (Physician Task Force, 1985, p. 183). Poverty is a crucible. Caution is required when judging its victims.

What does widespread poverty mean to the larger society in which it exists? To some, it may mean a betrayal of democratic values and a loss of optimism. Poverty weakens the image of the United States as a world leader. If we cannot resolve our own domestic problems, how can we expect developing countries to believe we are a model worth emulating? Poverty undermines the spirit and strength of a nation, and the magnitude of poverty reveals something about the heart of a society, especially one claiming to be the best and most affluent in human history.

What is this persistent malady? How do we comprehend it? Are our methods of defining and measuring it appropriate?

Once it is defined and measured, can we control or eliminate it? How does poverty fit into the larger scheme of American society? Finally, is poverty universal and inevitable?

Ranking Each Other

Social scientists use the term "social stratification" when referring to the ranking of people in a hierarchy relative to income, wealth, occupation, and education. A society's stratification system serves as a type of sociological "map," and poverty is an aspect of this system. Once an individual's position is located within a stratification system, the odds are favorable that, to a large degree, the behavior, aspirations, motivations, joys, and fears of that individual can be described and predicted. Because they have very little—if any—income, wealth, or power, people living in poverty are usually thought to be at the bottom of a social stratification system. Therefore, to effectively understand poverty and its consequences, they must be considered against the backdrop of the larger system of stratification.

Most Americans usually don't consider the United States to be a highly stratified country, at least not as stratified as European countries, and certainly not as stratified as underdeveloped, Third World countries. Nevertheless, a preoccupation with upward social mobility and the endless pursuit of material possessions dominate the lives of most American citizens. Many Americans think of themselves, and the majority of U.S. citizens, as starting the race for upward mobility from a basically "middle-class" position. Teachers constantly remind schoolchildren that anyone can grow up to become president, and any goal or ambition can be reached. After all, according to the prevailing ideology, in America there are no legal or social barriers to individual success; the only limits are those which are self-imposed.

Although rags-to-riches anecdotes abound, and many individuals do move up the social ladder, the reality of American stratification is somewhat less endearing. To illustrate the point, if each story of a building was represented by $10,000, then one of America's richest individuals, Sam Moore Walton (founder of the Wal-Mart chain, who, according to Forbes 400, is worth $13 billion) would be represented by a building at least 1,300,000 stories tall! But, because the median U.S. family income is only $29,460, the average American family, according to income, would be a mere two-, three-, or four-story building. Those at the very bottom of the income structure, the homeless, would be exactly where they are—in the street. The social and economic distances between multimillionaires and some of the desperate homeless, who literally have nothing but the tattered clothes on their backs, outdistances the distinction between the richest of kings and the poorest peasants and slaves of the past. Perhaps for psychological as well as political reasons, middle-class America refuses to recognize the highly visible stratification in the country. Refusal to acknowledge the existence and intensity of American stratification constitutes one of the great evasions of our time. The goals of the American dream may be offered to all, but due to social and economic stratification, not everyone has the same means available to achieve those goals.

Do We Have Any Class?

In recent years there has been much clamoring over the "shrinking" or "disappearance" of the middle class. We are all familiar with the middle class, and most of you who are reading this book undoubtedly consider yourselves members of that class. Ironically, the very fact that many Americans view themselves as middle class implies at least an unconscious recognition of the existence of an American class system. For, in order for some to be in the "middle" requires that others exist at the top and bottom.

Most social scientists agree that industrial societies are essentially stratified into social classes. And, like all other industrial nations, the United States is class-stratified. Although there are many different definitions of social class, most contain certain common features, which usually include criteria such as income, wealth, power, and status in determining a person's or family's social class. Social classes may be defined, therefore, as *large groups of people with relatively similiar incomes, amounts of wealth, life conditions, life chances, and lifestyles.* These "determinants" of social class, however, should only be used as guidelines. Our definitions cannot encompass all the complexities of reality. And even though social classes can be distinguished from one another, there are more than a few fuzzy areas where the criteria of one class overlap that of another.

Income refers to pre- or posttax sources of money. The origin of income varies. It may come from hourly wages, salaries, interest earned, dividends, rent, grants, inheritance, allowances, and so forth. When the total U.S. population is divided into fifths, we find that the top fifth receives 46.1 percent of all income whereas the bottom fifth receives less than 4 percent of all income—the lowest percentage since 1954 (U.S. Bureau of the Census, 1987). An impeccable source, *Fortune* magazine, claims the current income gap has resulted from income differences which have widened since 1969 (Burck, 1988, p. 48). Since 1981, the income share of the top fifth has increased by 1.8 percent. Focusing more closely on the top fifth, we find a further concentration of income. The top 5 percent of the population receives 16.7 percent of all income. That amount equals more than the combined income of the bottom two-fifths of the population.

These relative income differences have persisted since the end of World War II. Contrary to public perception, social class entails much more than varying degrees of income. Class also includes *wealth*, which takes several different forms. It may include property, such as homes, vehicles, furniture, artwork, and land. However, in addition to personal types of property, wealth also includes property not necessarily used for everyday purposes, but rather that which is employed to generate income and profit. This kind of wealth may entail ownership of businesses, factories, utility companies, large farms and ranches, and even multinational corporations. Once again, dividing the population into fifths, the top fifth of the population owns 79 percent of all the wealth in the nation. A study conducted by the Joint Economic Committee of Congress found that one-half of 1 percent of the population owned one-third of all American assets (U.S. Congress, 1986).

Contrasting *life conditions* also distinguish different social classes. The availability of resources, whether natural, material, social, political, or economic, determines the parameters of a person's life conditions. Closely related to the availability of resources are the opportunities to have access to and utilize those resources. Social scientists use the term *life chances* to describe these opportunities. Finally, *lifestyles* are defined as the patterns of use of income, wealth, resources, and opportunities which shape people's social activity, attitudes, motives, and aspirations. Generally speaking, there is a strong association between individual behavior and consciousness and one's social class membership. Even something as seemingly individual and personal as one's speech pattern is influenced by class membership. The infamous "Brooklyn accent" is a working-class German-Yiddish accent, while the accent of someone like William F. Buckley, Jr., reflects an elite, Yale, upper-class, New England influence. It is reasonable to expect that similar life conditions, chances, and styles would produce similar—but not necessarily identical—interests, concerns, motivations, and behaviors.

Power often manifests the degree of one's income and wealth. The ability to force or influence other people into doing what they otherwise may not want to do constitutes a significant dimension of power. Access to many options, or freedom of choice, which is made available by increased opportunities that are facilitated by high income and wealth, represents another aspect of power. The rank of one's position within a stratification system, coupled with the degree of respect and deference a society gives to that position, determines one's *status*.

Although a lot of disagreement surrounds the types and nature of social classes in the United States, there is some consensus that the American class structure would include at least the following recognizable social classes.

The *upper class*, composed of individuals and families with annual incomes of at least $500,000, own and control a disproportionate concentration of personal and corporate wealth. They constitute approximately 1 percent of the population or about 2.5 million people (Liazos, 1989:280). Real-life examples of upper-class families would include the Trumps, Rockefellers, Kennedys, DuPonts, and Mellons. Two of the other richest individuals in the United States, besides Sam Walton, who was mentioned earlier, are John Kluge of Charlottesville, Virginia, and H. Ross Perot of Dallas, Texas—each worth about $2.5 billion. Fortune 500 and Forbes 400 publish lists of many leading upper-class individuals and families. The mass media often fictionalize the lives of such families in television programs such as *Dallas* and *Dynasty* and in movies like *Wall Street*.

The *middle class* contains a wide variety of occupational and status groups. Indeed, all social classes contain various *strata*. Qualitative differences in income, wealth, and power define class, and different degrees of the distinguishing characteristics of a class determine strata within that class. For example, a well-established and experienced medical doctor may earn $200,000 or more annually and own shares in a medical clinic and lab, while a high school teacher, who probably earns less than $40,000 annually, will likely own no property other than a home. However, both the doctor and teacher are considered members of the middle class, although they belong to different strata within that class. Although many Americans like to think of themselves as middle class, and the mass media constantly lump many different occupations and income groups into the middle class, social scientists use several criteria to determine middle-class membership, including a wide annual income range of between $35,000 and $400,000, lack of controlling ownership in large businesses and corporations, and above average educational attainments. Of course, in reality, the criteria and lines between classes and strata are not clear cut. Other types of middle-class members would include owners of small businesses and shops, midlevel managers, many lawyers, college professors, and various types of teachers. Members of the middle class comprise about 40 percent of the population.

There has been much discussion in recent years about the erosion of the middle class. It is believed that a substantial minority (about 25 percent) of the lower middle class have suffered income losses that have dropped them into working-class lifestyles. Home ownership, once a sure indicator of middle-class status, has—since the early 1980s—become increasingly out of reach for a growing number of citizens. During the last decade, home ownership rates dropped from 44 percent to 36 percent among people in the 25–29-year-old age group, and from 61 percent to 53 percent among those in their thirties (Burck, 1988). Some analysts have suggested that the "success" of the upper middle class requires a redefinition of the income criteria for entrance into the middle class. *Fortune* magazine contends that the "real price of admission" to the middle class is a minimum income of $53,000 (Burck, 1988, p. 48). Using that figure as a determinant, less than one-fourth of American families can be considered members of the middle class!

The majority of Americans, at least 45 percent, receive their income from work they perform for someone else. Working people, or the working class, are identified by a lack of ownership or control over major types of wealth and corporate or business property. Incomes usually range from $10,000 to $35,000 annually, and are largely derived from wages. Once again, many different strata exist within this class. Some highly skilled workers earn incomes in the lower middle-class range, while unskilled and uneducated workers try to survive on minimum wages. As with the upper class, the mass media, especially television, often portray the life of working people in television comedies and dramas. *All in the Family* and its leading character, "Archie Bunker," was a prevailing working-class stereotype projected on national television in the 1970s. *Laverne and Shirley,* and the "Fonz" from *Happy Days* provide examples of programs and characters that were centered around the life problems of working-class people. More recently, TV shows such as *Roseanne* and *Married . . . with Children* fulfill the same function.

Below the working class there exists the lower class. The various strata of the lower class often are the subject of a great deal of political, criminological, and sociological investigation. Frequently described as "a nation apart" or "out of the economic and social mainstream," some strata within this class have been identified with derogatory labels such as the "underclass," "homeless," "lumpen working class," "chronically unemployed," "skid row denizens," "street people," "derelicts," or "welfare recipients." Further removed than any other class from the American Dream, people stuck at the bottom are likely to be more frustrated, angry, and hostile than anyone else. They could be described as living the "American nightmare." Although minority groups represent a disproportionate number of its members, the lower class is comprised of people from all races. Long periods of unemployment or underemployment, lack of any wealth (though sometimes personal property may include an extremely modest home), little opportunity for education, substandard housing, and virtually no private health care insurance denote membership in the lower class. Annual incomes may range from zero to approximately $10,000 to

$12,000. A perpetual cycle of joblessness, broken families, shattered dreams, and haunting despair characterizes the lifestyles of those in the lower class. During the time when I was the live-in manager of a shelter for the homeless, a young man who was barefoot and wore nothing but a ragged pair of cut-off jeans applied for shelter; he literally had nothing, not even a shirt on his back.

Most people restrict their conception of the poverty population to the lower class and one of its strata, the underclass. Certainly, most members of the lower class are poor; however, the poverty and near poverty populations extend well into the working class. The poverty population encompasses the entire lower class and crosses over into as much as one-third of the working class.

Moving On Up . . .

The ideal of children surpassing their parents in income, occupational prestige, and lifestyle represents an important aspect of the American Dream. And while social mobility of one kind or another is not uncommon, it is more likely that a person will move into a more prestigious occupation or experience an increase in income rather than shift into a higher social class. Movement between class strata—occupational mobility—occurs more frequently than movement between classes. In fact, most upward mobility is simply a matter of small degrees, not qualitative jumps. Of course, some groups have fewer opportunities to move up than others. The rate of black or Hispanic upward social mobility is significantly lower than that of whites, and, generally, the same is true for women.

All things considered, despite the large amount of propaganda, chances of upward social mobility in the United States are actually lower than in several European countries.

The Measure of Poverty

Poverty can be defined and measured in various ways. Whether defined or measured in "absolute," "relative," or "administrative" terms, poverty in the United States endures. The inability to adequately secure the basic necessities of life, which include food, clothing, and shelter, constitutes absolute poverty. Relative poverty is conceptualized as a condition of material and social existence that is far below the average requirements of a particular culture. Administrative definitions of poverty often serve political ends. Currently, the U.S. government determines the "poverty line" by multiplying the cost of a minimally nutritious diet by three. This figure is then adjusted for the number of individuals living in a household. As a point of reference, the 1990 poverty line for an urban family of four was $12,675. However, this method assumes that the cost of all other necessities will remain constant relative to the cost of an adequate diet. This assumption is questionable in today's highly inflated housing, clothing, and health care markets. By adjusting poverty criteria to raise or lower the poverty line, and thus the number of people who are considered "statistically poor," politicians are able to manipulate statistics and make them serve whatever political ends they desire. Recently, for example, the U.S. Census Bureau concluded that if the definition of income was calculated to include benefits from such programs as Medicare, Medicaid, rent subsidies, and food stamps, the official number of poor Americans would drop from 32.5 million to 27.6 million. Nevertheless, no matter how poverty is operationalized, it currently afflicts an increasing number of citizens.

The issue of poverty transcends simple economics and statistical manipulation. A society's determination of what constitutes poverty must include cultural standards and political considerations. The question of numbers is not simply an abstract, academic issue; the creation of social programs and the allocation of funds to support them are based, to some extent, on estimates of the poverty population. Ultimately, behind the numbers lies the reality of the existence of the people living in poverty.

Prior to the early 1960s, the federal government had no standardized method of measuring poverty or counting the number of poor Americans. The current federal definitions of poverty were derived from the work of a Social Security Administration employee, Mollie Orshansky, during the years 1963–65. Basically, Ms. Orshansky conceptualized poverty as "the lack of enough income to purchase a minimally adequate *market basket* of goods and services" (Committee on Ways and Means, 1983:2). However, the data required to determine the price of such a market basket did not exist. The cost of the entire plan, therefore, was based around one commodity—food—because that price could be established. As a result, the method of calculating the poverty line was constructed around the Department of Agriculture's (USDA) 1961 "economy food plan." Adjustments were made according to family size, inflation as reflected by changes in the Consumer Price Index (CPI), and whether the family was a farm or nonfarm family. Beginning in 1969, farm families were allotted only 85 percent of the cost of the economy food plan. This practice was based on the assumption that farm families could grow some of their own food. In 1980, however, the separate farm family poverty threshold was eliminated.

Currently, the government uses the Orshansky definition of poverty for two purposes. The Census Bureau relies on the definition to determine a "statistical" approach for counting the poor, and the Office of Management and Budget (OMB) sets eligibility standards for welfare benefits using an "administrative" approach based on the definition. Both uses involve "annual income amounts" that determine the parameters of what is variously termed the poverty guidelines, poverty thresholds, poverty level, or poverty line (Committee on Ways and Means, 1983:1).

Number Games

Numerous issues can be raised concerning the adequacy and accuracy of the current governmental criteria that are used for determining the poverty line.

Critic Robert Sheak (1988) succinctly outlined the government's attempt to minimize the extent of poverty in America. Arguing that the federal government's method of estimating poverty inherently reflects a conservative ideological bias, Sheak suggests five major flaws in the current procedures used for determining poverty.

First, the foundation of the current criteria for estimating poverty rests on the use of the cost of an "emergency" minimally nutritious diet. This diet was originally designed by the Department of Agriculture to be used by families for a temporary period of time; for instance, if they had been victimized by an emergency such as a fire, flood, or earthquake. The original diet included a lot of cheese, peanut butter, crackers, and the like. The current diet deviates from the normal diet of most Americans, and does not reflect any individual variation for nutritional requirements related to age, gender, body size, health, physical activity level, allergies, or various climatic conditions, i.e., harsh winters. When purchasing and preparing food for this diet, the poor must shop and cook selectively, and are not allowed much variety in their meals (Sheak, 1988:283–84).

Second, it is assumed that multiplying the cost of the emergency food diet by three provides an appropriate index of the poverty line. This assumption is based on an outdated USDA consumer expenditure survey which found, in 1955, that low-income families spend one-third of their income on food. Sheak points out that a more recent USDA survey provides information which indicates that multiplying the cost of the diet by four would more accurately reflect the poverty line than does the current number, three. Such an adjustment would more than double the number of Americans who are officially considered to be living below the poverty line.

The third problem Sheak finds with the present formula is that it is based on pretax income. If federal and state tax deductions were considered, the after-tax income of millions of Americans would place them below the poverty line.

The fourth issue demonstrates that inflation adjustments to the poverty line criteria are made relative to the price of the emergency food diet based on the Consumer Price Index. A more sensitive adjustment would be one which reflects changes in the median family income.

The fifth and final problem lies with the high probability that the U.S. Census Bureau figures undercount the actual number of poor people. Up until 1989, the homeless were not counted because they had no address. Others may be living in institutions such as jails, mental hospitals, and nursing homes. Also, undocumented persons who live and work in this country would not be included in the Census report (Sheak, 1988: 283–86). Furthermore, those individuals who may have no, or very little, income during portions of the year (and would therefore be poor during a particular period of time) are not added into the official figures. The Census Bureau projects the total number of people living below the poverty line from the sample basis of only 60,000 households. Probability samples only represent good guesses, not precise data. At the very best, they are statistical artifacts that may or may not accurately reflect the real situation.

Investigations have been conducted regarding whether or not poverty budgets are adequate to purchase the necessities they are supposed to include. One such study found that the given poverty budget for basic items such as food, housing, clothing, and the like covered only two-thirds of the actual costs of these items (Currie & Skolnick, 1988, p. 11).

Conservatives also criticize the official measure of poverty. Basically, they believe the current measure produces an exaggerated number of poor people. They attribute this "overestimation" to the underreporting of income by recipients and the exclusion of the cash value of in-kind benefits (food stamps, Medicaid, housing allowances, and the like) from budget figures. If these items were included, the official number of people living below the poverty line would decrease. The U.S. government computes and publishes estimates of the poverty population which are based on the inclusion of in-kind benefits, as well as estimates of the same population using 125 percent of the current poverty-level budget as their basis. If calculated on what is termed the "recipient and/or cash equivalent approach," which includes the value of food, housing, and medical benefits, the poverty population decreases from 13.6 percent to 11.6 percent of the total population, the equivalent of 5 million people (U.S. Bureau of the Census, 1987, p. 437).

This recipient and/or cash equivalent approach presents a paradox. Regarding the accusations of underreporting, even if they are valid, there is no way to estimate the amount involved. Furthermore, the public generally turns a blind eye toward this same practice when it is engaged in by middle-class and upper-class individuals for income tax purposes, although the amount of lost revenue is probably far greater than what may be lost from any underreporting engaged in by welfare recipients. Even more puzzling is the fact that, according to this approach, people who receive benefits must initially live below the poverty threshold in order to qualify for benefits. However, if the value of the benefits is included when determining criteria for qualification, then 5 million people (who initially met the criteria) will no longer qualify for benefits, because the value of the benefits will raise them above the calculated poverty level. Consequently, those 5 million people will be forced to remain in "official" poverty, with no chance of obtaining assistance from the government to help alleviate their situation or provide them with opportunities to improve their living conditions.

The poverty line must be drawn somewhere. However, if a family earns $50, $100, $1000, or $2500 above the official poverty level, does this mean they are not, in reality, poor? After all, no one would deny that incomes that are only slightly greater than the amount which delineates the poverty threshold constitute "low-budget incomes." The low-budget or near-poor population undoubtedly experiences economic and social insecurity in ways which, if not identical, must be very similar to those who are considered "officially" poor.

There are alternative concepts and definitions of the official determination of the poverty line. Some critics suggest that the poverty line should be designated at one-half of the median family income level. That would put the poverty threshold at approximately $15,000 for a family of four. A closely related approach would be to raise the upper limit of the poverty line by 25 percent, which would increase the amount to $15,843 for a family of four.

According to Bob Cleveland, of the Income Statistics Branch of the U.S. Census Bureau, in 1989 there were 94 million Americans with incomes less than $15,000. In addition, another 11.5 million Americans have incomes between $15,000 and $17,499 (Cleveland, 1990).

TABLE 1.1. Number of Americans below the Poverty Line and Number of Americans with Incomes Less than $15,000

Number in millions	
32.5 million	below poverty line ($12,675 for a family of 4)
94 million	at incomes below $15,000

Source. Bob Cleveland, Income Statistics Branch, U.S. Census Bureau, telephone conversation with the author, December, 1990.

Although the 32.5 million Americans who are below the official poverty line are included among the 94 million with incomes less than $15,000, that still leaves over 61 million Americans with incomes not very far above the official poverty line. These Americans might be called the "near-poor." The proportions of subpopulations among the near-poor—whites, blacks, Hispanics, women, children, and the elderly—remain basically the same as in the poverty population.

2

Who Are the Poor?

It's Not in the Stars

Does poverty randomly afflict just anyone? The answer is an unequivocal no. Some citizens have a much greater probability of falling victim to poverty than others. Undoubtedly, the social class into which an individual is born serves as a fairly accurate predictor of whether or not that person will succumb to a lifetime of economic insecurity. The demographics of the nation's poverty population identify those who are most vulnerable to poverty. Contrary to the prevailing stereotypes regarding the poor, more than 80 percent of the poverty population consists of children (40 percent), the elderly (11 percent), and women (30 percent); and most (77 percent) of the poor live in families (Figure 2.1). Although a disproportionate number of poor Americans are nonwhite, the majority (69 percent) are white. One-sixth of this nation's poor children have at least one parent who works full-time, year-round. Society cannot hold these children responsible for the problems of their parents. Furthermore, those adults who are most vulnerable to economic insecurity—women and the elderly—are entitled to society's assistance when the "safety net" fails.

43

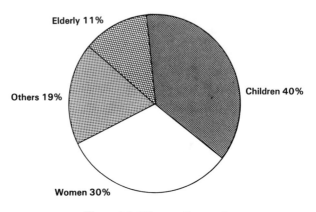

Figure 2.1. Who are the poor?

The Children

Most tragic of all are the children who live in poverty. Billy's story illustrates the appalling influence poverty can have on a child.

When all of Billy's worldly possessions were gathered together, they did not even fill a plastic garbage bag. His father deserted the family when Billy was six years old. Although he had to give up the pet cat he loved so much in order to move into a Seattle emergency shelter, Billy Todd Jr., 15 years old, was dismayed that he and his mother and brother were leaving the shelter. Billy had made friends at the shelter. Mack Litton, an out-of-work welder with a wife and kids of his own, taught Billy how to play ball and became a kind of substitute father to him. Mack described Billy as "a nice, quiet kid . . . a boy who worried whether other people would laugh at him. He didn't have nice clothes, and he had never had a father to teach him how to do things. He didn't know how to throw a baseball or a football right, for example. No one had ever showed him how." The housing Billy's mother found was "nothing more than a shack."

Billy called it a "raggedy house." On the Sunday before they were to leave the shelter and move into the "raggedy house," Billy hanged himself in a closet (Greene, 1989).

In 1990, one out of every five American children lived in poverty. If current trends continue, it is predicted that by the year 2000, one out of every three children will live in poverty. Many other children (15.6 million) live in conditions (25 percent above poverty line) which are virtually similar to the living conditions of the official poor, but they are not technically considered to be living below the official poverty line. A 1990 study, conducted by the National Center for Children in Poverty at Columbia University, examined families with children that were living in near-poverty conditions. The study found that "many of these families have as much difficulty as officially poor families. When we look closely at children living in near-poverty, we find they are often indistinguishable from children living in poverty" (UPI, 1990, April 16).

For minority-group children the situation is even more drastic. An astonishing 43 percent of black and 37 percent of Hispanic children live below the poverty threshold. Eighteen and a half million children live in the central cities; 29 percent of them live in poverty. The majority (71 percent) of poor children live in families with two parents present, and with one or both parents working.

A recent 300-page report by the House Select Committee on Children, Youth, and Families (Report: Children locked in poverty, 1989, October 3) found that children comprise the largest segment of the U.S. poverty population. Among children, the poverty rate has risen from 15 percent in 1970 to 20.5 percent in 1989.

A case in point is New York City. Seven hundred thousand, or nearly 40 percent, of the children in New York City live in poverty (Stein, 1986). According to a story in *The New York Times*,

> The living conditions of tens of thousands of children have deteriorated sharply in the last decade, in neighborhoods scattered across

New York City, where weedy lots flank abandoned buildings, and
broken-down schools, where young crack dealers loiter on many
street corners and few children know what it is like to have two
parents at home (Barbanel, 1989).

Former New York Mayor Edward Koch believes the causes
of New York poverty go beyond the control of the city and are,
to a large extent, the fault of the Republican administration in
Washington, D.C. William J. Grinker, New York City's Human
Resources administrator, estimates that "one-third of the nearly
half-million children on public assistance were living in isolated
pockets of such intense poverty that they are cut off from the
world of work and independence" (Barbanel, 1989).

Current estimates of the number of homeless children in
America range from 50,000 to 3 million. Whatever the exact
number, documentation now exists which indicates high rates
of disease and malnutrition plague homeless children. Also,
learning disabilities among homeless children have been linked
to these conditions (Homeless kids, 1989; United States GAO,
1989, June).

The Women

Over half (58 percent) of all the individuals who are poor
are female. Women comprise the majority (65 percent) of all
adults among the poverty population. Nearly half (48.5 percent)
of the families in poverty have a female head of the household.

Diana Pearce's research on poor women provides an outline
of the distinctive nature of women's poverty. Maintaining that
the poverty of women is "fundamentally different from that of
men," Pearce points out that there are two distinctly *female*
causes of women's poverty:

1. Women overwhelmingly bear the economic as well as

the emotional burdens of raising children when the parents do not live together.

2. Women enter the labor market handicapped by their
   gender, and thus earn considerably less than men
   (Pearce, 1984).

Working women in America, on average, make only 60 percent of what men are paid in almost all professions. Black wom-
en are more likely to be affected by these factors. Furthermore,
the plight of black males in the labor market contributes to the
disadvantaged condition of black women. In "The racialization
of poverty" (1989), Wilkerson and Gresham contend:

> Currently, the most critical problem relating to the plight of
> black unwed mothers is the massive unemployment of the males
> who would otherwise be potential mates for them. . . . In view of
> the astronomical levels of black males who are excluded from the
> labor market, the plight of black children must be examined in light
> of the circumstances of both their mothers and fathers, even
> though the mothers are usually left with the responsibility of car-
> ing for the children after the fathers depart under economic duress
> (126).

The Elderly

In the past, people 65 years old and older—the elderly—
constituted the largest specific age category among the poor.
Over three decades ago, in 1959, the poverty rate among the
elderly was 35.2 percent; today that rate has dropped to a histor-
ic low of 12 percent.

Certainly, cost of living adjustments for Social Security, the
establishment of Supplemental Security Income (SSI) in 1974,
and the expansion of private pension programs have all contributed to the reduction of poverty among the elderly. Nevertheless, some subgroups of the elderly population remain at high

risk for entering the ranks of the poor. Again, gender and race play a role in producing disproportionate rates of poverty in some groups. Among the poor, the percentage of elderly women (15 percent) is almost double that of elderly men (8 percent). Compared to elderly whites, elderly Hispanics are two and one-half times (and elderly blacks over three times) more likely to be poor (Gabe, 1989:29).

Although the number of elderly who live below the official poverty line has dropped, the economic position of millions of America's elderly citizens is, at best, very precarious. In addition to the elderly who fall below the poverty line, another one-fifth of the elderly hover just above it, existing at 125 percent of the poverty threshold.

Representative Edward Roybal, Chair of the House Select Committee on Aging, summed up the conclusions of a study on those elderly who are at risk for descending into poverty due to medical expenses thus:

> In America today, we are finally awakening to the huge financial risk faced by Americans needing long term care. The risk is especially great for the elderly living alone. Unless concrete action is taken quickly, all lower- and middle-income elderly Americans will remain at great risk of impoverishment due to the high and sustained cost of long-term care (Prolonged illness may cause poverty among elderly in U.S., 1987).

Minorities

A popular stereotype depicts most of the poor as nonwhite. Technically, that stereotype is false. The basis for it, however, stems from the fact that a disproportionate percentage of the poverty population is nonwhite. In other words, the majority (69 percent) of poor people are white, yet only 12 percent of the entire white population is poor. On the other hand, 28 percent of the poverty population is black, but blacks make up only 11.9 percent of the entire general population. People of Spanish origin comprise only 6 percent of the general population, but 12.5 percent of the poverty population is Hispanic. These disproportionate differences have persisted since the government began collecting poverty data.

According to the National Research Council report released in 1989, "the economic status of Blacks relative to whites has, on average, stagnated or deteriorated" (U.S. Blacks lag in status, 1989). Citing the decrease in industrial jobs that has had disproportionate impact on blacks, the report goes on to state:

> Under conditions of increasing economic hardship for the least prosperous members of society, Blacks because of their special legacy of poverty and discrimination, are afflicted sooner, more deeply and longer. . . . The status of Black Americans today can be characterized as a glass that is half full—if measured by progress since 1939—or as a glass that is half empty—if measured by the persisting disparities between Black and White Americans since the 1970s. . . . Even though Blacks' real per capita income in 1984 was about six times its 1939 level, their 1984 income is still only 57 percent of white income.

Native Americans

Most contemporary discussions of poverty in the United States omit any reference to the status of Native Americans. Their military defeat and subsequent concentration on "reservations" has forced generations of Native Americans to exist in desperately miserable living conditions.

Even the conservative magazine *U.S. News and World Report* published an article in the early 1980s entitled, "America's Indians: Beggars in Our Own Land" (Huntley and Witkin, 1983). Describing Indian reservations as America's own "Third World," the report went on to state that

> more than 100 years of federal programs have not improved the lives of Indians. . . . After more than a century of federal supervision and dashed hopes, the first Americans find themselves still at

the bottom of the ladder—high in unemployment, health problems . . . low in wealth and education.

Furthermore, sociologist James Vander Zanden observes:

> Native Americans are the most severely disadvantaged of any population within the United States. By adolescence, Indian children show high rates of suicide, alcoholism, and drug abuse. The suicide rate among young people is often more than 10 times the national average, and nearly 50 percent of all young Native Americans have serious alcohol or drug problems (1990: 202).

A 1989 U.S. Department of Commerce study reported that about 28 percent (400,000) of the total Native American population lives below the poverty line, and one-fourth of them still live on reservations. Among certain Native American populations, poverty rates are even higher. For example, within the American Eskimo population living in Alaska, the poverty rate is 31 percent. Recently, while testifying before a congressional select committee on Indian Affairs (United States Senate, 1989), Janie Leask, president of the Alaskan Federation of Natives, remarked:

> Most Alaska Natives live in communities in which the local economies cannot provide a life-sustaining standard of living without substantial on-going public subsidies. . . . What is clear from all of this is that there has been a fundamental failure of public policy toward Alaska Natives and rural Alaska (13).

In Cedar City, Utah, where I presently live, there is a Paiute Indian reservation with approximately 162 residents, 75 percent of whom live below the poverty line. As of October 1989, the unemployment rate among these people was 57 percent, and the median family income amounted to $6736.

The Working Poor

Some people distinguish between what they term the "deserving poor" and the "undeserving poor," a distinction based on whether or not the poor person is working or willing to work. The person who works full- or part-time is often regarded more sympathetically by society and considered to be more "deserving" of assistance than a poor person who is unemployed. In the United States, approximately 9 million people could be classified among the working poor. Of these working poor, 2 million work full-time, an increase of 50 percent since 1968. Although the majority of the poor are children, women, and the elderly, 60 percent of able-bodied, poor adults work full-time, part-time, or seasonally (Whitman et al., 1988:19).

Even among the homeless, research demonstrates that a significant minority work full- or part-time. For example, a major study of the homeless in Los Angeles, which has one of the largest homeless populations in the United States, reported that 6 percent worked full-time and 14 percent worked part-time (Ropers, 1988: 43). The *New York Times* reported a similar finding in an article titled "In affluent towns the working poor are filling shelters" (Loecher, 1990). Pam Hyman, director of the Operation Hope shelter for the homeless in Westport, Connecticut, described the new type of clients she is admitting to the shelter: "We've noticed we're getting more people who are working. About half the men at our shelter work" (Leocher, 1990).

During the last decade, the number of people who work, yet remain poor, has burgeoned; this fully discredits the common, comfortable stereotypes often used to depict the poor. Furthermore, from 1979 to 1984, 60 percent of all new jobs that were created payed less than $7000 a year, suggesting the causes of poverty are not to be found in the personal characteristics of those who are poor, but reach far beyond their control.

The Rural Poor

Poverty remains a predominantly urban problem, if for no other reason than the fact that 75 percent of the general population lives in urban areas. Rural poverty, however, is becoming a growing concern. Indeed, the poor, inner-city black represents another common stereotype of American poverty. Yet, the poverty rate in America's rural areas is as great as that in the central cities, and 50 percent higher than that of the entire urban population (O'Hare, 1988). In the late 1980s, 17 percent of rural Americans lived below the official poverty line. These statistics indicate a reversal of the 20-year trend toward declining rural poverty and increasing urban poverty. One out of every four children in rural America lives in poverty. Again overrepresented, blacks constitute 44 percent of the rural poverty population. This fact contradicts the stereotype that black poverty is a problem that is confined to the inner cities.

According to a report by the Center on Budget and Policy Priorities, one-fourth of the rural poor live in the Midwest, more than one-third in the South, 14.5 percent in the West, and less than 7 percent in the Northeast. Also, the rural poor, when compared to the urban poor, are more likely to be elderly, employed, and live in families with two parents (Report: 17% of Rural Americans live below poverty line, 1989).

By the year 2000, the number of American farms will be reduced to 1.25 million, a reduction of approximately half the current number. The mid-1980s witnessed one of the most severe farm crises since the Great Depression of the 1930s. As the *New York Times* put it:

> Economic problems of a size not seen by generations of Americans are wrenching farm life and rural communities across the country's principal food-producing regions. Evidence is mounting that fear and despair are spreading among hundreds of thousands of farmers who are looking at losses of millions of acres, farms either already lost or likely to fall into the hands of creditors soon. (Robbins, 1985)

Despite the large amount of media attention given to the farm crisis in the mid-1980s, the driving forces behind increased rural poverty are found primarily in the nonfarm sectors. Because the farm population represents less than 10 percent of the total rural population, the current economy of rural America depends heavily on nonagricultural industries. Service and trade industries offer the majority (63 percent) of job opportunities in rural areas, and the remainder are found in industries such as forestry, fisheries, mining, manufacturing, and construction. The following three factors, which are related to the latter industries, have contributed to increased rural poverty: declining population growth, rising unemployment, and diminishing incomes.

Representative George Miller of California, Chair of the House Select Committee on Children, Youth and Families, which held hearings in 1989 on the issue of growing poverty in rural America, summarized the committee's findings this way:

> In hundreds of small towns and rural communities, economic insecurity plagues millions of hard working families. . . . And in addition to the economic costs, the social costs they bear are eroding families and communities alike. . . . People are working but need some partial assistance to bridge the gap. (Hawkings, 1989).

3

A Tale of Two Countries

According to an article in *Psychology Today,* the criminal activities of some super-rich business tycoons are often motivated by the "thrill of peak performance" (Landi, 1989:28). Convicted Wall Street inside stock trader Ivan Boesky and young millionaire Martin Siegel, also convicted for insider trading, serve as *Psychology Today's* examples of "Type T" (thrill-seeker) personalities. The article maintains that Boesky and Siegel broke the law not for the mere acquisition of wealth but for the excitement of beating the system. As psychoanalyst Abraham Zaleznik explains, "It's the artistry, more than the desire for monetary gain, that provides the fuel." Perhaps an appropriate label for this genre would be "con-art."

Zaleznik further explains that Boesky and company violated the law "in pursuit of their own peculiar genius." Psychologist Frank Farley adds, "If you do things strictly according to law, you will not do many creative things. . . . It just so happens they're doings things that are negative." The *Psychology Today* article suggests that this thrill seeking by the criminal super-rich may be inborn, and possibly gives them a "benign high" (Landi, 1989, p. 28).

This same article also describes the personalities and behavior of the noncriminal rich by citing examples like Donald Trump, who "epitomized the more-more-more mentality of the '80s." In addition to thrill-seeking genes and personalities, social climate plays a role. Described as the "roaring '80s," the Reagan years will be remembered as a time when it was, "not only okay to be rich: it [was] okay to flaunt it." This spirit is symbolized by the release of a new board game, modeled on Monopoly, called Trump the Game; the objective of which is to beat your competitors and win all the money.

Somehow, when applied to welfare mothers and some of the homeless who violate the law, these same explanations appear less valid. In 1984, I appeared in court as an expert witness on behalf of Penny Benjamin, a homeless, unemployed housekeeper. Ms. Benjamin had been accused of habitating in a vehicle, a violation of Los Angeles Municipal Code 85.02. Based on the psychological research presented in *Psychology Today*, perhaps I should have testified that Ms. Benjamin had a "Type T" personality—the result of an inherent thrill-seeking condition which forced her to manifest an artistry for creative adventure by living a homeless lifestyle and sleeping in her truck. Sounds pretty ridiculous, doesn't it? Actually, I testified that she was a victim of large economic and social forces beyond her control which caused her to be unemployed and homeless. She was found not guilty on the basis of necessity.

Why does the thrill-seeking explanation sound more plausible when applied to the super-rich who violate the law, but not to the poor? Not too long ago, *Fortune* magazine ran a story titled "Toward Two Societies," which maintained that "the gap between rich and poor is wider mainly because the poor don't have the tools they need" (Burck, 1988). It is difficult to imagine any other explanation regarding the growing chasm between the haves and the have nots from a magazine like *Fortune*. American society subscribes to the cultural mythology that the wealthy somehow are more virtuous, more industrious, and more intelligent than everyone else. After all, isn't their wealth a product of their character? Nonetheless, a growing body of evidence suggests that the rich are getting richer and the poor are getting poorer due to large-scale political, economic, and social transformations that are occurring in the United States, not because of the unique features of any group or class of individuals.

The Concentration of Income

During the nine-year period between 1978 and 1987, the bottom one-fifth of the population's share of income declined by 8 percent, while the share of income earned by the top one-fifth of the population increased by 13 percent. One disturbing aspect of this growing inequality is that it mainly impacts people with jobs (Reich, 1989). Real income (adjusted for inflation) for nonsupervisory workers was lower in 1987 than it had been in any other year since 1966. Also, almost 60 percent of the people who were living below the official poverty line had at least one family member who was working full- or part-time.

Many Americans would like to think that the United States is not as stratified as other industrialized nations. However, a study conducted by the World Bank that compared the proportion of income received by the bottom one-fifth of the population in each of the leading 17 noncommunist industrial countries shows otherwise. The study found that the bottom one-fifth of the U.S. population receives a lower proportion of income than does the corresponding segment of the other nations' populations (Farley, 1990:240).

Robert Reich, writing in *The New Republic*, suggests that while the "economic recovery" of the late 1980s was good for those at the top, it wasn't very good for those at the bottom. He explains:

> So when General Motors, say, is doing well, that probably is good news for a lot of executives in Detroit, and for GM shareholders across the globe, but it isn't necessarily good news for a lot of assembly-line workers in Detroit, or anywhere else in America (Reich, 1989: 26).

Numerous government reports fully document the gross discrepancies in the distribution of income in the United States. Table 3.1 illustrates the distribution of pretax income by dividing the population into fifths. Keeping in mind that the median U.S. family income is about $30,000, the bottom fifth of the population receives only 3.8 percent of the total U.S. income, while the top fifth receives 46.1 percent of all income. The second fifth (from the top down) receives 24 percent of all income, the third fifth receives 16.4 percent, and the fourth fifth receives 9.7 percent (U.S. Department of Commerce, 1988, December: 5). However, by increasing the focus on the top fifth, we find that the very top 5 percent of that category receives nearly 17 percent of all income. In other words, 5 percent of one-fifth of the population receives more income than does the entire bottom 40 percent of the population.

When we examine the distribution of income among whites, blacks, and Hispanics (Table 3.2) we find, not surprisingly, that over half of both the black (60.4 percent) and Hispanic (53 percent) populations fall into the lowest and second lowest categories, while only a little over one-third (37.6 percent) of whites fall into these same categories.

TABLE 3.1. **Distribution of Income before Taxes in the United States**

Income share (%)	Households
46.1	Top fifth
24.0	Second fifth
16.4	Third fifth
9.7	Fourth fifth
3.8	Bottom fifth

Source. Based on *Measuring the Effect of Benefits and Taxes on Income and Poverty: 1986* (1988, December). Washington, D.C.: U.S. Department of Commerce, Bureau of the Census.

TABLE 3.2. **Pretax Income by Population Fifths and Race**

	White (%)	Black (%)	Hispanic (%)
Lowest fifth	18.1	37.6	28.3
2nd fifth	19.5	22.8	24.7
3rd fifth	20.5	17.5	20.4
4th fifth	20.5	13.5	15.6
Top fifth	21.3	8.7	11.0

Source. Based on *Measuring the Effect of Benefits and Taxes on Income and Poverty: 1986* (1988, December). Washington, D.C.: U.S. Department of Commerce, Bureau of the Census.

In a summary of the shifts of national income from the poor, the working people, and the middle class to the rich during the decade between 1980 and 1990, The National Coalition for the Homeless reported the conclusions of an August 1990 Congressional Budget Office study:

> [T]he gap between the very rich and other Americans has become so great that the richest 2.5 million Americans will have nearly as much after-tax income in 1990 as the 100 million poorest Americans. At the same time, the share of the national income going to middle-income Americans has fallen to the lowest level since the end of World War II. . . .
>
> Between 1980 and 1990, households in the top one percent of the population will receive an average increase of more than $90,000 in capital gains income, after adjusting for inflation. Those in the bottom 90 percent of the population, on the other hand, will receive an average increase in capital gains income of just $12 over the same period (Safety Network, 1990: 1).

The Concentration of Wealth

The Joint Economic Committee of the U.S. Congress (1986) compiled a study on the concentration of wealth in the United

States over a twenty-year period. The study described the distribution and concentration of wealth in America by dividing the population into four segments. For purposes of description, the four groups were designated as (1) "the super-rich" who make up 0.5 percent of American households; (2) "the very rich" who make up an additional 0.5 percent; (3) "the rich" who constitute 9 percent; and (4) "everybody else"—the bottom 90 percent of the population (U.S. Congress, 1986, July).

This congressional report defined wealth as "stored-up purchasing power." Wealth can be measured "by the value of what could be purchased if all of a family's debts were paid off and the remaining assets turned into cash" (p. 5). Therefore, homes, cars, appliances, saving accounts, corporate stocks, real estate, and the like can all be considered different forms of wealth. Again, as is true with income, the distribution and concentration of wealth in the United States is extremely unequal.

The very top one-half of one percent of the population (about 420,000 households)—the super-rich—owns 35 percent of the nation's wealth; the average value of the wealth of each one of these households amounts to $8,851,736. Excluding the equity from personal residences, the super-rich own 45 percent of the wealth, which includes 58 percent of unincorporated businesses, 46.5 percent of personally owned corporate stock, 77 percent of trusts, and 62 percent of state and local bonds (p. 23).

Much media attention has focused on Donald Trump lately (especially since he and his wife Ivana separated), which has provided the public with glimpses into the lifestyles of the super-rich. The Trumps epitomized what sociologist Thorstein Veblen once called the "conspicuous consumption" of the wealthy. *People* magazine summed it up as follows:

> In a decade of glitz, they were the glitziest; in a decade of
> greed, they were the greediest: He the scrappy investor who made
> a fortune wheeling and dealing real estate, she the gregarious,
> Czech-born outsider who charmed and clawed her way into New

> York's most refined social circles. . . . So when, only six weeks into 1990, Donald and Ivana Trump announced they were calling off their 12-year marriage, it seemed the perfectly scripted end to a decade of flash and cash. In a fitting coda, a few days later Drexel Burnham, the brokerage house whose junk bonds had fueled the '80s with gushers of debt, declared bankruptcy. The Age of Trump seemed over, and a shaken New York peered curiously at the wreckage.

The congressional study concluded that the second one-half of the top one percent (another 420,000 households), the *very rich*, were found to be "decidedly less well off" when compared to the super-rich. The average very rich families held net assets ranging from $1.4 million to $2.5 million, which amounts to only one-fifth as many assets than the super-rich hold. When viewed in the context of overall national wealth, the assets of the very rich account for only about 7 percent of the national wealth, compared with the assets of the super-rich, which total approximately 35 percent of the nation's wealth.

About 7.5 million households make up the next 9 percent of the population—the *rich*. The rich own another 30 percent of all American wealth with the average value of their wealth amounting to $419,616. Therefore, 72 percent of the net wealth of all American families is owned by 10 percent of the population, the super-rich, the very rich, and the rich. Everyone else, the remaining 90 percent of families, owns only 28 percent of the nation's wealth. The average household value of their wealth amounts to only $39,584. And if home equity is excluded from these calculations, we find that the combined amount of wealth owned by 90 percent of American families equals a mere 16.7 percent of the nation's wealth (U.S. Congress, July 1986).

It must be added that the people at the very bottom of the current American stratification system own literally zero income or wealth. The U.S. stratification system is not one of moderation or of degrees. The discrepancies between income and wealth groups are dramatic and extreme.

What About Welfare for the Rich?

One factor that certainly contributes to the increased disparities in income and wealth in the United States is the inequity in the tax system. Citing a Congressional Joint Committee on Taxation report that indicates 83 percent of the benefits of President Bush's 1990 capital gains tax cut proposal would reduce taxes only for those people who make $100,000 or more, Representative Dan Rostenkowski, Chair of the tax-writing House Ways and Means Committee, asked, "Where is the economic justice in that?" (Zaldivar, 1990). Bush wanted to lower the capital gains tax from 28 percent to 15 percent, but Congress did not go along with him.

In 1981, when Reagan cut taxes and increased tax shelters for the rich, the concentration of wealth accelerated. A tax study prepared by the Congressional Budget Office in 1990 revealed that in the decade between 1980 and 1990, the real income of the poorest one-fifth of the population dropped by 3 percent, but the net federal tax rate for this income group increased by 16 percent. Meanwhile, the richest one-fifth of the population, with an average pretax income of $105,209, experienced a 32 percent increase in real income, and a 5.5 percent cut in their tax rate (Zaldivar, 1990).

Tax rates have a significant impact on altering the distribution of income. As Table 3.3 indicates, the disproportionate burden of taxes imposed on the bottom three-fifths of the population decreases their share of the total national income. However, the income share, after taxes, of the top one-fifth of the population actually increases to over 50 percent, while the income share of the second one-fifth remains the same. These shifts in the tax rates, which in effect redistribute income in favor of the rich, continue despite tax reforms that were implemented in 1986. Economist Ravi Batra aptly summarized the consequences of the 1986 tax reforms:

> In the so-called Tax Reform Act of 1986, tax shelters were virtually annihilated, but the top tax rate affecting the richest households

TABLE 3.3. Distribution of Income
Less Federal Taxes in the
United States

Income share (%)	Households
50.6	Top fifth
24.4	Second fifth
15.7	Third fifth
8.2	Fourth fifth
1.1	Bottom fifth

Source. Based on *Measuring the Effect of Benefits and Taxes on Income and Poverty: 1986* (1988, December). Washington, D.C.: U.S. Department of Commerce, Bureau of the Census.

came down from 50 percent to 28 percent—a 44 percent reduction in the marginal rate. Ostensibly, the law also dramatically benefited the poor, because several million penurious families were removed from the tax rolls. But this was and is a smokescreen without which the law itself would not have passed. Taxes rose sharply for corporations, which always pass them on to those who buy their products, and the vast majority of such buyers are lower-income individuals. Once again the rich came out ahead in the tax revision of 1986, while others were fooled by the seeming drop in their tax bill (1988:229).

The results of a 1989 Gallup Poll indicate that many Americans perceive the tax system as being unfair, despite the 1986 tax reforms. Asked if there was an equitable distribution of the tax load among all taxpayers, only 13 percent of the respondents believed the tax system was fair (Gallup, 1989).

There is also another way that taxes benefit the well-to-do. This is done through their ownership of corporations which receive government subsidies. In his article, "Corporate welfare state is on a roll" (*Los Angeles Times*, 1990, March 5), Ralph Nader contended that:

> From bailouts to outright giveaways and from military procurement fraud to bloated subsidies, our national government has

become a golden accounts receivable for hordes of organized, corporate claimants who lobby daily to get something for nothing or a lot for a little. . . . Hundreds of billions of dollars in taxpayer assets have been squandered. It is time to give taxpayers the means to correct these injustices. After all, they pay the bills.

Examples of these types of government handouts are:

1. *Bailouts.* Over the last two decades major bailouts have included a $250 million Lockheed loan guarantee, a $1.5 billion Chrysler loan guarantee, a half-trillion-dollar savings and loan bailout, and a $100 billion nuclear weapons waste cleanup for Du Pont and Rockwell.

2. *Resource Depletion.* Use of public lands for nominal fees by the mining, timber, and oil industries. Corporate farms and ranches use public lands and pay rock-bottom leasing fees.

3. *Taxpayer-Funded Research and Development.* Corporations often benefit from free or minimal cost research, which is funded by government departments or government-subsized firms. For example, the drug AZT which is used in the treatment of AIDS was developed by the National Cancer Institute (NCI) with taxpayer dollars. NCI then granted the drug company Burroughs Wellcome, Inc., an exclusive patent to market AZT without requiring the company to pay the government a dime for the free research and development that NCI conducted. Furthermore, between 1982 and 1987, federal and state government agencies paid Burroughs Wellcome, Inc., $2.4 billion when they purchased the AZT from them.

Possible Consequences of the Concentration of Wealth

Batra has written two significant books (1987, 1988) on the relationship between the increasing concentration of wealth and increasing poverty. His study of the concentration of wealth in America concludes that the current period is characterized by one of the highest concentrations of wealth in U.S. history. The only other period in U.S. history when the concentration of wealth at the top equaled that of today's occurred in 1929, just before the Great Depression. In 1929, the top one percent of the population owned 36 percent of the nation's wealth; currently, the top one percent of the population owns as much or more of the nation's wealth.

The acceleration of the concentration of wealth that began in the early 1970s has been accompanied by increasing numbers of Americans falling below the poverty line along with growing masses of homeless. Economic recovery and prosperity in the mid-1980s appears to have been measured by the rich getting richer and the remainder of the population being left further and further behind. Between 1973 and 1986, the number of poor Americans increased by 33 percent, while the amount of wealth owned by the top one percent of the population grew from 24.9 percent in 1969 to 36 percent in 1987. Indeed, there is some indication that the rate of concentration of wealth increased during the latter part of the 1980s. The number of billionaires in the United States in 1985 totaled 14. However, that number increased to 49 billionaires, or 250 percent, in 1987 alone (Batra, 1988:233). Consequently, the extreme ends of the stratification system polarized, and the middle class shrank.

As Batra sees it, the increasing concentration of wealth causes the "number of persons with few or no assets" to rise. Thus, more poverty and homelessness is a direct consequence of the concentration of wealth. But just as significant is the negative impact of wealth concentration on the entire economic and social structure.

Batra lists what he calls the eight "dire consequences" of wealth concentration as follows:

1. It creates business takeovers and monopolies and hence destroys free enterprise.
2. It hurts incentives to work and increases speculation.
3. It increases domestic debt.

4. It raises interest rates.
5. It creates a trade deficit.
6. It creates a shaky banking system.
7. It eventually leads to depressions.
8. It is usually a prerequisite for violent upheavals (1988: 235).

Batra argues that corporate concentration may be fatal to the financial system, because it limits competition and creates monopolies that "usually charge higher prices for often inferior products." Without competition there is no motive for the workers employed by a monopoly to work efficiently, or to produce quality products (1988:236). As the upper classes increase their wealth they become more willing to engage in risky, speculative investments. A prime example of this type of speculation is corporate raiding. Motivated by the possibility of gaining large profits quickly, raiders stimulate "wealth disparity without generating any increase in goods and services that would be of public benefit" (p. 238). Evidence of this type of activity was brought to the public's attention with the collapse of the Wall Street investment house of Drexel Burnham Lambert.

Time magazine called the collapse of the 152-year-old investment house the "predator's fall, marking the end of a money-mad era" (February 26, 1990). Under the direction of Michael Milken, who was then under a "98-count fraud and racketeering" indictment, Drexel Burnham Lambert led Wall Street in the pursuit of superprofits through the promotion of "junk bonds"—very risky investments that yield high profits. As *Time* described it:

> Thanks in part to Drexel, the 1980s became the decade of the deal. In 1986 alone, 3,973 takeovers, mergers, and buyouts were completed in the United States, at a record total cost of $236 billion. While some takeovers shook up overly complacent managers and led to useful restructuring, much of the raiding served only to distract corporate America from its real work of improving products and services. . . . The resulting riches created a whole new spending culture as Wall Streeters found new ways to dispose of

their wealth, buying multimillion-dollar Manhattan apartments, building lavish estates in Connecticut and on Long Island, commuting to work in limos, seaplanes, and helicopters. (p. 47).

As a result, the majority of Americans (63 percent), according to a *Time*/CNN poll, have little or no trust that Wall Street bankers and brokers do what is best for the country (p. 47).

Wealth inequality has direct and indirect links to growing domestic debt. The combined debt of consumers, corporations, and government (about $6.5 trillion) is the highest it has ever been in U.S. history. The government's debt results largely from expenditures for social service programs to aid the poor and on defense spending. This government spending has not been matched by a sufficient intake of taxes, especially taxation of the well-to-do. As an increasing proportion of the population faces tough economic times, people tend to borrow more, thus increasing the consumer debt. Corporate takeovers and mergers increase corporate debt.

Interest rates are determined "in the market of loanable funds." Simply put, as wealth inequality increases, those in the lower stratum of the income and wealth distribution scale have a greater need to borrow money, resulting in a greater demand for loans. When demand is greater than supply, interest rates go up (Batra, 1988:247).

The trade deficit, which is the difference between what it costs foreign consumers to purchase products that are manufactured in America compared to the prices Americans pay to purchase imported products, "crossed the $100 billion mark for the first time in history" (Batra, 1988:252).

The epidemic of bank failures demonstrates another consequence of the extreme concentration of wealth. In 1980, ten banks failed; in 1988, the number rose to 200. How does the concentration of wealth relate to bank failures? As the wealthy increase their bank deposits, banks become more willing to lend money in order to increase their return on investments. Those borrowing from this increased pool of deposits, however, represent a disproportionate number of people who come from the lower end of the wealth and income distribution scales and, therefore, stand a greater probability of defaulting on their loans. Thus, the domino effect comes into play—with an abundance of money to invest, banks become willing to make risky loans that result in a higher percentage of defaults and, ultimately, more bank failures.

All of the above factors lead to the possibility of a severe recession or even a major economic depression. Batra argues that, because of the exaggerated concentration of wealth, the United States is racing toward economic and social disaster in the 1990s.

With an epidemic of social problems ranging from domestic violence to the plague of gang and street violence, American society is already tremendously strife-torn. Batra also warns that violent upheavals by the have-nots have often been triggered by extreme discrepancies in wealth. Difficult as it may be to imagine, if the United States experiences a severe economic depression in the latter part of the 1990s, we cannot afford to dismiss the possibility that increased frustration over finances among growing numbers of citizens could result in mass violent upheaval.

An example of the incipient violence of the have-nots was indicated in a report by *Time* magazine:

> Mesmerized by the prospect of a business boom that could produce thousands of new white-collar and service jobs, Milwaukee's civic leaders never gave much thought to the possibility of civil unrest. So it came as a shock when Alderman Michael McGee proclaimed earlier this month that he was forming a Black Panther militia that would resort to "actual fighting, bloodshed, and urban guerrilla warfare" unless the city did more to improve the lot of impoverished African-Americans. Inner-city blacks, warned McGee, were fed up with white officials spending money on shopping malls and skyscrapers while prosperity passed them by. "It's been 25 years since Martin Luther King, and things have gotten worse for black people," said McGee, "I'm not going to let it go any further than this" (Gwynne, 1990:26).

4

Those at the Very Bottom

The New Homeless

The emergence of millions of homeless Americans has rendered all prior discussions, debates, and controversies regarding the poor, poverty, and welfare obsolete.

Prior to the mid-1980s, homelessness was considered an emergency situation—by definition, short-term. However, since then, for the poor and the nation, it has graduated from an emergency to a long-term crisis. The homeless have become the most conspicuous among the poor. According to a *New York Times* poll, 76 percent of those who live in big cities "said they see the homeless on their daily routine." The majority of those polled (65 percent) supported increased government spending to help the homeless, and a half said they were willing to pay $100 more a year in federal taxes to aid the homeless (Toner, 1989).

A subsequent *New York Times*/CBS survey, conducted in January 1990, showed a dramatic 10 percent increase in the number of Americans who believe that homelessness is the most important problem currently confronting the nation (The homeless: A growing priority, 1990).

"Homeless people are not wanted in our country," eu-

logized the Reverend George Kuhn at the funeral of an uniden-
tified homeless man who was murdered by Rodney Sumter, a
New York City subway passenger. While on a subway platform,
Sumter beat a homeless person, who had spat on him and
punched him on the head, to death. Social commentator Myron
Magnet stated in the *New York Times:*

> How many subway riders, wary of the deranged homeless who
> make the subterranean world so menacing, have not fantasized
> responding to assault with violence? (Painton, 1990:15).

What kind of society have we become? Apparently homelessness, the most vivid and cruel form of poverty, has become a
painful daily reminder of some of the hideous social and economic contradictions in American society of the 1990s. The most
recent and valid research demonstrates that the majority (80
percent) of the homeless are not chronically mentally ill, drug
addicts, or derelicts (Ropers, 1989). Rather, they represent the
victims, or fallout, of an increasing polarization in the American
stratification system. And now the homeless face double jeopar-
dy. First, they have already fallen victim to large-scale social and
economic transformations that are beyond the control of any
single individual. Second, they are becoming the victims of the
anger and frustration of middle-class citizens who must walk
around, over, or past homeless Americans who beg for money
in the streets, public buildings, and transportation centers.

A familiar and pervasive feature of the nation's urban landscape, homelessness is, in a sense, becoming institutionalized in
America. Those in power basically dismiss the problem as one of
the individual pathology of bums, nuts, drunks, dope addicts,
and the lazy. Former New York City Mayor Edward Koch told
New Yorkers to stop giving money to homeless beggars because
he believed that many "just don't want to work for a living"
(Painton, 1990:14). According to *Time* magazine:

> People who maybe a year ago would simply have walked away
> really snap back at panhandlers and homeless people who are

acting aggressively," says Robert Kiley, chairman of the Metropolitan Transportation Authority. "Just in the past four or five
weeks, I've seen a couple of near physical confrontations." Peter
Harris, the MTA's director of research, says his "eyes kind of
bulged" in October as he listened to the complaints of subway
riders who participated in a focus group. One woman said, "I've
spent my whole life in New York, I've grown up on the Upper West
Side, and I consider myself a liberal. But I'm sick and tired of
feeling guilty." Says Harris: "This thing has really turned" (Painton, 1990:14–15).

Of course, middle-class citizens should be disturbed by this
manifestation of poverty. However, the homeless, regardless of
how they became that way, are also U.S. citizens and are entitled to the rights inherent within that citizenship. Perhaps the
blame for poverty as manifested in homelessness does not belong to any one group of citizens, but should instead be placed
on misguided political priorities and long-term contradictions in
the economy and the low-income housing market.

How Many Millions?

In 1984 the Department of Housing and Urban Development (HUD) conservatively estimated, from a highly flawed
study (Appelbaum, 1988), that only 250,000 people were homeless. By 1989, HUD increased its homeless estimate to 600,000.
Advocacy organizations for the homeless, on the other hand,
maintain that, on any given night, 3 million people are homeless. Although it is difficult to arrive at an exact number of
homeless during a specific amount of time, the average 30 percent yearly increase in the demand for emergency shelter indicates the magnitude of this tragedy. A 1989 report issued by
Partnership for the Homeless in New York City, based on a
survey of 46 cities, found that between January 1988 and April
1989 the national homeless population grew by 18 percent. Sixty
percent of the cities included in the study reported that the lack

of affordable housing was the major cause of homelessness, followed by unemployment and underemployment (UPI, 1989, October). Another national study by the National Coalition for the Homeless, also released in October 1989, revealed that "homelessness is a growing problem across the nation. No corner of America is untouched by the problem of homelessness." (UPI, 1989, October, 5).

In some cities like Los Angeles, where the homeless problem is massive, researcher Paul Tepper has identified the magnitude of the problem as follows:

> At least 100,000 and as many as 160,000 people were homeless for some period in Los Angeles County between July, 1988 and June, 1989. This figure, which is far above previous estimates, is based primarily upon an analysis of State of California Department of Social Service and L.A. County Department of Public Social Service statistics for the target period.
>
> These numbers do not include:
>
> - the estimated 40,000 families living in garages in the City of Los Angeles.
> - the tens of thousands of individuals sleeping on the couches of friends and family.
> - the families and individuals who are doubling or tripling up in apartments designed for far fewer and the people living in substandard apartments throughout the County.
>
> Nor do they include:
>
> - the estimated 150,000 Los Angeles City households who are paying 50% to 90% of their income for housing. This population is merely "one personal crisis" away from being on the streets (Tepper, 1990 & Stewart, 1990).

Can the U.S. Census Count of the Homeless Be Valid?

No one came to Byron Case's place to count him for the 1990 census. It bothers him. "I think I deserve to be counted. Maybe I don't deserve anything else, but I deserve to be counted," he said.

> Earth Day 1990 came and Case did what he always does for the
> environment—but not intentionally. He went through the garbage
> looking for food to eat. He collected aluminum cans and sold them
> (Christian, 1990).

Byron is one of the homeless the U.S. census missed. He lives in a tent in a wooded area just outside of Provo, Utah.

The federal government's 1990 census count included an attempt to count the homeless with the consultation of prominent sociologists like Peter Rossi. Rossi was considered to have done "important beginning work" on the methods of counting the homeless, according to U.S. Census Bureau official Cynthia Taeuber (Taeuber, 1990, June 21). Census counts of various populations are potentially significant in terms of determining the distribution of government funds to meet the needs of communities. Attempting to arrive at an accurate count of the U.S. homeless population is worthwhile, if the attempt is conducted objectively.

Advocates for the homeless, however, hold the Republican administrations partially responsible for the homeless problem, and contend that they cannot be objective in conducting a count of the homeless. To quote the late homeless advocate Mitch Snyder, "I think it is politically naive not to understand that coming in with a small number is going to be misused. It's going to be used to try and drive down appropriations" (AP, 1990, March 20).

In New York City, critics of the attempt to count the homeless "call it poorly designed and doomed to undercount the homeless." According to Associated Press information, "City officials and advocates for the homeless have a long list of complaints about the count's timing, organization, the data to be collected and the recruitment of people to do the counting" (AP, 1990, March 12).

But the Census Bureau has already offered a disclaimer:

> "We are deliberately staying away from defining this as a census of
> the homeless," said Kenneth Meyer, assistant census regional man-

ager. "Nor are we saying that we expect to get a 100 percent count
of the homeless. It's going to give us some idea of the characteristics of this group but not necessarily the true size of it" (AP,
1990, March 12).

If the purpose of the census count of the homeless is not to
obtain accurate figures, then millions of tax dollars are being
wasted because hundreds of valid scientific surveys of who the
homeless are have already been concluded.

It is difficult not to suspect the objectivity of Homeless Census consultant Rossi's social science methodological skills and
his ideological biases. His previous studies of the homeless in
Chicago have been discredited by other social scientists due to
his methods, his blaming the victim interpretations, and his
ideological biases. Rossi (in collaboration with James D. Wright)
concluded in a previous study that the city of Chicago had an
estimated homeless population of only 2000 to 3000 people, a
range far below even the conservative and flawed HUD study's
estimate of 20,000. Rossi's low numbers were based on two samples of homeless people. One sample, collected in the fall of
1985, contained only 23 homeless individuals; the other, collected in the winter of 1986, contained only 30 homeless individuals! (Rossi & Wright, 1986). Maintaining that only the "literally homeless" should be counted, Rossi limited his search for
Chicago's homeless population to shelters and individuals who
were in the streets between the hours of 1:00 and 6:00 AM, and
who admitted to being homeless.

Since Rossi was a key consultant to the 1990 U.S. Census
count of the homeless and the author of two different, but frankly redundant, books on the homeless which were based essentially on his Chicago study (1989a, 1989b), it is worth the effort to
examine in more detail his past work on this issue. Professor
and Chair of the Department of Sociology at the University of
California, Santa Barbara, Dr. Richard P. Appelbaum (1986)
summarized the flaws of the Rossi/Wright study:

I believe there are two major flaws with this approach. First is the assumption that people interviewed were forthcoming in telling whether or not they were homeless. It should be recalled that only about one in ten of those who were at all willing to talk admitted to being homeless. What were the other nine doing on the street between 1:00 and 6:00 AM? Is it not possible that at least a few of them were also homeless but understandably reluctant to admit being so to their early morning interrogations? And what of the people who refused to be screened at all [79 percent of those approached]? Isn't it likely that most if not all of these were homeless?

These questions are important, since when you are projecting from a base of only 20–30 people, another 20–30 who somehow escaped your net will double your total projection. For example, if we assume that half of those who refused to be interviewed were homeless, and that half of those who claimed they were *not* homeless were lying to the interviewers, then the fall projection nearly triples—from 2,300 to 6,300. If we assume that 90 percent of those encountered were in fact homeless, regardless of what they said or didn't say to the interviewers, then the total more than quadruples to 10,000. The point is that given such a minuscule number of people who make up the baseline for the projection, tiny fluctuations in the number of homeless encountered will produce enormous differences in the citywide total.

This raises the second problem with the study, by now familiar to us; the definition of homeless. The Chicago study's definition excluded people in rooming houses, SRO's, jails, halfway houses, and detoxification centers. It did not survey people riding the buses and trains, an important haven for homeless people in Chicago, especially in the winter. It could not account for those who saw the interview team approaching and left the block. And it declined to define as homeless those who were temporarily sleeping in other people's homes (Appelbaum, 1986: 7–8).

One can only wonder how accurate the 1990 census count of the homeless was when influenced by the likes of a partisan such as Rossi.

Another problem with Rossi's work on the homeless is the conservative ideological use to which it has been put. William Tucker, an analyst for the right-wing think tank, The Cato Institute, based in Washington, D.C., uses Rossi's research to support blaming the victim explanations of homelessness, i.e., explanations that blame homeless individuals for their own condition (see Chapter 6). For example, Tucker writes:

> Rossi speculates that the increasing failure to form families among blacks has led to an increase in both male and female homelessness.
>
> The profile developed by Rossi appears quite accurate from anecdotal experience. The homeless, he said, are people who have exhausted the patience and resources of family and friends, either through their long dependency or anti-social behavior. Family break-up and high levels of drug use and alcoholism among low-income blacks have also obviously played a part (1990: 31).

In late 1986, I had the opportunity to meet Rossi and discuss the homeless problem with him during a conference on the homeless crisis which was held at George Washington University in Washington, D.C. When the issue of the political policies of the Reagan Administration was mentioned as at least having contributed to the increase in homelessness, Rossi emotionally and vehemently argued that the idea that politics played any role in aggravating the homeless crisis was ridiculous. I wondered then, as I do now, just how nonpartisan and methodologically objective Rossi is.

Rossi's collaborator, James D. Wright, also authored two short books on homelessness and a score of articles which have influenced the social science literature on the topic. Citing Rossi's study, Wright believes the best estimate of the number of homeless in Chicago is about 3000 persons (1987: 9). And like Rossi, Wright appears to focus on the alleged characteristics of homeless people as an explanation for their condition. Wright says, for example, that homeless people "do not maintain 'normal' levels of contact with other persons," and their unemployment status is often the result of "physical, mental, and social disabilities as well as from inadequate 'work motivation' " (1987:8). Rossi and Wright's writings have reinforced negative stereotypes of the homeless and obscured the social, economic, and political causes of this terrible American tragedy.

Social Science Hoax

It took years to undo the damage caused by those who, in the early 1980s, initiated and perpetuated negative stereotypes of the homeless. The prevailing stereotype that all of the homeless were "lazy, crazy, drunk, and doped" has been replaced by the recognition that the majority of the homeless are just like other Americans who are down on their luck. The attempts by some psychiatrists to "medicalize" a complex social, economic, and political problem such as homelessness constitute one of the social "scientific" hoaxes of the latter part of this century (see Chapter 6 for a more detailed discussion). By contending that the majority of the homeless were deinstitutionalized mental patients or individuals who should be institutionalized, some psychiatrists became unwitting pawns in President Reagan's ideological game (Farr, 1982; Lamb, 1984; Bassuk, 1984; Torrey, 1989). Throughout his presidency, Reagan attempted to whitewash the homeless crisis by attributing it to the mental disorders or "free choices" of homeless individuals (Homeless by choice? 1987; Toner, 1989). Contrary to administrative opinion, research has revealed that, although all homeless people suffer from the psychological distress of not having jobs and homes, the vast majority are not former mental patients nor do they need to be institutionalized (Ropers, 1988).

The fact that a disproportionate number and, in many cities, a majority of the homeless are black, Hispanic, or Native American raises some very significant questions about the status of race relations in this country. Nevertheless, the racial character of the homeless population is frequently ignored during discussions about the causes of homelessness.

In response to the homeless crisis, more emergency shelters, soup kitchens, and indigent medical clinics have been opened; more volumes of research documents have been produced; and more congressional hearings regarding the issue have been held than at any time since the Great Depression of the 1930s. However, it required the organizational and public relations skills of homeless advocates, coupled with the political organizing, demonstrating, and lobbying by the homeless themselves, to generate enough public and political concern before the "band-aid" programs currently aiding the homeless were implemented.

Unfortunately, the attempt by conservatives to stigmatize the homeless as predominantly alcoholic and drug addicted continues into the 1990s. *U.S. News & World Report* published a major story entitled, "The return of skid row: Why alcoholics and addicts are filling the streets again" (January 15, 1990), in which it claimed that almost half (44 percent) of the homeless were substance abusers and that the personal pathologies of the homeless were largely responsible for their homelessness. It is certainly true that many of the homeless use and/or abuse substances, but U.S. News did not mention that, among the general population, one-third of those who drink alcohol are "heavy drinkers." The issue of cause and effect was also neglected. It simply is not logical to argue that substance abuse alone causes anyone to become homeless; after all, 95 percent of the alcoholics in the United States have jobs and homes.

The facts are, as most valid research studies indicate, that the majority of the homeless are minority-group members of the working or lower classes, and are victims of job and housing discrimination, a lack of low-income housing, unemployment and underemployment, and government policies and corruption (Ropers, 1988; Ropers, 1989; General Accounting Office, August, 1989; U.S. House of Representatives, 1985).

Other studies also indicate that as the number of American farms declines, the number of rural homeless people increases. In a *New York Times* article entitled, "As farms falter, rural home-

TABLE 4.1. A Select Comparison of Rural and Urban Homeless in Utah and Ohio

Characteristic	Utah		Ohio[c]	
	Rural[a]	Urban[b]	Rural	Urban
Age				
40 years or younger	—	—	72%	60%
60 years or older	—	—	5%	7%
Mean age	34 years	35 years	—	—
Gender				
Male	82%	78%	68%	84%
Female	18%	22%	32%	16%
Race				
White	82%	87%	92%	59%
Black	5%	13%[d]	6%	35%
Hispanic	4%	—	2%	4%
Native American	9%	—	—	1%
Other	—	—	—	1%
Employment status				
Unemployed, but looking for work	77%	67%	62%	44%
Veteran				
Yes	34%	29%	24%	33%
Receiving public assistance				
Yes	11%	8%	61%	40%

[a]Data from intake forms of the Cedar City Iron County Care and Share shelter, January–September 1987, while under the author's management. Sample size 104. Analyzed with the assistance of Dr. Oakley Gordon, Southern Utah University.
[b]From a personal memo to the author from Judith T. Maurin, R.N., Ph.D., Professor and Associate Dean for Academic Affairs, University of Utah, and coauthor of *Utah's Homeless: Preliminary Report*. Salt Lake City, UT: Mayor's Task Force for the Appropriate Treatment of the Homeless Mentally Ill, June 1986.
[c]Ohio, *Homelessness in Ohio: A Study of People in Need*. Ohio Department of Mental Health, Office of Program Evaluation and Research, 1985. Sample size 979.
[d]All nonwhites combined.

lessness grows" (Wilkerson, 1990, May), Bill Faith, head of the Ohio Coalition for the Homeless, stated:

> Rural homelessness is growing faster than we can keep track of it. . . . People are living in railroad cars and tarpaper shacks. Shelters in tiny towns we've never heard of are operating at or above capacity and are turning people away (Wilkerson, 1990:A1).

Dr. Fredric Solomon of the National Academy of Sciences views the increase in rural homelessness as caused by downturns in farming and related businesses. He states, "Rural homelessness is a more clearly economically caused homelessness" (p. A14). The rural homeless population is composed not just of dispossessed farm families but also of migrant farm workers and workers in farm subsidiary industries who are out of work because of the economic down-turn of American farming. The rural homeless are basically similar in their characteristics to the urban homeless. When compared to the national homeless profile, however, in most cases, there are fewer non-whites among the rural homeless (see Table 4.1).

Homelessness: The American Nightmare

Despite the enormous increase in the number of emergency shelters in the past few years, some of our most impoverished citizens literally live and sleep in streets and alleys. Americans are accustomed to the "third world" homelessness in places like India and various African and Latin American countries. But, unquestionably, there now exists a "third world" American poverty.

As the decade of the 1990s began, The National Coalition for the Homeless published a research document, *American Nightmare: A Decade of Homelessness in the United States* (1989, December), which was based on a survey of the homeless problem in 26 cities. It summarized the highlights of the homeless crisis in the 1980s and gave a prognosis for the 1990s. The document concluded:

> Once perceived to be exclusively the plight of substance abusers, homelessness is now widely viewed as an extension of poverty in the United States, and a complex problem requiring a more comprehensive solution. . . . One alarming finding of the survey is that not only are current housing needs not being addressed, but the rate of homelessness in most cities is growing. . . . Virtually every community reported that its housing needs were increasing. In most urban and rural communities the waiting list for public housing or rental assistance (known as Section 8) are often years long.

A case in point regarding the condition of the homeless and the status of emergency shelters is the situation in Los Angeles. Based on a study by Shelter Partnership, Inc. (1989, October), Los Angeles shelters operate at 100 percent capacity, and each shelter averages over 13 turnaways every night. The total average number of turnaways throughout Los Angeles is at least 1800 individuals a night! The majority of the shelter operators (73 percent) believe "that the need for their services will increase in the coming year and that homelessness is increasing; not one shelter said that homelessness is on the decline" (p. 4).

As for the causes of increasing homelessness in Los Angeles, the report concluded:

> The overwhelming number of shelters cited increasing poverty (92%), lack of low cost housing (85%), inadequate public financial resources to support needed services (85%), and lack of adequate public assistance (79%) as the reasons for increasing homelessness (p. 4).

Despite the increasing demand for emergency shelter, 33 percent of the shelters "were actually forced to cut back or close programs due to lack of adequate funding" (p. 5).

The McKinney Act

The Reagan Administration resisted every attempt by the federal government to assist the homeless. This policy was based on the insistence that homelessness is a manifestation of individual pathology and essentially a local problem. Although every local community has its own local homeless population, the national economic and social trends and policies which have produced homelessness have been firmly documented (Ropers, 1988). Late in his presidency, Reagan finally gave in to congressional pressure and reluctantly signed into law the McKinney Act of 1987, which provided limited funding for various programs designed to aid the homeless.

However, even with Bush's more sympathetic position on the homeless crisis, government bureaucrats left over from the Reagan Administration found various ways of crippling the release of funds for homeless programs. More interested in enhancing Reagan's image on social issues than in implementing programs, some HUD bureaucrats actually impeded the distribution of McKinney funds. In 1987, Title 2 of the McKinney Act established the interagency Council on the Homeless. This council replaced the Federal Task Force on the Homeless that had been created by the Department of Health and Human Services in November 1983. The interagency Council, which included representatives from all eleven cabinet posts, was designed to coordinate all federal programs and activities relative to the homeless problem. There is evidence, however, that the council failed to facilitate state and local government access through the maze of McKinney Act red tape (Green, 1989).

On March 5, 1989, the United States General Accounting Office released the testimony that John M. Ols, Jr., Director of Housing and Community Development Issues, gave before a House subcommittee. Regarding the efforts of the Interagency Council on the Homeless, Ols stated:

In summary, our work to date indicates that the Council has been slow to react to what the Congress said was an immediate and unprecedented homelessness crisis. In fact, the Council did not start to fully function until approximately June 1988—almost one year after its creation—and never has been fully staffed. Although the Council has engaged in numerous activities to meet the requirements of the McKinney Act, such as the issuance of annual reports and newsletters, these efforts have been largely inadequate and ineffective. The Council's most recent annual report did not make any recommendations as to the level of federal assistance needed to address the problem of homelessness; thus its usefulness to the Congress is limited.

In addition, the Council has not successfully met its requirement to disseminate information regarding McKinney Act programs to state and local providers of homeless assistance, possibly precluding providers from receiving federal assistance. Further, although more than a year and a half has passed since its creation, the Council still has not developed detailed policies and guidance to direct its activities (United States General Accounting Office, 1989).

The HUD Scandal

During his presidential campaign, Reagan launched an attack on government waste, fraud, and abuse. Nevertheless, by mid-1989 evidence revealed that, while a record number of Americans were homeless, the cabinet-level agency Housing and Urban Development (HUD) (whose task it is to oversee housing issues) was the most fraudulent and corrupt of all the Reagan agencies. When Inspector General Paul Adams compared the findings of his investigation with the Pentagon procurement scandal investigation, he released the names of several former top-level HUD officials, and those of some top Reagan Administration officials, who had been raking in big profits from their involvement in awarding contracts for the rehabilitation of subsidized housing for the poor (Welch, 1989).

The investigation discovered that favoritism and insider information had been used to direct HUD awards for the rehabilitation of 35,780 low-income housing units over the five-
year period from 1984 to 1988. Consultants, who charged fees
up to $1.3 million, included James Watt, former interior secre-
tary; John Mitchell, Nixon's attorney general; Edward Brooke, a
former senator; and Louise Nunn, a former governor. One HUD
official, while commenting on former government officials making big bucks, remarked, "You come in here and work for a few
years and then get out and make millions in mod-rehab" (Welch,
1989). *Time* magazine put it this way:

> If you can't kill a Government program, why not milk it? . . .
> The most effective way to get a housing project approved under
> President Reagan's HUD Secretary, Samuel Pierce, was for the de-
> veloper to hire a prominent Republican as a "consultant" and pay
> him a substantial fee (It's who you knew at HUD, 1989).

Time summed up the scandal thus: "HUD took care of the
greedy instead of the needy."

Does Rent Control Cause Homelessness?

In 1990, the ultraconservative CATO Institute published *The
Excluded Americans: Homelessness and Housing Policies,* by William
Tucker. Without a doubt, this book is one of the most blatant
right-wing ideological tracts regarding the subject of homelessness. Writing from the perspective of the "landlord class,"
Tucker shamelessly attempts to reduce the many complex factors that cause homelessness down to one—rent control. According to Tucker, rent control puts the landlord class out of the
business of creating "housing opportunities."

Tucker uses a statistical technique called "regression" to
attempt to demonstrate that rent control is the only variable that
has a significant "correlation" to homelessness. The regression
charts he presents (which, as he states, are based on the regres-

sion analyses someone else ran for him) correlate, one by one, various factors including unemployment and poverty rates, the rate of public housing, race, rent control, and so on with homelessness. Out of a host of possible factors that were run through several regression analyses he eliminated all, except rent control and median house price, as contributing to homelessness. To the individual not trained in elementary statistical techniques, these regression charts undoubtedly appear impressive. However, his method of proving the landlord class's position is seriously flawed.

Regression analysis, or any other statistical technique, is not a magic wand that turns any data into scientific truth. Regression, as well as any other statistical technique, is only as good as the quality of the data put into the model. The first mistake in Tucker's strategy is his measure of the rate of homelessness for various cities. The basis for the rate of homelessness that he correlates with other variables in each of the regression analyses is derived from the highly flawed 1984 HUD study. HUD's methodology has been thoroughly discredited elsewhere (Appelbaum, 1988) by competent social scientists. For example, Tucker claims there are only 525 homeless people each night in Salt Lake City, Utah. But I live in Utah and am a member of the Utah Governors' Committee on the Homeless. Thus, I know from firsthand experience that 500 homeless people receive emergency shelter every night at the Traveler's Aid Shelter alone, which is just one of several shelters in Salt Lake City. Furthermore, the number of homeless in Salt Lake City who are turned away because the shelters are filled are evidence of an even higher number of homeless.

Tucker's sample of cities used to study the relationship of homelessness to rent control was not randomly selected and, therefore, violates one of the most elementary requirements of inferential statistics (statistics that attempt to generalize information which is gained from samples onto entire populations). Without some type of random selection, statistical findings—no matter what they reveal—cannot be considered valid. Tucker found no significant correlations between homelessness and factors like poverty, unemployment, race, and housing availability because these factors were also measured and analyzed incorrectly.

Tucker finds no "correlation" between the rate of homelessness and rates of poverty and unemployment in various cities because the overall poverty or unemployment rate of a particular city cannot be properly compared to a presumed rate of homelessness. All demographic studies on the characteristics of homeless populations clearly demonstrate that homelessness does not randomly affect just anyone located anywhere in a city. Again, certain demographic groups, members of the working and lower classes, minority groups, the poor, and the unemployed are disproportionately represented among the homeless. Tucker, or whoever ran the regression analyses for him, should have measured the correlation of the unemployment and poverty rates for working- and lower-class blacks and Hispanics with each specific group's rate of homeless. If he had, he would have found, as the author did (Ropers, 1988), that homelessness is indeed "correlated" with poverty, unemployment, and race.

Finally, and most curious of all, is the fact that Tucker used only nine cities to correlate rent control with the rate of homelessness, but he used numerous cities to correlate the rates of the other various factors.

Since Tucker provides the raw data of the various regression models presented in his book, it was possible to reanalyze them and see if his presentation and interpretations were accurate. With the collaboration of Professor Oakley Gordon, psychologist and statistician at Southern Utah University, Tucker's data on the rate of homelessness in various cities and its relationship to the different variables, such as, unemployment, race, rent control, housing value, and the like were reanalyzed in a "forward stepwise regression" (see Figure 4.1). Tucker had incorrectly analyzed each variable separately with rate of home-

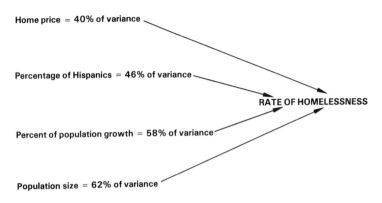

Figure 4.1. Stepwise regression.

lessness. He should have analyzed all the possible "predictors" of homelessness simultaneously in what is called a multiple regression, which would have demonstrated the relative contribution of each variable to the prediction of homelessness. Basically, the statistical technique of stepwise regression selects from a group of variables the ones that are the best predictors of the main variable under consideration, in this case a city's rate of homelessness. The results of the reanalysis of Tucker's data indicate that rent control is not a predictor of homelessness; instead, the best predictors are median home prices, the percentage of Hispanics, the percent of growth in a population, and population size. A city's median home price was the strongest predictor of homelessness, accounting for 40 percent of the variance in the rate of homelessness. This makes good sense and matches the findings of the majority of studies on the causes of homelessness. It is the lack of low-cost housing and not the lack of housing in general which is the leading factor causing low-income people to become homeless. It follows, therefore, that the higher the median home cost in a particular city, the more likely it is that that city will have a higher rate of homelessness. The next contributing variable is the percentage of the population that is Hispanic. This variable combined with home price accounts for 46 percent of the variation in homelessness. This also makes sense, since all homeless populations are disproportionately nonwhite. The percentage of population growth of a city contributes another 12 percent of the variance and, combined with home price and percentage of Hispanic residents, explains 58 percent of the variance in homelessness. Finally, city population size combined with the other three variables accounts for 62 percent of the variance of homelessness. These findings are not surprising. Large and increasing populations in an area produce greater competition for available housing and low-cost housing in that area, thus increasing the probability of homelessness. When rent control was added to the other predictor variables, it only contributed less than one percent to the explanation of the variance in the rate of homelessness. This reanalysis completely refutes Tucker's claim that rent control is the leading cause of homelessness.

Free Enterprise Zones?

In an era dominated by a "me first–get rich" mentality, the tragedy of homelessness has revived awareness of the "other America," which is characterized by poverty and deprivation. Even the Bush Administration has acknowledged the magnitude of the homeless crisis and has made a limited attempt to address the issue.

Ironically, Bush's appointment of archconservative Jack Kemp to head HUD turned out to be an improvement over the Reagan Administration's approach to homelessness and poverty. Kemp adheres to the dogmatic ideological position that "enterprise zones"—areas targeted for job creation and investment through tax abatement—are the ultimate solution to poverty and homelessness.

Institutionalizing Homelessness

Prompted by advocates for the homeless, it took nearly a decade before Washington seriously acknowledged the reality of the homeless crisis and initiated modest programs to help. The result, however, can only be described as the "institutionalization" of homelessness. Although emergency programs have provided much needed immediate aid, they have also had the effect of making homelessness a permanent feature of American society. The root causes of homelessness—the crisis in low-income housing stock, the deindustrialization of U.S. industry, and high underemployment, to name a few—have not been dealt with effectively. And the fundamental long-term economic, social, and political processes that have polarized the socioeconomic structure of America remain in place. Instead of implementing programs that address these basic issues (for instance, mandating construction of permanent low-income housing on a national scale), the government's response, though well intended, has contributed to the institutionalization of homelessness.

For example, in May 1988, New York City's welfare hotels housed over 3350 homeless families, including 7400 children. In 1987, New York City spent $81 million on welfare hotel payments. The city paid an average daily hotel room rate of $65, or about $2000 per month. Families stayed an average of 13 months in these hotels. Some families, however, have stayed for up to three years. Obviously, those who benefit most from welfare monies used to house the poor are the private owners of these hotels. In New York, the federal government matches Aid to Families with Dependent Children (AFDC) and Emergency Assistance (EA) funds by about 50 percent. Funding from both of these agencies contributes to the payment of welfare hotel rates. According to the U.S. General Accounting Office:

> Fraudulent schemes and violations of procurement laws have been found by local audit agencies examining fiscal matters relat-

ing to hotel use. For example, almost 17 percent of checks New York City issued in September 1986 to families for emergency hotel shelter were cashed by the hotels even though the families were not registered at the hotels for the periods the checks covered. This was reported by the New York City Comptroller's Office in January 1988. Projecting the results of their random sample to a full year, the auditors estimated that checks totaling almost $1.4 million were issued to families who were not registered. Either hotels are cashing checks for families without providing rooms, the report concluded, or providing rooms without registering families, then substituting the check for cash received from other nonwelfare families to reduce reported revenues for tax purposes (January 1989:33).

This method of sheltering the poor and homeless is obviously wasteful and inefficient. Permanent low-income housing at "fair market rents" would cost taxpayers much less. Four areas—New York City; Westchester County, New York; Essex County, New Jersey; and Washington, D.C.—compared the price of emergency housing in hotels with the price of rent for existing two-bedroom houses. It currently costs taxpayers about 300 percent more to shelter the homeless in hotels than it would to provide them with permanent low-income housing. Furthermore, the condition of these welfare hotels and the services provided, if any, are usually inadequate and often criminal. Deficiencies in security, plumbing, heating, and sanitation are often found in such places. Thus, the process of institutionalizing homelessness through emergency housing not only avoids any real solution to the problem but is also an incredibly expensive and foolish social policy.

Discussion

The reality of homelessness has led to a new look at the causes and nature of American poverty in the 1990s. Homelessness, in many cases, is such a brazen and cruel form of deprivation that few individuals voluntarily choose it, and most do everything they possibly can to avoid or get out of it. It can no longer be said that America's poor are more affluent than people in third world countries. To the contrary, desperate third world poverty currently exists in America.

Almost a century ago Robert Hunter, while writing about America's homeless, summarized the major causes of homelessness that still seem to persist today:

> So long as the wages of certain classes of workmen are only sufficient to keep them during the period when they are employed, so long as there is an ebb and flow of industrial activity, so long as certain trades employ men at certain seasons only, so long as those who close the factories continue to have no responsibility for the outcast workers, so long as the laws of competitive industry make industrial depressions necessary, and so long as the system of industry demands a surplus of labor which may be but casually employed, so long indeed, as there is such a thing as enforced unemployment—just so long will the sources of vagrancy be ever active (1904:139).

The emergence of homelessness in the 1980s and its continued growth in the 1990s raise serious questions regarding the soundness of American economic and social structures, and require a new focus on the causes of poverty and its victims.

5

Welfare

Not Even Treating the Symptoms

> I'm a little discouraged and irritated at the welfare-recipient fami-
> lies growing in size all the time and those of us who work and pay
> taxes all the time having to pay for them. . . . It is far better to
> prevent a person from coming into the world unwanted and facing
> a bleak future. That is really not fair to the child. . . . Requiring
> sterilizations, abortions, or other forms of birth control could ac-
> complish two things: It would keep some people off welfare and
> break the continuing cycle. . . . We've got generation after genera-
> tion on welfare.

So stated Hilmar G. Moore, chairman of the board of Human
Resources and Mayor of Richmond, Texas. Moore chaired the
agency which administered welfare programs in Texas during
1980 (Sterilizations urged to cut welfare cycle, 1980, February 28).

Michael Milken, an employee of the investment firm of
Drexel Burnham Lambert, received $554 million in salary and
bonuses in 1984–1986 and $550 million in 1987. In early 1989
Milken was indicted by a federal grand jury on 98 felony courts
of stock manipulation, insider trading, and racketeering. If convicted he could be sentenced to 520 years in prison (Taking it all
back, plus interest, *Time*, April 10, 1989, p. 42). Ultimately,

Milken pleaded guilty to six felonies, agreed to pay $600 million in fines, and was sentenced to ten years in prison (Guest, 1990). No subsequent articles appeared urging that dishonest stockbrokers and their families be sterilized.

Why does society direct these vehemently hostile reactions and biases toward welfare recipients and not toward corrupt stockbrokers? Surely, the cost to taxpayers of prosecuting one individual like Milken, whether he is innocent or guilty, amounts to significantly more than the amount that would be lost in tax dollars due to the combined cheating of a thousand welfare recipients!

Perhaps the stereotypes regarding welfare recipients remain pervasive partly because of statements made on the subject by some prominent politicians. As far back as the mid-1960s, when Ronald Reagan was campaigning for governor of California, he commented, "From now on the able-bodied will work for their keep or take job training to fit themselves for jobs, and there'll be no pay for play." Later, in his state inaugural address, he said:

> But we are not going to perpetuate poverty by substituting a permanent dole for a paycheck. There is no humanity or charity in destroying self-reliance, dignity, and self-respect . . . the very substance of moral fiber (Quoted in Feagin, 1973: 5).

One of the legacies Ronald Reagan left for the 1990s was the enactment of new "workfare" rules for welfare eligibility. The workfare rules reflect Reagan's philosophical stance on welfare. In his 1986 State of the Union message, Reagan argued that many of America's leading domestic problems—increasing crime, child poverty, the breakdown of family values and structure, and the weakening of American education—were the result of a "welfare culture."

Over a two-decade period, from 1968 to 1988, federal expenditures for various welfare programs increased (in constant

1988 dollars) from $51.7 billion to $147.9 billion. But, as a result of Reaganite reforms, per capita spending on welfare after 1981 fell 3 percent. For the first time since 1973, welfare spending failed to keep pace with inflation (Burke, 1989: 5).

One of the major Reaganite reforms of the welfare system, which was enacted into law during the 1980s, was the 1981 Omnibus Budget Reconciliation Act (OBRA). OBRA essentially tightened eligibility criteria and placed special restrictions on the earned income of applicants. Because of the new criteria, by mid-1984, at least 442,000 families were taken off of AFDC. The Congressional Research Service, in summing up the goals of Reagan's reforms, stated:

> The general thrust of the 1981 welfare changes was to concentrate benefits on those with lowest incomes. Thus, the new law lowered income ceilings for some benefits; reduced benefits for those with earnings, virtually ending financial incentives for work by AFDC recipients and reducing them for food stamp enrollees; imposed new categorical eligibility limits; required (or permitted) States to count more of an AFDC family's potential income as an offset to benefits. In reference to work incentives, it stressed work requirements, authorizing States to require able-bodied recipients without young children to work off their AFDC and food stamp benefits or to establish alternate AFDC work programs. In nutrition programs, Congress delayed several cost-of-living adjustments that would have increased benefits (Burke, 1986:10).

Nevertheless, in 1988, despite all attempts to get people off welfare, the federal government spent $173 billion on social relief programs—an amount equal to 3.6 percent of the gross national product and an all-time record! Yet today, despite these huge expenditures, there are more poor Americans, on and off welfare, than there were before the "Reagan revolution."

When we probe beneath all the rhetoric and stereotypes surrounding welfare, we discover a reality quite different from the popular images. A 1988 cost-of-living study conducted by the New York State Department of Social Services found that the welfare benefits of 1.3 million New York state residents would have to be raised 30 percent in order to meet their minimum needs. That increase, however, would bring the benefit levels up to only 98 percent of the poverty threshold (Barbanel, 1988).

Nationally, hundreds of thousands of people who are eligible for welfare or Medicaid benefits are denied assistance because their applications are entangled in bureaucratic red tape. A study sponsored by the Southern Governors' Association and the Southern Legislative Conference found that 26.7 percent of those who apply for welfare are turned down.

Although the percentage of children living in poverty in New York City rose from 25 percent in 1975 to 37.5 percent in 1987, welfare benefits fell more than a third (Barbanel, 1989). As reported in the *New York Times*, "In 1975, a combination of food stamps and welfare benefits brought a typical family of four to 116 percent of the poverty level. By last year [1988], it had dropped to 83 percent."

Conservatives often complain about welfare abuses, but there is much evidence to support the claim that most of the abuse occurs in the administration of welfare programs rather than in the recipients' use of welfare.

What Is Welfare?

Four major welfare programs account for over 60 percent of government spending on welfare. In addition to these four, a variety of 66 other less extensive assistance programs exist. The four major welfare programs are called "means-tested," meaning that recipients must prove that they lack the means to support themselves. All welfare programs can be divided into two categories: (1) cash payment programs and (2) noncash assistance programs.

Cash Payment Programs

The two major cash payment programs are Aid to Families with Dependent Children (AFDC) and Supplemental Security Income (SSI). Approximately 11 million persons in about 4 million families receive AFDC. The federal government assumes the cost of about 54 percent of AFDC expenditures; the remaining 46 percent is covered by the individual states. In fiscal year (FY) 1988, for example, the total AFDC bill amounted to $16.6 billion, of which the federal government paid $9.1 billion.

According to the Congressional Research Service, eligibility criteria for AFDC include:

1. A parent is absent from home continuously.
2. Families must be "needy" by State standards and must meet a test of counted resources, established by the States within outer Federal limits. State need standards for an AFDC family of three persons ranged in January 1989 from $218 per month in Kentucky to $1169 in Maine.
3. Federal law requires almost all able-bodied AFDC recipients to register for training and employment services (which may include job search for no more than 8 weeks per year) unless they are school children or mothers of preschool children. States also may require AFDC applicants to engage in job search. Effective October 1, 1990, the Family Support Act requires States to replace the Work Incentive (WIN) work and training program with the JOBS, an education, work, and training program (Burke, 1989:55–56).

As of January 1989, AFDC payments for a family of three ranged from a low of $118 per month in Alabama to a high of $809 in Alaska.

The other major cash assistance program, Supplemental Security Income (SSI), provides monthly payments to the "needy aged, blind, and disabled persons," enabling them to come up to the federal poverty level. The federal government pays 78 percent of the $14 billion cost of SSI benefits that go out to 4.5 million recipients. Average benefits payments in 1989 were $197 to the aged, $319 to the blind, and $306 to the disabled (Burke, 1989: 61).

Noncash Welfare Programs

Most recipients of AFDC and SSI also qualify for Medicaid. The federal government matches, by "means of a variable matching formula," the cost to the states of medical services to the needy. Two categories of recipients currently in use are the "categorically needy" and the "medically needy."

The categorically needy recipients of Medicaid are in general persons who have qualified for either AFDC or SSI. The medically needy are those with incomes slightly above the poverty line, but with medical bills that would put them below it. Medicaid costs for FY 1988 were $54.3 billion (Burke, 1989: 34).

Food stamps are the other well-known noncash benefits. They are redeemable for food for individuals and families whose incomes amount to 130 percent of the poverty line. The Congressional Research Service describes the benefit levels as follows:

> The Food Stamp Act specifies that a household's maximum monthly food stamp allotment shall be the cost of a nutritionally adequate low-cost diet, as determined by the U.S. Department of Agriculture's Thrifty Food Plan, adjusted periodically (each October) for changes in food prices, and increased by certain percentages set forth in law. A participating household's actual monthly allotment is determined by subtracting, from the maximum allotment of its size, an amount equal to 30 percent of its counted monthly income, on the assumption that it can afford to spend that amount of its own income on food. Minimum benefits for households of one and two persons are legislatively set at $10 per month; minimum benefits for other household sizes are generally somewhat higher (Burke, 1989:89).

There are approximately 19 million food stamp recipients, and each recipient averages approximately $50 a month in food stamp benefits.

Further on in this chapter, examples of barriers in the administration of localized welfare programs, especially cash assistance and housing allowances, will be highlighted.

Who Are Welfare Recipients?

The demographics of the welfare population are, as one might expect, similar to the demographics of the poverty population. Remember, over 80 percent of the poor are children, women, and the elderly. The pattern is similar among welfare recipients.

A U.S. Department of Commerce report, issued in 1989, documented the characteristics of persons receiving benefits from major assistance programs during a 32-month period. The major assistance programs referred to in the report were (1) AFDC, (2) general assistance, (3) SSI, (4) Medicaid, (5) federal food stamps, and (6) federal and state rent assistance. Eighteen percent of Americans received some form of major assistance during the 32-month period.

Women made up the largest category of welfare recipients. One-fifth of all women, regardless of age, benefited from one or more of the major welfare programs. This high percentage of women receiving welfare reflects the disproportionate percentage of women among the poverty population, and is due also to the fact that poor women are likely to live in a family with no husband present. The poverty rate for persons in a family without a spouse is four times higher (34.6 percent) than for persons (7.1 percent) in married couple families.

Race was also found to be strongly related to receiving welfare. Almost half (48.5 percent) of those who received some form of welfare in the 32-month study were black.

When grouped by age, children under six were the most likely (30.1 percent) beneficiaries of one form of welfare or another, while among all children under 18 years old, 27 percent benefited from welfare. Persons 65 years or older amounted to 18 percent of the recipients.

Welfare: Perpetuating or Alleviating Poverty?

Charles Murray, in his controversial book, *Losing Ground* (1984), argues that welfare is responsible for perpetuating poverty. According to Murray, welfare has created an underclass which has become dependent on welfare for generation after generation, especially among blacks. He contends that the welfare underclass is trapped in a vicious cycle of unemployment, undereducation, and unwanted pregnancies because its members are content to live off of taxpayer dollars. Between 1950 and 1980 federal welfare spending was increased and eligibility criteria were "liberalized." The attempts may have been well intended, but the result was that "we tried to remove the barriers to escape from poverty, and inadvertently built a trap" (p. 9). Says Murray:

> It is indeed possible that steps to relieve misery can create misery. The most troubling aspect of social policy toward the poor in late twentieth-century America is not how much it costs, but what it has bought (1984: 9).

Although it is statistically true that over the last 20 years there has been an increase from 15 percent to 25 percent of AFDC recipients who remain on the program continuously for at least five years, the majority of AFDC recipients stay on the program three years or less (O'Hare, 1987:7). A disproportionate number of long-term AFDC recipients are indeed young unmarried black women and children, but this is the result of changing demographics and employment opportunities in the black inner-city communities (this issue will be explored further in Chapter 7), rather than the result of some kind of moral pathology which leads to laziness and welfare dependency.

Los Angeles: A Case Study in the
Failure of Public Welfare

An aspect of the "widening gap" between the rich and the poor in Los Angeles is the way the welfare system deals with the poor and homeless. The following account is based on my direct, personal experience with this issue while I was a consultant for the Legal Aid Foundation of Los Angeles.

One of the persistent problems of the welfare system is its inability to provide effective assistance to those in need. Indeed, some evidence exists that certain rules for welfare eligibility and maintenance may actually contribute to making and keeping people poor. As Robert Chaffee, former director of the Bureau of Assistance Payments, Los Angeles County Department of Public Social Services, put it, "The welfare application process . . . was designed to be rough. It is designed, quite frankly, to be exclusionary" (Rensch, 1986). Due mainly to lawsuits against the Los Angeles welfare system, some reforms have been implemented to meet the needs of the poor. Some of the litigation involved the failure and, in some cases, the unwillingness of one of the largest local welfare administrations in the nation, the Los Angeles County Department of Public Social Services (DPSS), to provide various forms of welfare to those in need. While my direct experience with the Los Angeles welfare system took place in the mid-1980s, updates for 1990 have been provided. The cases presented here offer tragic examples of welfare programs that fail to meet the needs of the poor, and that actually contribute to the increase of poverty.

The Los Angeles County DPSS has a cash welfare program called General Relief (GR). Currently, the GR basic allowance is $312 for one person living alone and $504 for two people living together (Fast, 1990). This welfare program is intended for destitute individuals who are ineligible for other cash welfare programs. According to a study by the Los Angeles County DPSS, the typical male employable recipient of General Relief is a 37-

year-old black who "most likely turned to General Relief due to lay-off or expiration of unemployment benefits" (Los Angeles County, 1983). In conjunction with GR, there is a "60-day penalty" stipulation intended to provide GR applicants with "incentive" and "to encourage self-respect and self-reliance and to develop and maintain good work habits." Individuals in the process of applying for or receiving GR could be placed on the 60-day penalty (during which time they are denied GR benefits) as punishment for various infractions of welfare regulations, or for disobeying the oral directives of welfare workers. Being late for or missing an appointment with a case worker, not completing the required 20 job searches per month, "tardy" documentation, and refusal to take an assigned work project constituted some of the grounds for being placed on the 60-day penalty. In 1985, a lawsuit was filed against Los Angeles County (Bannister, 1985) that claimed the GR 60-day penalty provision actually caused some poor people to become homeless. According to the Legal Aid Foundation of Los Angeles, in that same year, an average of 2500 people a month were placed on the 60-day penalty.

Rather than providing GR applicants with "incentive," encouraging "self-respect and self-reliance," and developing and maintaining "good work habits," Legal Aid argued that the reality of putting someone out on the streets for 60 days did nothing for the individual's work ethic. To the contrary, implementation of the penalty actually reduced a person's chances of finding employment and permanent shelter. The suit resulted in a court order demanding that Los Angeles County be more prudent and selective in its implementation of the policy. However, as of February 1990, the 60-day penalty remains in effect (Fast, 1990). And, according to one Legal Aid attorney, about 4000 individuals "at any one time" remain on the 60-day penalty (Blasi, 1990).

In another lawsuit involving General Relief (Blair, 1985), it was alleged that the monthly GR allowance of $228 (of which

$143 is supposedly allotted to housing) was insufficient to secure the basic necessities of life in Los Angeles, and resulted in "enforced homelessness" for thousands of GR recipients. Evidence was submitted that demonstrated that no housing of any kind was available in Los Angeles for $143 a month. Consequently, many homeless GR recipients had to utilize the nonhousing allotment to supplement the $143 housing allotment. By doing so, they were using up the remainder of their $228 allowance, which was intended for other necessities. As a result of the Blair suit, Los Angeles County was ordered to raise its GR monthly allowance from $247 to $312, effective July 1, 1987.

The experience of one GR recipient, Henry Clark, is typical of the Catch-22 situation confronting many welfare clients:

> I am 47 years old. I have lived in Los Angeles County for 17 years. For years I worked as a journeyman carpenter. I belonged to Local 1437 of the Carpenter's Union. I worked as a framer. In 1980, I developed a blood clot on my brain. I had to have surgery on my brain. I have had seizures ever since. I have been receiving GR checks for about a year now. I get $228 per month. Right now I'm staying at the Union Rescue Mission. I've got a bed there for five nights. Before that, I was sleeping in the plastic chairs in the Chapel at the Union Rescue Mission. The last real place I had to stay was the Bixby Hotel. The monthly rent there is $225. The weekly rent is $60 a week. It costs three or four dollars to cash my check, so I never had enough money to pay for a full month. The only other place I've had this year was a hotel in Compton. The rent there was $225 a month. I've looked as hard as I can to find a place I can afford. I've looked in Compton. I've looked in Long Beach. I've been all over Skid Row. The cheapest place I ever heard of was $195 a month, but it was gone by the time I got there.
>
> For the last three or four months, I've been homeless for at least part of each month, because I can't afford to pay the rent any place. I also need money to try to keep my clothes clean, to take care of myself. But there is not enough money for that. Everything I have goes to rent when I do have a place. The rest of the time I'm on the streets or in the missions.
>
> I don't know if I can make it much longer on GR, living on the streets and in the missions (Blair, 1985).

Presently the monthly GR allowance is only $312, and Los Angeles Legal Aid currently maintains that that amount is totally inadequate to purchase even the basic necessities of life in Los Angeles during the 1990s (Blasi, 1990).

In addition to the General Relief program, the DPSS administered an emergency housing assistance program which was proven to be inadequate in meeting the needs of applicants. Up until mid-1984, DPSS dealt with persons requiring emergency housing by issuing vouchers that could be exchanged for a room in a rundown single room occupancy (SRO) hotel. These hotels are primarily located in the downtown Los Angeles skid row area. During January 1984, on average, SRO hotels accommodated 1211 persons a night utilizing county vouchers (Robertson, Ropers, & Boyer, 1984, p. 46). When the available spaces in SRO hotels which held contracts with the county were exhausted, the county would issue $8 emergency housing checks. Between February and April 1984, an average of 50 emergency housing checks was issued daily.

Allan Heskin of UCLA's Graduate School of Architecture and Urban Planning completed a study of costs and vacancy rates in low-cost hotels and motels in Los Angeles County during the week of May 7, 1984 and concluded:

> This research established that there is virtually no possibility that a person whose only resource is a County warrant in the amount of $8 will actually find shelter in the hotel/motel market in Los Angeles. This is the case primarily because there are virtually no vacancies in those relatively few hotels and motels with rates in the designated range (1984).

Various restrictions regarding eligibility for receiving a housing voucher or an emergency housing check also existed. Eligibility for this form of welfare required identification, and even then there was often a waiting period of several days before any assistance was given. Many homeless persons often lacked identification because all of their belongings had either been lost or stolen. And some applicants for emergency shelter often became homeless due to the waiting period the DPSS required before rendering any assistance!

A related lawsuit (*Ross* v. *County Board of Supervisors*) alleged that the $8 emergency housing checks were insufficient to obtain shelter. Los Angeles County was enjoined from issuing these checks. Currently, the county is no longer issuing such checks. The county did respond, however, by increasing the rates paid to SRO hotels by 45 percent, but did not improve the quality of the accommodations. This presented a golden opportunity for some landlords. Within three months of the increase, the number of hotels participating in this program increased from 77 to 151 (Blasi, 1984: 6). The private owners of SRO voucher hotels were making as much as $15,000 a month from the vouchers issued by the county; and at least one proprietor, who owned several SRO hotels, made nearly $1 million from the program during the year. Investigations by Legal Aid found that most of these hotels were in violation of fire, safety, and health codes and, in some cases, found that long-term SRO tenants were being evicted so that the hotels could become county voucher hotels in order to ensure guaranteed profits which were paid for by welfare dollars.

One recipient of the DPSS's housing vouchers, Frank Csapla, described his experience in a SRO hotel that was supported with welfare housing assistance funds:

> When I unlocked the door and walked in the room I could not believe the mess. The room's only light was from a street light that shined in the broken window. There is no electricity at all in my room. Nor is there any heat. The room is real cold, especially with the broken window.
>
> I asked the manager for a blanket. I was told there is none. I was given one dirty old ripped sheet. It rips more and more each day. I asked for a new one, I was told they were all out.
>
> There is a sink in my room but it doesn't work. There is a bathroom in the hallway. I went in there once and I walked out. There was shit on the walls, on the toilet seat and on the floor. I can't use the bathroom. I go over to another hotel to use their

toilet. There are showers in the hallway but they don't work either. I take my showers at another hotel.

There are holes in the wall of my room. The walls are cracked with plaster crumbling. There are roaches everywhere. I bought some roach killer but it seems the more you kill them they come back three times greater.

There are mice in the hallways. You can see them anytime of day. I have seen at least 20 mice. It was disgusting to see mice in the place I have to stay. Growing up I had never seen mice in our house.

I don't feel good living in that dump. I have never lived like this before. I don't think anyone wants to live like this (Paris, 1984).

As a consequence of these findings, a lawsuit was filed to stop taxpayer funds from supporting hotels that were operating in open violation of health, safety, and fire laws (Paris, 1984). The litigation succeeded in bringing modest improvements to the conditions of Los Angeles' downtown, skid row, SRO welfare hotels. All of these hotels now operate on a nonprofit basis, and all now have heated rooms, although it required yet another lawsuit to force these hotels to heat their rooms.

The Homeless Litigation Team, composed of attorneys from six public-interest law firms and headed by Gary Blasi from the Los Angeles Legal Aid Foundation, provided evidence in still another suit that the mentally and developmentally disabled, indigent, and homeless citizens of Los Angeles have been effectively excluded from GR because of an "exceedingly and unnecessarily complex and convoluted application process" (Rensch, 1986). Many of the poor and homeless who suffer from the debilitating psychological and physical consequences of unemployment and homelessness and those who suffer from chronic mental disorders were denied the last hope of emergency welfare relief because they could not negotiate the hurdles of the welfare bureaucracy. Maintaining that "the General Relief program is the basic 'safety net' for the needy and is, in essence, the program of last resort, beyond which there is nowhere else to turn," the litigation team filed a motion which partially contended:

> This motion for a preliminary injunction is filed on behalf of mentally and developmentally disabled indigent and homeless residents of Los Angeles County who seek meaningful access to the basic necessities of life—food, shelter, and clothing. State law mandates that the County provide for these essential survival needs of those not otherwise supported. Pursuant to that mandate, the County operates a program of General Relief. It is the meager assistance afforded by General Relief that, in theory, provides for the subsistence needs of the disabled poor of the County and permits them to avoid a life of complete and utter destitution. In fact, however, they are effectively excluded from General Relief by an exceedingly and unnecessarily complex and convoluted application process. That process presents to the mentally disabled a barrier as insurmountable as is a staircase to a person in a wheelchair. For the mentally disabled poor of Los Angeles County, the consequences are severe: deprived of the means to obtain food, shelter, and clothing, they are consigned to wander our streets begging for food and shelter, seeking refuge in alleys and doorways, under bridges, in abandoned cars, and in already overcrowded churches and missions (Rensch, 1986).

Dr. Kevin Flynn, a Los Angeles psychologist, provided testimony based on his work with poor and mentally disabled individuals, regarding the consequences for individuals unable to negotiate through the welfare application process. One example of the types of problems individuals face when dealing with the welfare office is described in Dr. Flynn's statement concerning a female client.

> Ms. H.C., age 55, was diagnosed as paranoid schizophrenic. She related that she applied for General Relief and was given emergency shelter and instructed to supply her social worker with documentation going back five years. She was unable to comply with the request and was terminated and told by the worker to reapply. She subsequently reapplied and was assigned to the same worker who then told her that she would be terminated. . . . For the past ten months she has been sleeping on a bench at a bus stop on

Wilshire Boulevard. . . . She clearly has been a destitute and impoverished person living on the kindness of people who would
stop at the bus station and give her food and clothing.

This lawsuit resulted in a court order requiring Los Angeles
County to provide more assistance during the application process for those who were deemed mentally disabled. According
to Paul Fast, research director of the Los Angeles County DPSS,
a "needs special assistance" program has been implemented to
facilitate the approximately 3700 applications that are submitted
monthly by people suffering from various mental disabilities
(Fast, 1990). However, Legal Aid attorney Gary Blasi maintains
that in 1990 the number of mentally disabled and poor individuals in Los Angeles County who are not receiving help because they are still unable to negotiate the welfare application
process is double that of the number of applicants receiving
assistance with their applications (Blasi, 1990). Litigation was
still in progress in early 1990 against Los Angeles County for not
facilitating the application process of all qualified mentally disabled welfare applicants.

As of this writing, Los Angeles County is once again the
defendant in a comprehensive lawsuit regarding its GR welfare
program. But this time the leading plaintiff is the City of Los
Angeles in conjunction with Legal Aid and other public advocacy law firms (*City of Los Angeles* v. *County of Los Angeles*, Case
No. C 655 274). Although the rulings regarding all of the above
cases were found in favor of the plaintiffs, it is currently alleged
that the county fails to meet its legally mandated welfare responsibilities. This particular lawsuit attempts to consolidate
complaints against the county's administration of welfare programs (including, once again, most of the complaints of the
lawsuits discussed above, since the original complaints have not
been satisfied); and goes so far as to contend that county welfare
policies actually contribute to increased poverty and homelessness among certain groups. One of the nation's largest welfare administrations has been accused of not serving its clients,

but, rather, of increasing their misery. The legal brief of this case
highlights the issues:

> The California Legislature has mandated, through the *Welfare
> and Institutions Code,* that it is the duty of the County of Los An-
> geles to provide care and support for the homeless indigent resi-
> dents of this County. This action challenges Defendants' failure
> and refusal to fulfill that statutory duty.
>
> Defendants have established and administer a program of
> general assistance to the poor known as General Relief. The Gener-
> al Relief Program, although purportedly designed to provide last
> resort welfare for the homeless and indigent, is in fact designed to
> deny emergency shelter and other essential assistance to substan-
> tial numbers of eligible homeless indigent residents.
>
> As a condition of receiving General Relief assistance, Defen-
> dants require that eligible persons meet unreasonably detailed and
> onerous application, reporting, documentation, and verification
> requirements, in addition to undertaking unduly burdensome
> work assignments, job searches, employment registration, and
> medical and psychiatric examinations. Failure by an eligible person
> to comply with any of Defendants' unreasonable procedural re-
> quirements, for any reason, results in the denial or revocation of all
> General Relief benefits. . . .
>
> The requirements imposed . . . operate as a system that
> serves the County's budgetary objectives rather than the needs of
> the indigent homeless with whose care the County is statutorily
> charged. This system bears no rational relationship to the legisla-
> tive purpose of providing care and support for the poor. It is in-
> stead designed to limit County expenditures without regard to the
> actual numbers of persons who need assistance or the actual needs
> of those persons. Thus, after the County stipulated to entry of an
> order of this Court requiring an increase in the amount of General
> Relief assistance to be provided to each eligible person, Defendants
> promptly imposed additional procedural requirements which func-
> tion to increase the number of eligible persons denied such
> assistance. . . .
>
> As a consequence of Defendants' unlawful policies and prac-
> tices, thousands of indigent persons are denied the basic human
> services to which they are entitled. They are compelled to live on
> the City's streets, in alleys, under bridges, and on the beach, with-
> out adequate food or clothing. Children are separated from their
> parents because the parents, unable to obtain federal AFDC bene-

fits and deprived of General Relief assistance, are unable adequately to provide for them.

The resulting presence of a large and growing homeless population in the streets and other public places of the City of Los Angeles has created a continuing situation of civic urgency (City of Los Angeles, 1990).

In the opinion of Gary Blasi, the minimal improvements in the Los Angeles County welfare system, achieved after years of litigation are being overwhelmed by the increasing numbers of poor people in Los Angeles and the even greater demands put on an inadequate welfare system (Blasi, 1990). Almost 25 percent of all individuals who are eligible to receive GR don't even apply (Tepper, 1990).

As Los Angeles entered the last decade before the twenty-first century, the California Department of Finance reported that the number of persons living in poverty in the state had increased from 16.8 percent in 1980 to a current rate of 21 percent. The United Way, in the Executive Summary of its Los Angeles *Environment Scan 1990,* reported:

Growing poverty characterizes the urban underclass in Los Angeles, and declining demand for low-skill workers could make matters worse. Fifteen percent of the population—over 1.3 million persons—are mired in poverty. Projections are for this situation to get worse as the century ends. Poverty has increased most among Hispanics, especially those who are immigrants. Not surprisingly, poverty is greater in families headed by women. There are also substantial numbers of elderly poor, with many others vulnerable to poverty in an economic downturn. Recipients of Aid for Dependent Children (AFDC) are increasingly Hispanic, as proportions of white and Black recipients have declined since the beginning of the '80s (p. 13).

In addition, a recent survey of Los Angeles shelters for the homeless found "increasing poverty was cited by 92 percent of the shelters as one of the major factors contributing to homelessness" (Shelter Partnership, 1990: 9).

Increasing poverty goes hand in hand with a diminishing

low-income housing stock, exacerbating Los Angeles' problems even further. As Shelter Partnership researcher Paul Tepper concluded:

> As poverty has increased, the stock of affordable housing has diminished and the cost of existing housing has skyrocketed. The City of Los Angeles Blue Ribbon Committee for Affordable Housing found that the City's population is growing faster than its housing and there is an annual shortfall of 10,000 units per year. They noted that "Soaring costs of a decent place to live causes a chain reaction resulting at the extreme in thousands of homeless families and individuals." The Committee concludes that "the gap between wages and housing costs . . . threatens to change the character of the city."
>
> Clearly, the distinction between a "homeless person" and a "poor person" has become blurred as it becomes harder to be poor and maintain a decent, secure life (1990).

All of these problems exist in what is considered to be one of the strongest welfare "safety nets" in the nation. Given the "holes" in the Los Angeles safety net, imagine the problems facing welfare systems in other cities across the nation.

Conclusion

Controversy over welfare programs is not new. Nevertheless, the welfare issue has gained significance as the United States experiences one of the largest increases in its poverty and homeless populations since the Great Depression of the 1930s. The way in which a society responds to the needs of its most vulnerable members indicates the values and priorities of that society. Will we not be judged by the way we care for our needy children, women, and elderly rather than by the number of fast-food restaurants we franchise or the glories of a few multimillionaires?

The reality of American society in the 1990s is that about half of the nation's households receive government benefits in the form of means-tested welfare or social insurance programs. The stereotype that most welfare recipients are able-bodied black males living off the dole and racing to the liquor store in their pink Cadillacs to cash their welfare checks is nothing more than political ideology which has obscured the reality of poverty and welfare in America today.

Although there is no question that the poor would be worse off without the meager assistance they receive, current social welfare programs do little to lift most recipients out of their poverty. The fact that so many are poor and homeless gives some credence to the argument that poverty today is mainly a result of large-scale demographic, economic, occupational, and political trends and conditions, not simply caused by the moral, biological, or familial pathology of those who require public assistance. Are the majority of the women, children, elderly, and disabled who receive welfare not deserving? Furthermore, it is unrealistic to determine the potential income-generating capabilities of impoverished women who are raising children by the same criteria we use for able-bodied males who are not single heads of households.

As the case study of the Los Angeles County welfare system revealed, the alleged "safety net" of some localized welfare programs is riddled with holes. The cost to taxpayers in terms of law enforcement programs to handle the fallout from failed welfare systems should be sufficient motivation to make welfare more "cost effective." Similar problems exist in the administration of the major national welfare programs. For example, the National Association of Children's Hospitals and Related Institutions claims that Medicaid covers only one-half of all the children in poverty and skimps on preventive care and that the application process is so complex that one-fourth of the applicants are determined ineligible because they can't complete the application process (Painter, 1989). The social and moral costs of those needs which are left unmet by the welfare system diminish the quality of life not just of the poor, but of us all. Are we not socially and morally uncomfortable when, as we commute to work, attempt to enjoy public parks and areas, or walk our city streets, we are confronted with the appalling misery of the poor and the homeless?

It simply is not necessary, financially or politically, that the basic necessities of life be denied to any American citizen due to inadequacies in our welfare system. What we require is a welfare system which doesn't contribute to the maintenance of poverty, but one which can truly serve as a bridge out of poverty, and enable the poor to enter and participate in mainstream American life. Piven and Cloward concluded in their book, *Regulating the Poor: The Functions of Public Welfare* (1971) that "relief arrangements . . . have a great deal to do with maintaining social and economic inequities." (p. vxii).

The welfare system does indeed need to be reformed. Such reform, however, should be focused in the direction of adequately meeting the needs of the poor. Certainly, for many who attempted to negotiate the hurdles of the Los Angeles County General Relief program, welfare was not relief. Instead, it was a living hell. Is it conceivable that some welfare administrations are actually structured with the intent to humiliate and punish applicants and recipients for being poor? The evidence and court rulings of the various lawsuits filed against Los Angeles County appear to support that possibility.

As long as we live in a socioeconomic system that produces large-scale poverty, near poverty, and homeless populations, we will require a welfare system. Therefore, the best we can hope for, under present circumstances, is the development of a system that functions properly and meets the needs of those members of society for whom it was created.

6

Blaming the Victim

How do we explain the persistence of poverty? What are the appropriate evaluations of its victims and its consequences? There are, of course, no lack of explanations. One could easily become lost in the myriad theories surrounding poverty. However, despite the many different assumptions, concepts, and focuses of the various explanations, they can all be lumped into one of two major camps: blaming the victim or blaming the system. This chapter will review some representative blaming the victim theories of poverty.

Two issues generate controversy regarding blaming the victim theories: one issue is their scientific validity, the other their ideological role. In *Blaming the Victim* (1971), William Ryan suggested that there is a category of explanations which is used to account for various social problems that focus on the characteristics, attributes, and behaviors of the people who suffer from a particular social condition in order to determine the source of the problem. Ryan calls this blaming the victim approach a "process of evasion." The evasion distracts attention away from the social and economic structural causes of social problems, leaving primary injustice untouched.

An inversion of cause and effect, such as attributing the

lifestyles of those afflicted by a social condition to be the cause of that condition, is the essence of the blaming the victim ideology.

What follows is an introduction to some representative examples of contemporary blaming the victim theories and research studies. Where possible, summary statements on the positions of the advocates of various blaming the victim theories are presented.

Social Darwinism

In 1859, Charles Darwin published *The Origin of Species*, in which he presented his version of evolution, called the "theory of natural selection." Basically, natural selection works like this: Nature selects those members of a species that can best adapt and survive in particular environmental conditions, and that can continue to reproduce and pass on their characteristics to their offspring. As an illustration, imagine a population of giraffes living 100 million years ago on the savanna plains in Africa. Within this population of early giraffes (as in almost any population of organisms), there is a lot of individual variation in coloring, leg size, weight, height, and neck length. The giraffes obtain one of their main sources of food by grazing on the leaves of various trees. Once the animals have eaten all of the leaves on the lower branches of the trees, those giraffes with slightly longer necks and legs will still be able to reach up a bit higher and consume the leaves on the upper branches. When leaves are scarce—during times of drought or as a result of changing environmental conditions—the individual giraffes that are able to survive, because they can obtain leaves that their shorter siblings cannot, stand a greater chance of passing their longer necks and legs on to their offspring. This process is repeated many times over millions of years. Also, genetic mutations add to the changes. A giraffe may be born with an exceptionally long neck and exceptionally long legs; therefore, if environmental conditions demand it, this exceptional giraffe may survive over its siblings and pass on its genes.

Social Darwinism attempts to apply these concepts of natural selection to human social conditions. This theory claims that those classes and races which are most successful economically, socially, and politically succeed because they are biologically superior, both as individuals and as groups. Thus, social stratification reflects the "survival of the fittest." Social institutions and the distribution of income, wealth, and power are viewed as manifestations of biological laws. Since the laws of nature, and consequently their reflection in society, cannot and should not be altered, inequality remains an inevitable feature of human societies.

Reductionism

Most blaming the victim explanations of poverty share a common thread of one variety or another with Social Darwinism. Social Darwinism has been dismissed by the majority of contemporary social scientists as a type of *reductionism*. Theories characterized by reductionism attempt to explain complex phenomena with explanations from less complex levels. For instance, radical vegetarians, who believe that most human behavior is primarily the result of what people eat, often contend that major social problems such as crime, aggression, and wars could be eliminated if humans would stop eating meat. Certainly the food we ingest affects our chemistry and metabolism, and it influences our moods and behavior. To maintain, however, that all the complexities of social life and society are simply the products of biology and chemistry creates an incomplete and inadequate explanation of human affairs: it is an example of reductionism. Lewontin, Rose, and Kamin in *Not in Our Genes: Biology,*

Ideology, and Human Nature (1984), which is a critique of biological determinism and Social Darwinism, state:

> Broadly, reductionists try to explain the properties of complex wholes—molecules, say, or societies—in terms of the units of which those molecules or societies are composed. They would argue, for example, that the properties of a protein molecule could be uniquely determined and predicted in terms of the properties of the electrons, protons, etc., of which its atoms are composed. And they would also argue that the properties of a human society are similarly no more than the sums of the individual behaviors and tendencies of the individual humans of which that society is composed (p. 5).

Social Darwinism is reductionist because it attempts to explain the complexities of social stratification and poverty, not in a social context, but rather in terms of the biological factors and characteristics of individuals or families.

Genetic Stupidity and Poverty

One variant of the blaming the victim perspective, which is a blatant type of neo-Social Darwinism, focuses on the alleged lower intelligence of the poor, particularly poor blacks, as an explanation for their poverty. Black people were alleged to be less intelligent than whites long before contemporary "mental measurement professionals" claimed they could scientifically explain that the disproportionate number of blacks among America's poor is due to "inherently inferior" black intelligence. For example, a popular nineteenth-century U.S. school geography textbook informed students:

> The home of the black or "Negro" race is central and southern Africa and some of the Australian islands. The peoples of this race have coarse woolly or kinky hair, protruding lips, and dark brown or black skin. The black race includes some of the most ignorant people in the world (Redway & Hinman, 1898, p. 29).

Craniology

Craniology, the science of comparative measurement of skulls, brains, or the volume of the empty brain cavity of a human skull, was a popular nineteenth-century "scientific" method of demonstrating that nonwhites (again, especially blacks) and women were naturally inferior to white men. One of the methods used to measure brain capacity was to stuff mustard seeds through the opening at the base of the skull (the foramen magnum). Comparative measurements could then be taken by comparing the weight of the removed mustard seeds from one skull with those from another skull. Leading scientists (Broca, Le Bon, Spitzka) of the latter part of the nineteenth century made conclusions based on these methods that blacks, other nonwhites, and women had smaller cranial capacities than white males, and that their smaller brain size was proof of inferior intelligence (Gould, 1981).

The theories, methods, and logic of craniology have been largely dismissed by the scientific community because they are considered less than scientific by today's standards. For example, in one instance it was discovered that when the mustard seeds were put in the skull of a white man, the seeds were packed in tightly, while the skull of a black man was filled loosely. Of course, the careful measurements of the mustard seeds from the two skulls revealed that the white skull had a superior cranial capacity. In addition, modern scientists know that brain size, without consideration of it's relative size to overall body size, bears no relation to intelligence.

One nineteenth-century craniometrician, French psychologist Alfred Binet, published nine journal articles on the value of craniometry before his studies of the measurements of the heads of schoolchildren led him to lose faith in brain size as an index of intelligence. He had found that the differences in the "cerebral volume" of children who had been labeled dumb or

smart were negligible (Gould, 1981: 146). The French government asked Binet to devise a method of determining which children were likely to fail in school so that steps could be taken to
prevent their failure. Since he had given up on brain size as a
determining factor in measuring intelligence, Binet turned to
the study of photographs of children's faces in an attempt to
discover correlations between types of faces and school failure.
When the face method also proved unsuccessful, he turned to
palmistry—the reading of lines in the hands—to predict intelligence (Blum, 1978: 56).

Characterology

In 1921 Rand McNally and Company published a set of
booklets, authored by L. Hamilton McCormick, on the "science"
of characterology. McCormick described characterology as

> an exact science for the reason that by observing the rules and
> tenets herein formulated all possible combinations of features, cra-
> nial as well as facial, can be analyzed and the traits to which they
> refer named, and if errors are not made in the application of such
> rules, mistakes in diagnosis cannot occur. . . . By means of this
> science he can obtain a more nearly complete knowledge of the
> personality of an individual in a few moments. . . . Judged by its
> utility, Characterology ranks with mathematics, economics, chem-
> istry, medicine, and law (1921:12–13).

What this now discarded "science" alleged was that traits
like "honesty, dishonesty, crime, insanity, aptitude for music,
science, and art" could be linked to the physical features of
individuals. Characteristics such as ear, eye, and nose shape;
the configuration of the head; skin complexion; thinness or
thickness of the lips; or hair color and texture were claimed to be
scientifically linked to various social behaviors, including occupational status and material success.

An example of characterology's claim to infer behavioral

and cultural attributes from physical features is the following description of the relation of lip thickness to cultural traits:

> Excessively thick, protruding lips, unless there are counter-balancing signs, refer to grossness, slothfulness, love of food, sensuality, lack of breeding, and an unenterprising, indolent disposition.
>
> Negroes whose lips are large and thick are fond of brilliant colors which harmonized with their bronze complexions, and furthermore, they have the sense of taste highly developed; they consequently excel in cooking, knowing instinctively the kind and amount of flavoring required. Negroes and natives of tropical countries, as the fullness of their lips indicate, are affectionate, musical, and religious (McCormick, 1921: 7–8).

Regarding skin complexion, McCormick goes on to state:

> The black (or dark brown, as pure black skin does not exist) complexion of the African and certain Oriental races implies affection, lethargy, music, love of brilliant colors, and lack of initiative (p. 25).

IQ Tests: Old Wine in New Bottles

Alfred Binet, the former craniologist, is better remembered today as the creator of the first "IQ" test in 1908. Its contemporary version is known as the Stanford-Binet Intelligence Scale, because of updates conducted at Stanford University. Binet's IQ test was composed of questions he believed reflected various tasks normal children should be able to perform in school. To Binet's credit, he never contended that a student's IQ score was anything other than an indication of what a student had learned in class and how well that information had been applied. Nevertheless, the idea that "intelligence" tests measured innate fixed intelligence became widespread. By 1917, American psychologist Robert Yerkes had administered IQ tests to 2 million army recruits.

In the 1920s, Stanford University Professor Lewis M. Terman revised and updated the Binet test, resulting in the current popularity and wide spread use of the Stanford-Binet IQ test in the United States. Terman summed up his views on intelligence differences between the races in *The Measurement of Intelligence*, which he dedicated "To the Memory of Alfred Binet":

> Their [nonwhites'] dullness seems to be racial, or at least inherent in the family stocks from which they come. The fact that one meets this type with such extraordinary frequency among Indians, Mexicans, and Negroes suggests quite forcibly that the whole question of racial differences in mental traits will have to be taken up anew and by experimental methods. The writer predicts that when this is done there will be discovered enormously significant racial differences in general intelligence, differences which cannot be wiped out by any scheme of mental culture (Terman, 1916: 91–92).

Terman also believed that intelligence differences between social classes resulted primarily from biological differences. As he put it, "That the children of the superior social classes make a better showing in the tests is probably due, for the most part, to a superiority in original endowment" (1916: 72).

Furthermore, he wrote,

> the common opinion that the child from a cultured home does better in tests solely by reason of his superior home advantages is an entirely gratuitous assumption. Practically all of the investigations which have been made of the influence of nature and nurture on mental performance agree in attributing far more to original endowment than to environment. Common observation would itself suggest that the social class to which the family belongs depends less on chance than on the parents' native qualities of intellect and character (p. 115).

These ideas were popularized by many other books, including S. J. Holmes' *Human Genetics and Its Social Import* (1936). In Chapter 14, titled "The Social-Problem People," Holmes summarized the view of geneticists regarding the relation of low intelligence to social problems:

> Low mentality tends to go along with poor education and an inferior economic and social status. Pauperism, vagabondage, il-

> legitimacy, and intemperance tend sooner or later to become a part
> of the traditional mores of the group. People of this class are prone
> to mate with their own kind, and as a result whole communities
> grow up characterized by a large amount of consanguinity which
> brings out undesirable recessive traits (p. 186).

Current theories which attempt to explain contemporary American poverty and stratification as stemming from inborn differences in intelligence rely heavily on results from the Stanford-Binet test. At this point, a brief review of how IQ scores are calculated is appropriate. IQ is an abbreviation of *Intelligence Quotient*, which is derived from the following original formula of Binet: IQ equals mental age (which is derived from "IQ" test scores) divided by chronological age and multiplied by 100 or:

$$IQ = \frac{MA}{CA} \times 100$$

For example, if a ten-year-old child scores a "mental age" of 13 years, as measured by a standard IQ test such as the Stanford-Binet, then we would calculate the child's IQ as follows:

$$\frac{13}{10} \times 100 = 130$$

This child would have an above average IQ, since a "normal" ten-year-old should have at least a ten-year-old mental age. The normal ten-year-old's IQ would be figured this way:

$$\frac{10}{10} \times 100 = 100$$

Consequently, an IQ score of 100 is normal. However, if the ten-year-old scored a mental age of eight years, his IQ score would be 80, which is below normal.

$$\frac{8}{10} \times 100 = 80$$

Arthur R. Jensen, a self-described "mental measurement professional," is undoubtedly one of the most infamous advocates of the ideology that social stratification results from innate IQ differences. One of the basic tenets of Jensen's position proposes that "there is no rational basis for the *a priori* assumption of racial equality in any trait, physical or behavioral" (1981:197). He attributes the observed differences in average group IQ scores between American blacks and whites to "genetically conditioned behavioral differences between human races that show many other signs of evolutionary divergence" (p. 199).

Throughout his research, Jensen has contended that the average black/white IQ difference is about 15 points. Based on his review of identical twin studies that were conducted by British psychologist Cyril Burt, Jensen concluded that 80 percent of IQ is inherited and the remaining 20 percent is influenced by environment. However, after his death in 1971, Burt was "accused of fraud, of having faked much of his research, of reporting tests that were never done, and of signing fictitious names as coauthors" (Eitzen, 1982: 294).

Furthermore, Jensen believes that American society has bent over backward to do everything possible to remove all social, cultural, and legal barriers that inhibit black achievement. In addition, the federal government has funded numerous remedial programs, like Head Start, to help black children. Despite society's efforts, blacks continue to represent a disproportionate number of poor people, welfare recipients, and criminals, and their IQ test scores remain lower than do those of whites. If the fault does not lie in the structure of U.S. society, then the only explanation left is that the fault lies in the genetic structure of blacks.

Jensen summarized his position as follows:

> The plain truth is that compensatory programs have not resulted in any appreciable, durable gains in IQ or scholastic achievement for those youngsters who have taken part in them. This is an important discovery, and the fact that we do not like this outcome

or that it is not what we expected neither diminishes its importance nor justifies downplaying it.

The error lay in believing that the disadvantage with which many poor or culturally different children entered school—and the disadvantage that compensatory education was intended to remedy—was mainly a deficiency in knowledge.

I suspect that a substantial part of the individual variance in IQ and scholastic achievement—probably somewhere between 50% and 70% according to the best evidence on the heritability of IQ—is not subject to manipulation by any strictly psychological or educational treatment. The reason for this, I assume, is that main locus of control of the unyielding source of variance is more biological than psychological or behavioral (1981).

Other writers have taken Jensen's claims even further than merely attempting to explain poverty in America. For example, Stanley Burnham, in *Black Intelligence in White Society* (1985), writes:

This high correlation between IQ and SES [socioeconomic status] seems entirely relevant, then, in finding a cause for the pervasiveness of black poverty throughout the world. A lower standard of living among blacks is not just an American problem, but may be found across the globe from Tanzania to California. For in no country, nor in any recorded epoch of history, has the overwhelming majority of the black population even known anything except hand-to-mouth survival at a subsistence level (p. 48).

Sooner or later it must be recognized that the responsibility for black poverty should be primarily traced to blacks themselves, in large part resulting from their problem of cognitive deficiency (p. 51).

Today, the social and economic disadvantage of blacks seems, if anything, worse than before, very powerfully suggesting that the bimodal distribution in brain size and IQ test measurements . . . might indeed bear its bimodal equivalent in social deprivation (p. 54).

Richard Herrnstein helped popularize Jensen's views. Herrnstein summarized his argument by means of a syllogism, wherein he reasoned:

1. If differences in mental abilities are inherited, and
2. If success requires those abilities, and
3. If earnings and prestige depend on success, then
4. Social standing (which reflects earnings and prestige) will be based, to some extent, on inherited differences among people (1971: 58).

Herrnstein contends that because an ideology of egalitarianism dominates our society, we are under constant pressure to eliminate social barriers to status mobility. Thus, as social barriers to mobility decrease, the only remaining obstacles to social mobility must be inborn. In addition, the gap between the rich and poor will increase because, if there are any intelligent people in the lower classes, they will naturally drift up into the higher classes. Herrnstein points to Edward Banfield's book *The Unheavenly City* (1970) (which will be discussed below) as an example of one alert social scientist's description of the consequences of the innate inferiority of the lower class. Herrnstein concludes:

> Greater wealth, health, freedom, fairness, and educational opportunity are not going to give us the egalitarian society of our philosophical heritage. It will instead give us a society sharply graduated, with ever greater innate separation between the top and the bottom, and ever more uniformity within families as far as inherited abilities are concerned (1971: 64).

Herrnstein suggests we greet the ascent of an IQ meritocracy with enthusiasm because such a system will result in a society in which natural abilities will match social functions. When asked in an interview what he thought of Herrnstein's prediction regarding the rise of a meritocracy in the United States, Jensen responded, "I think his prediction . . . is quite right" (1976: 66).

Nobel prize-winning scientist William B. Shockley expanded on the "lower intelligence as the cause of social stratification" argument. In the 1970s, Shockley and four other prominent scientists joined millionaire physicist Robert K. Graham in establishing a "sperm-bank" as a depository for "superior sperm." The purpose of the bank was to create a "master race" which would solve America's leading social problems. The sperm bank, officially called the Repository of Germinal Choice, is located in Escondido, California. The *New York Post* described the events as follows:

> Three super intelligent women were impregnated last year with the frozen sperm of the scientists in an experiment which is likely to become the most controversial in the nation's history. . . . Each woman was able to choose the sperm of her "mate scientist" on the basis of his IQ, age, weight, height, skin, hair, color of eyes, and history of bearing healthy children (Seifman, 1980).

Shockley explained to the *Post* that his efforts were directed at "saving the human race from the genetically disadvantaged." He also stated that he believed "genetic defects in blacks are responsible for their criminal tragedies" and that he was "endorsing the concept of increasing the people at the top of the population" (Seifman, 1980: H13).

From Inferior People to Unheavenly Cities

Edward Banfield, who was appointed by President Nixon to head the task force on model cities during the early 1970s, carried the inferiority of race explanation one step further. Once again, poverty—especially black poverty—and, in Banfield's opinion, nearly all other urban social problems can be explained by the unique characteristics of the people who are poor. Banfield's *The Unheavenly City* (1970) is a controversial blaming the victim ideological tract that lacks any pretense of humanitarian heart-bleeding. According to Banfield, poverty is caused by a combination of inferior biology and a "culture of poverty," i.e., a belief system of negative personal and moral values. Banfield's analysis of poverty viciously proposed the idea that a possible solution to the perpetuation of poverty would be to reduce the children of the poor to marketplace commodities.

> As a matter of logic, the simplest way to deal with the problem—and one which would not involve any infringement of parents' rights—would be to permit the sale of infants and children to qualified bidders both private and public (1970: 231).

Banfield arrived at such a conclusion through a curious theory of social class. Rather than defining social class by some set of objective social criteria, as most social scientists do, Banfield defines it as "one primary factor, namely, psychological orientation, toward providing for the future." Banfield further explains: "The more distant the future the individual can imagine and can discipline himself to make sacrifices for, the 'higher' is his class" (1970: 47). Based upon this one factor, he came up with a description of the stratification of American society and its heavy concentration of blacks in the lower and working classes (see Table 6.1). Banfield believes that poor people enjoy their conditions; he states:

> The lower-class individual lives in the slum and sees little or no reason to complain. He does not care how dirty and dilapidated his housing is either inside or out, nor does he mind the inadequacy of such public facilities as schools, parks, and libraries: indeed, where such things exist he destroys them by acts of vandalism if he can. Features that make the slum repellent to others actually please him (p. 62).

According to Banfield's logic, the source of our serious urban social problems originates from lower-class blacks. Crime, youth gangs, the drug problem, racial tensions, welfare fraud, urban decay, and just about all other urban problems can be attributed to the culture of poor blacks in the central cities. In a provocative statement Banfield says:

> So long as the city contains a sizable lower class, nothing basic can be done about its most serious problems. Good jobs may be offered to all, but some will remain chronically unemployed. Slums may be demolished, but if the housing that replaces them is occupied by

TABLE 6.1. Blacks, Whites, and
Social Class

	Blacks (%)	Whites (%)
Upper class	1	12
Middle class	4 .	21
Working class	37	50
Lower class	58	17

Source. Based on Banfield (1970), p. 266.

the lower class it will shortly be turned into new slums. Welfare payments may be doubled or tripled and a negative income tax substituted, but some persons will continue to live in squalor and misery. New schools may be built, new curricula devised, and the teacher-pupil ratio cut in half, but if the children who attend these schools come from lower-class homes, they will be turned into blackboard jungles, and those who graduate or drop out from them will, in most cases, be functionally illiterate. The streets may be filled with armies of policemen, but violent crime and civil disorder will decrease very little (pp. 234–35).

Therefore, isn't it the right and the responsibility of society to protect the interests of the majority? Hasn't the United States previously been required to infringe upon the rights of a minority to protect the majority? As Banfield puts it:

[I]f abridging the freedom of persons who have not committed crimes is incompatible with the principles of free society, so, also, is the presence in such society of persons who, if their freedom is not abridged, would use it to inflict serious injuries on others. There is, therefore, a painful dilemma. If some people's freedom is not abridged by law enforcement agencies, that of others will be abridged by law breakers. The question, therefore, is not whether abridging the freedom of those who may commit serious crimes is an evil—it is—but whether it is a lesser or a greater one than the alternative (p. 184).

Unfortunately, the urban crisis now confronting the United States requires a similar response. Realizing that selling infants probably wouldn't be acceptable, Banfield proposes the following five-point program:

1. Encourage the black person to realize that he, himself—and not society or racism—is responsible for his ills.
2. Get him out of school at age 14, and place the ones who are unable to get jobs into the army or a "youth corps."
3. Give cash subsidies to the "competent" poor, but only goods to the "incompetents"; and encourage or force the "incompetents" to reside in an institution or a semi-institution, such as a "supervised public housing project."
4. Provide "intensive" birth control "guidance."
5. Increase police powers in black areas and toward black people, including more "stop and frisk" procedures and similar tactics, including jailing those persons "likely" to commit violent crimes (p. 246).

Banfield's use of the idea of a "culture of poverty" as a partial explanation for the condition and behavior of lower-class blacks is derived from the theory developed by anthropologist Oscar Lewis.

The Culture of Poverty

Oscar Lewis first suggested the concept of a culture of poverty in *Five Families: Mexican Case Studies in the Culture of Poverty* (1959). By the midsixties, with the publication of *La Vida: A Puerto Rican Family in the Culture of Poverty* (1965), Lewis attempted to systematically clarify a concept of a culture of poverty, and to address issues regarding the proper use of this concept. He defined the concept in the following way:

The culture of poverty in modern nations is not only a matter of economic deprivation, of disorganization or of the absence of something. It is also something positive and provides some reward without which the poor could hardly carry on. . . . [T]he culture of poverty transcends regional, rural-urban and national differences and shows remarkable similarities in family structure, interpersonal relations, time orientation, value systems and spending pat-

terns. . . . [T]he culture of poverty is both an adaptation and a
reaction of the poor to their marginal position in a class-stratified,
highly individuated, capitalistic society. . . . [T]he culture of poverty, however, is not only an adaptation to a set of objective conditions of the larger society. Once it comes into existence it tends to
perpetuate itself from generation to generation because of its effect
on the children (1965: xlvii).

According to Lewis, the culture of poverty is evident on
three levels: the individual, the family, and the community. The
characteristics of individuals living in a culture of poverty include

strong feelings of marginality, of helplessness, of dependence and
of inferiority. . . . [O]ther traits include a high incidence of mater-
nal deprivation, of orality, of weak ego structure, confusion of
sexual identification, a lack of impulse control, a strong present-
time orientation with relatively little ability to defer gratification
and to plan for the future, a sense of resignation and fatalism, a
widespread belief in male superiority, and a high tolerance for
psychological pathology of all sorts (1965: xlvii–xlviii).

Families in the culture of poverty are characterized by a
high incidence of abandonment by the fathers or other adult
males. Consequently, there exists a trend toward female- or
mother-centered families, and the children in these families do
not experience a "specially prolonged and protected stage in the
life cycle." At the community level, we find poor housing conditions, crowding and "gregariousness," but most important, a
minimum of organization beyond the level of the family.

This litany of the culture of poverty characteristics, if true,
is certainly enough to convince anyone that the poor are indeed
a pathetic and pathological horde. But, Lewis contends, the
culture of poverty actually has positive adaptive functions for
the poor. It provides adaptive mechanisms by helping to reduce
frustrations, thus making the deprivation of poverty tolerable.

Unfortunately, politicians, academics, and journalists who
adopted Lewis' culture of poverty concept failed to heed the
exceptions and qualifications regarding it. The culture of pover-

ty idea became a pivotal point around which many other theories attempted to explain why poverty persists. It also highly influenced U.S. government studies that were published on the topic. Nevertheless, Lewis admitted from the very beginning that although economic and material poverty are pervasive, the culture of poverty was not widespread. As he stated:

> [T]here is relatively little of what I would call the culture of poverty. My rough guess would be that only about 20% of the population below the poverty line in the United States have characteristics which would justify classifying their way of life as that of a culture of poverty (1965:li).

For the poor who do live in a culture of poverty, Lewis found evidence that

> when the poor become class-conscious or active members of trade-union organizations, or when they adopt an internationalist outlook on the world, they are no longer part of the culture of poverty, although they may still be desperately poor (1965:xlviii).

Despite the use of his concept by conservatives to maintain the status quo, Lewis voiced some very nontraditional views regarding the elimination of the culture of poverty

> by creating basic structural changes in society, by redistributing wealth, by organizing the poor and giving them a sense of belonging, of power and of leadership. Revolutions frequently succeed in abolishing some of the basic characteristics of the culture of poverty even when they do not succeed in abolishing poverty itself (1965:lii).

The Negro Family

Shortly after Lewis introduced the culture of poverty idea into discussions of poverty and social problems, the government published a document explaining the condition of black America in terms of a culture of poverty. In the context of over a decade of struggle for civil rights and black urban rebellions in

Children and women make up the majority of the poor.

Seventy-five percent poverty on the Paiute Indian reservation, Cedar City, Utah.

A victim of persistent poverty.

Hungry Americans on line for food handouts, Salt City Utah, 1990.

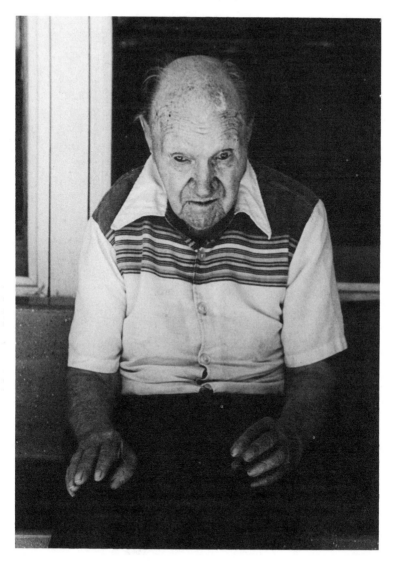

The forgotten elderly poor.

A working and poor American family.

The declining American farm.

The author with American Indian farm labor children.

Attempts by the poor to organize politically.

many cities during the early 1960s, Daniel Patrick Moynihan, then assistant secretary of labor, prepared the report *The Negro Family* (1965), which came to be known as the "Moynihan Report." Aspects of the report were also reflected in a number of significant speeches delivered by President Johnson that addressed the question of poverty and the state of black Americans during that time. In a speech delivered at Howard University on June 4, 1965, regarding the "widening gulf" between white and black America, Johnson, said:

> [F]or the great majority of Negro Americans—the poor, the unemployed, the uprooted and the dispossessed—there is a much grimmer story. They still are another nation. Despite the court orders and the laws, despite the legislative victories and the speeches, for them the walls are rising and the gulf is widening.

What was to become problematic was how the government and the nation understood why poor blacks seemed to be stuck in perpetual poverty. The Moynihan Report provided an explanation.

Although pointing out that the conditions of poor blacks are historically related to slavery, Moynihan nevertheless emphasized that "at the heart of the deterioration of the fabric of Negro society is the deterioration of the Negro family" (1965: 5). He derived his insights concerning the importance of the family from psychoanalytic theory. Consequently, his report placed much emphasis on personal and family pathology as the cause of the condition of poor blacks. The statistical basis of his argument was that one-fourth of urban black marriages had dissolved, one-fourth of black births were illegitimate, and one-fourth of black families were headed by females.

Although Moynihan did, in passing, mention the historical oppression of blacks, the fear many whites exhibit toward blacks, the lack of capital afforded blacks, and white organized crime as factors that contributed to the production of the "Negro condition," he maintained that blacks themselves are basically responsible for their status. As Moynihan stated:

> Nonetheless, at the center of the tangle of pathology is the weakness of the family structure. Once or twice removed, it will be found to be the principal source of most of the aberrant, inadequate, or antisocial behavior that did not establish, but now serves to perpetuate, the cycle of poverty and deprivation (1965: 30).

Based on this explanation, Moynihan's case for national action to correct the condition of poor blacks concluded:

> In a word, a national effort towards problems of Negro Americans must be directed towards the question of family structure. The object should be to strengthen the Negro family so as to enable it to raise and support its members as do other families (1965: 47).

In other words, the black family could be strengthened through psychotherapy. Once that was accomplished, blacks would be like other people, and many of America's social problems would be solved. Many civil rights leaders of the time objected strongly to Moynihan's analysis. James Farmer's response represents a good summary of the black community's reaction to the report:

> This well-enough intentioned analysis provides the fuel for a new racism. . . . [I]t succeeds in taking the real tragedy of black poverty and serving it up as an essentially salacious "discovery" suggesting that Negro mental health should be the first order of business in a civil rights revolution.
>
> Nowhere does Moynihan suggest that there may be something wrong in an "orderly and normal" white family structure that is weaned on race hatred and passes the word "nigger" from generation to generation.
>
> Nowhere does Moynihan suggest that the proper answer to a shattered family is an open job market where this "frustrated" male Negro can get an honest day's work.
>
> And nowhere does Moynihan suggest that high illegitimacy rates in the black community may be partly explained by the fact that birth control information and covert abortions are by and large the exclusive property of the white man.
>
> I say all this because I'm angry . . . really angry and I intend to spell out this anger in just one more effort to convince somebody, anybody, down in the places of power that the cocktail hour on the "Negro Question" is over and that we are sick unto death of being

analyzed, mesmerized, bought, sold and slobbered over while the same evils that are the ingredients of our oppression go unattend-ed.

It has been the fatal error of American society for 300 years to ultimately blame the roots of poverty and violence in the Negro community upon Negroes themselves. I honestly felt that the Civil Rights and Voting laws indicated that we were rid of this kind of straw-man logic, but here it is again, in its most vicious form, handing the racists a respectable new weapon and insulting the intelligence of black men and women everywhere (Rainwater and Yancey, 1967: 410).

Functional Inequality

One of the major schools of American sociology is known as *functionalism*. As the name implies, this perspective is derived from the approach that functionalists take toward the study of social phenomena, i.e., institutions, organizations, groups, and the like, by asking the question, "What is the function of this or that social condition or institution for society?" When func-tionalists attempt to explain poverty and inequality they pose the question, "What is the function of social stratification?"

What is now considered the "classical" position of func-tionalism on stratification was written over forty years ago by Princeton University sociologists Kingsley Davis and Wilbert E. Moore in "Some principles of stratification" (1945). There are, however, striking similarities between the propositions of Davis and Moore and current American ideology regarding inequality. David and Moore began their discussion with the premise that social stratification is a "universal necessity." In other words, stratification has always been present in human societies, it is present in all contemporary societies, and it will always be pre-sent in future societies.

They go on to argue that some social positions are more "functional" for society than others. This means that certain occupations are more vital or important to society than others. For example, a medical doctor's contribution to society is more significant than that of a ditch digger. The doctor's work involves saving lives and preventing illness, and requires many years of education and training as well as the application of expertise to difficult situations. In addition, not just anyone has the intelligence and discipline to become a doctor; only a few select individuals have that potential. In short, a doctor's position is more functional for "societal survival," whereas the work of digging ditches requires no education or expertise and can be performed by just about anyone.

Therefore, the function or purpose of social stratification, i.e., economic and social inequality, is to insure the proper allocation and distribution of social rewards (high income, wealth, prestige and power) and social punishments (low pay, low prestige, powerlessness). Consequently, the stratification system serves as a mechanism for placing and motivating the best individuals to fill the most functional positions. As Davis and Moore put it, "Social inequality is thus an unconsciously evolved device by which societies insure that the most important positions are conscientiously filled by the most qualified person" (1945).

Doctors receive high pay, prestige, and power because they have supposedly earned it the old-fashioned way—through hard work, dedication, sacrifice, and the market value of their services, i.e., the more functional nature of their occupation to society. Thus everyone in society ends up in the social position for which they are more or less fit and receives appropriate social rewards or punishments. Inequality is then not only functional for society, it is also morally just and fair.

Although the functionalist theory of inequality is allegedly a sociological viewpoint, Davis and Moore slip in a bit of biological determinism. They point out in passing that "inherent capacity" is one major source of the talents that are the root of why different individuals end up in high or low social positions (1945).

The ideological relevance of the functionalist theory of inequality is obvious. It is the basis for the popular conservative, man-in-the-street view that the rich are rich because they deserve to be, and the poor and homeless are exactly where they should be because they are lazy, unproductive, and pathological. One of the major American sociological paradigms, functionalism ends up in the blaming the victim category regarding poverty. The theory implies that, because inequality is inevitable and universal, the poor will always be with us, and that's fine, because poverty is functional for "societal survival."

Bad Personalities, Bad Brains, Bad Genes, and Bad Luck

> On July 7, 1986, a homeless Cuban refugee aboard a Staten Island ferry unwrapped a sword and began hacking and stabbing other passengers. Before he was subdued, Juan Gonzalez had killed two people and wounded nine others. After his arrest, he informed police God had told him to kill (Chapman, 1989).

This account of an obviously mentally ill homeless person typifies some of the highly distorted and biased images the mass media projects regarding the homeless crisis. They are images derived from the pronouncements of a select group of psychiatrists who have attempted to convince the public that the complex causes of homelessness and poverty can be simplistically reduced to a mental illness issue and, subsequently, to a genetic issue.

The newspaper commentary went on to present its analysis of the causes of homelessness, stating,

> One of the most durable myths about the homeless is that there is nothing wrong with them that cheap apartments wouldn't fix. . . . [M]any of the homeless are people who would have trouble keeping a roof over their heads if you gave them a mansion on Rodeo Drive (Chapman, 1989).

Where did this newspaper commentator get his information? He found it in the book *Nowhere to Go: The Tragic Odyssey of
the Homeless Mentally Ill* (1988), written by psychiatrist E. Fuller
Torrey, in which he claims that there are "vast hordes of mentally ill homeless persons" populating our cities. He describes
the bulk of the homeless population as "lazy individuals who
will do anything to avoid having to work . . . alcoholics and
drug addicts . . . newly arriving immigrants . . . [and] recently
released denizens of jails."

In December 1986, I participated on a panel with Torrey
during a national conference on the homeless held at George
Washington University in Washington, D.C. The panel attempted to address the causes of homelessness. Torrey's position was very clear cut: homeless people are mentally ill—they
have either been released from mental hospitals or should be
placed in them.

In a short article, Torrey asserted that three factors cause
homelessness: bad brains, bad genes, and bad luck. He maintains that one-third of the homeless have "bad brains," which
means they have mental diseases such as schizophrenia. Torrey
further speculates another one-third of the homeless are afflicted with alcoholism, drug abuse, criminal behavior, marginal
IQ's, and personality disorders. He argues that all of these conditions are evidence of "bad genes" (Torrey, 1988, March). The
remaining one-third, Torrey concludes, are victims of "bad
luck"; for example, individuals who have been displaced from
jobs due to changes in technology. Absolutely no scientific or
psychiatric research exists which can adequately document such
sweeping claims.

There is no consensus among the scientific research community that one-third of the homeless are schizophrenic or man-
ic-depressive. A review of the research literature on mental illness among the homeless shows that no more than 15 percent of
the homeless have a diagnosis of schizophrenia or bipolar disorder combined. Furthermore, the validity of these diagnoses is

questionable (Ropers, 1988). In fact, most of the research in the latter part of the 1980s and early 1990s, including the psychiatric research, indicates that the vast majority of the homeless do not suffer from any form of chronic mental illness, nor are they former mental patients or individuals who should be institutionalized.

The bad genes theory was dealt with in the section of this chapter that discussed Social Darwinism, and needs no further commentary.

As for the bad luck explanation, it suggests that random, haphazard events, which happen to selected individuals, cause some homelessness. The homeless, however, are not victims of chance occurrences; rather, they are victims of clearly identifiable and patterned national economic, social, and political trends, such as the lack of low-income housing, underemployment, and cutbacks in social welfare.

Torrey, however, is not alone. Throughout the Reagan years and into the Bush era, various "experts" have attempted to shift the focus on the causes of homelessness away from larger economic and social processes onto the alleged characteristics and attributes of homeless individuals. Most of the initial literature on the new homeless of the 1980s was well grounded in the blaming the victim tradition. Other psychiatrists have also played prominent roles in "medicalizing," "psychologizing," and "biologizing" the origins of homelessness. Perhaps unwittingly, these psychiatrists have succumbed to the ideological requirements of very conservative political administrations.

Ellen Bassuk, Harvard psychiatrist and Chair of the Better Homes and Gardens Magazine Foundation for homeless families, claims in a *Better Homes and Gardens* article that "homelessness is ultimately a local issue, dealt with by local organizations" (Daly, 1989). In 1984, she authored an article that appeared in the prestigious *Scientific American,* in which she offered the position that deinstitutionalization from mental hospitals and chronic mental illness were the primary causes of homelessness. The evidence Bassuk gave for these claims was weak, and the conclusions lack any solid scientific reliability or validity. According to her "homelessness is often the final stage in a lifelong series of crises and missed opportunities, the culmination of a gradual disengagement from supportive relationships and institutions" (1984: 43). Frankly, it is difficult to understand why such a notable scientific journal would have published this piece; it was clearly more speculative and ideological than scientific. Much of Bassuk's subsequent research focused on homeless families and children. Although more recently admitting that the lack of decent low-income housing plays a role in homelessness, she still basically concludes that homeless mothers and children suffer from "personality disorders" or "difficulties in relationships," which contribute significantly to their homelessness (Bassuk, 1986).

In 1988, the National Academy of Sciences published *Homelessness, Health, and Human Needs,* a book prepared by the academy's Institute of Medicine. The book contained a comprehensive review of research about who the homeless are, but it also included a disappointing explanation of the causes of homelessness. The Institute of Medicine apparently either forgot about or became confused regarding the meanings, distinctions, and relationships between *necessary* and *sufficient* causes in its discussion on the origin of poverty and homelessness. It claims, under a section titled "Health Problems that Cause Homelessness," that in many cases health problems *are* the cause of homelessness. The section states:

> Some health problems precede and causally contribute to homelessness . . . the most common of [which] are the major mental illnesses. In addition to accidents, various common illnesses such as the degenerative diseases that accompany old age can also lead to homelessness (1988: 39).

Certainly, mental illnesses and various other health problems occur among the homeless, but to maintain that they are either necessary or sufficient causes of homelessness constitutes poor logic, reductionism, and pseudoscience.

There is no question that a physical or mental illness may contribute to increasing an individual's vulnerability to becoming homeless. Illness, however, is neither a necessary nor sufficient cause of homelessness. In science, a necessary cause is one which *must* be present in order for the effect under study (in this case homelessness) to occur. For example, in order for a human to become pregnant she must be female; but not all females become pregnant. Therefore, being female does not *cause* one to become pregnant. A sufficient cause is one, which, when present, inevitably leads to the effect under study. So, although many of the homeless suffer from health problems, and some from serious psychological problems, illness of any kind does not inevitably lead to homelessness any more than being female inevitably leads to pregnancy. To argue otherwise is not science but ideology. In addition, such arguments unwittingly serve the function of perpetuating blaming the victim views of homelessness. These kinds of approaches obscure the real causes of homelessness and play into the hands of political reactionaries.

The public pronouncements of psychiatrists like Bassuk and Torrey regarding the homeless are based on highly flawed research or, in some cases, on no research at all. Undoubtedly, the prestige of the medical profession played some role in the early acceptance of these views. It is more likely, however, that the ideological role of these psychiatric positions accounts for their wide acceptance. Blaming homelessness on bad personalities, brains, and genes fits well into the extreme individualistic and entrepreneurial ideologies of the Reagan and Bush administrations. And contending that homelessness is primarily caused by mental illness opens the door to the argument that, in the final analysis, homelessness is biologically determined. Dr. David Tomb, professor of psychiatry at the University of Utah Medical School and Medical Director of the Western Institute of Neuropsychiatry, maintains that a genetic defect causes schizophrenia and that most of the homeless are schizophrenic; therefore, homelessness is caused by a biological pathology (Palmer, 1986).

Because they believe that one of the most severe manifestations of inequality in the United States today—homelessness—is mainly a mental health issue, many psychiatrists are caught up in a blaming the victim approach. They often advocate various forms of "psychotherapy" as a solution to the homeless problem, ignoring or dismissing the structural injustice of the U.S. stratification system.

On several occasions, I interacted professionally with Dr. Rodger Farr, who headed the Adult Psychiatric Consultation Services, Los Angeles County Department of Mental Health during the mid-1980s. Farr was personally responsible for perpetuating the myth that among the homeless in Los Angeles, "75 percent of the males and 90 percent of the females are suffering from chronic incapacitating psychiatric illness" (1982). When my 1985 UCLA study of the homeless (Ropers, 1985) (which demonstrated that the majority of Los Angeles' homeless were not mentally ill) was released, Farr went out of his way to attack and attempt to discredit the study's findings (Farr, Koegel, & Burnam, 1986), which have since been confirmed many times over.

Farr's views illustrate a transparent application of contemporary reductionist and blaming the victim ideology, which attempts to obscure the real nature of inequality in the United States. According to Farr, the rise of the homeless population is a result of the deinstitutionalization of mental patients from state hospitals. The homeless, he claims,

> are not the winos or derelicts of the past but are often men and women from middle-class families who have experienced chronic mental illness and because of their mental disability, have been unable to make it on their own (1986: 67).

Furthermore, the condition of the homeless in Los Angeles' skid row is blamed, in typical culture of poverty fashion, on the attitudes and beliefs of the homeless.

Farr explains that the homeless are unable to utilize social support programs because they "fear government agencies," they are "unable to live in a structured community environment," they have an "inability to seek medical care," and the "vast majority would rather live in filth and be subjected to beatings and violence than to be institutionalized, even in our finest mental hospitals" (pp. 67–71).

Farr proposed that the best method for dealing with increased poverty and homelessness in Los Angeles was to "provide mental health consultation, education, emergency crisis management, and evaluation and referral" (p. 77).

The stereotype that most of the homeless are undeserving bums and derelicts, or that some personal form of pathology (e.g., alcoholism, drug abuse, mental illness or retardation, divorce or separation) is the primary cause of homelessness, was used by the Reagan Administration to divert attention away from serious structural problems surrounding the economy and social system. The combination of political activity on the part of the homeless and their advocates and the culmination of scientific research presents a more accurate picture of who the homeless are and how they became homeless. This information clearly refutes the ideologically inspired stereotypes. It turns out the homeless are mainly displaced and unwanted members of the lower and working classes, victims of national social and economic trends well beyond the control of those afflicted. Compared to previous generations of the skid row homeless, the contemporary homeless have been found to be younger, better educated, and disproportionately nonwhite. And if there was one "institution" most of the homeless men had been in, it wasn't a mental hospital, it was the U.S. military. One-third to one-half of the men, depending on location, are veterans. One-fifth of the homeless are working full- or part-time, while another three-fifths are actively looking for work. The majority received no public assistance before becoming homeless and, at least through most of the 1980s, most received no assistance while they were homeless. Although approximately one-third of the homeless may have various problems with alcohol, the extent of this problem does not differ significantly from that which is found in the general population.

Then there are the homeless children. According to Education Department Secretary Lauro Cavazo, more than 65,000 homeless children are prevented from attending school on a regular basis because they lack transportation, clothes, or proper motivation. All together it is estimated that there are 220,000 school-age and 33,119 preschool children who are homeless (UPI, Homeless kids are often deprived of education too, 1989).

All of the blaming the victim theories reviewed in this chapter have several themes in common. All are reductionist in that they ultimately end up accounting for the complex social conditions of poverty, homelessness, inequality, and stratification in terms of genetic, biological, attitudinal, or personality defects and pathology. They are overly simplistic and limited in their scientific validity and lend themselves to supporting conservative and even reactionary right-wing politics. They are part of a great evasion of primary social and economic injustice in the United States.

7

Blaming the System

An alternative category of explanations for research findings regarding poverty and inequality shifts the focus away from the personal characteristics of individuals or groups and concentrates on external factors in accounting for poverty. These theories can be called "blaming the system" explanations. There are several varieties of blaming the system theories, some of which maintain that large-scale economic, social, and political trends are largely responsible for growing inequality. Other theories and studies look at more immediate environmental or situational conditions. Another variety points to temporary defects in the management or functioning of certain institutions or bureaucracies.

The following is an introduction to some representative types of blaming the system theories, which, in many cases, serve as a counterbalance and response to the blaming the victim theories.

Sweatshop America

The United States General Accounting Office (GAO) (1988, 1989), an investigative arm of the U.S. Congress, has docu-

155

mented that "sweatshops exist throughout the United States, in the opinion of the federal and state officials we surveyed" (USGAO, 1988: 1).

As defined by the GAO, a sweatshop is "a business that regularly violates both wage or child labor and safety or health laws" (1988: 1). Investigators found particular labor law violations that were similar to those which existed in the nineteenth century. Examples of violations reported in 1988 were

> failure to keep required records of wages, hours worked, and injuries; incorrect wages, both below the minimum wage and without overtime compensation; illegal work by minors; fire hazards; and work procedures that cause crippling illness. (p. 2).

Reportedly, thousands of sweatshops exist across the nation. The meat-processing, apparel-manufacturing, and restaurant industries are most frequently cited for multiple violations. The GAO report claims, for example, that approximately 2500 restaurants in Chicago (which employ 25,000 workers) and one-fourth of the apparel firms in New Orleans are violating multiple labor laws (p. 2).

A follow-up report, entitled *Sweatshops in New York City: A Local Example of a Nationwide Problem* (USGAO, 1989, June) revealed that the sweatshop problem in New York City "has not improved or has become worse over the last decade" (p. 1). Focusing in on the apparel industry, a senior of the New York State Labor Department stated that "7000 apparel firms operate in the city, and about 4500 of them are sweatshops by our definition, employing more than 50,000 workers" (p. 2).

The specific labor law violations of New York City sweatshops included paying workers between $2.00 and $2.50 an hour for a 12-hour day and violating child labor laws. Describing the work conditions of a 15-year-old boy who was employed by an apparel business, the report states:

> On the 12th floor of 333 West 39th street a 15-year-old boy works in conditions considered barbaric half a century ago. He could be

found by his table . . . sewing pleats into cheap white chiffon skirts. He hopes to make $1.00 an hour, even as winter winds swirl through a picture-window-size hole in the back wall and take all feeling from his fingers (USGAO, 1989: 8).

Government investigators gave a detailed illustration of a sweatshop in the apparel industry, and claimed their description was typical of sweatshops that operated in violation of various laws:

Working conditions were quite uncomfortable. The workplace was extremely small, approximately 20 feet long and 10 feet wide, and contained one long wooden workbench with sewing machines that were in fairly poor condition. Work space was crowded with five employees and the co-owner present. Our interview with the co-owner had to be conducted in the main aisle of the establishment because there was no place to sit.

The employees, all Hispanic, worked diligently at their stations as ethnic music combined with the roar of sewing machines. They worked under extremely warm conditions in dilapidated wooden chairs without padding. A large window at the end of the workbench had a garment scrap covering it, providing partial shade, but no ventilation.

The workplace contained numerous safety hazards. For example, electrical cords to the sewing machines were frayed. The work area contained many boxes that were piled in narrow aisles. Scraps of fabric and other debris were strewn on the floor and across the workbench where workers eat their lunch. An extension cord and rotten banana peel, partially hidden by fabric, were also lying on the floor. Plaster fell from the walls during our visit (p. 26).

Similar issues were reported by the *Los Angeles Times* in a story in which UCLA researchers claimed that sweatshops are turning Los Angeles into a "Third World City" (Hernandez, 1985). Major companies, especially in the garment and electronics industries, contract out their production functions, concluded UCLA researcher Goetz Wolff,

to smaller firms more willing to risk hiring illegal immigrants . . . and smaller firms that tend not to conform to accepted business practices such as complying with health and labor standards. . . .

As a result, all those things that Americans pride themselves in
having gotten rid of (such as child labor and underpaid workers)
are being reintroduced (Hernandez, 1985).

Wolff also believes that the sweatshops deflect the demands
for higher wages of workers in mainstream industries because
the sweatshop economy produces goods and services below
market prices. Thus, demands for higher wages are countered
with threats to replace traditional American blue-collar workers
with low paid sweatshop workers.

Exploitation of children in the workplace has once again
become such a serious problem that, in March 1990, the Labor
Department initiated "Operation Child Watch." *Time* magazine
described Operation Child Watch as "a nationwide three-day
sweep of 3400 garment shops, restaurants, supermarkets and
other businesses suspected of abusing young workers" (Suffer
the little children, 1990: 18). Outlining the problem, *Time* stated:

> In city after city, town after town, children are slipping into the
> work force to make up for a growing labor shortage, while the laws
> designed to protect them are widely flouted. In New York, it is the
> garment industry: in California, the fast-food restaurants; in Iowa,
> the farms; in Maryland, the door-to-door candy sellers. Violations
> of child-labor laws shot up from 8877 in 1984 to a record 22,508 last
> year, as ever younger children worked ever longer hours at jobs no
> one else would take for the pay (p. 18).

Additionally, in 1989 there were 25,000 child labor law violations of all types (e.g., hours standards, underage standards,
hazardous occupation, and the like)—an increase of 150 percent
since 1983.

Serious work-related injuries, including an increase in the
number of deaths, also resulted from violations of child labor
laws. For example, 31,500 work-related injuries and illnesses
were reported in 1988. In 1987 and 1988, ten children were killed
(United States General Accounting Office, 1990, March 16).

Utah, where I currently reside, has been reported to have
"more child labor law violations than any other state in the

Rocky Mountain Region," according to Labor Department investigators (Sanchez, 1990).

Capital versus Community

In *The Deindustrialization of America* (1982), Barry Bluestone and Bennett Harrison offer one of the most comprehensive contemporary explanations for growing poverty and the increasing polarization of the stratification system in the United States. They define deindustrialization as "widespread, systematic disinvestment in the nation's basic productive capacity" (p. 6). Disinvestment takes at least three forms. The first form involves multiindustry corporations "milking," i.e., diverting the profits from one industry and investing them in a totally different business or industry. One consequence of the milking of an industry is its eventual decline and abandonment. The second form "involves physically relocating some of the equipment from one facility to another, or selling off some of the old establishment's capital stock to specialized jobbers" (p. 7). The third and most blatant form of deindustrialization is to literally close down an industry and move it to a Third World country. The motive behind this practice is to cut production costs, specifically, labor costs, in order to increase profits. As a result of the disinvestment in American industries, there have been numerous plant shutdowns, high rates of hidden unemployment and underemployment, economic and social disruption of communities, and myriad psychological and health maladies afflicting millions of working Americans and their families.

Flint, Michigan, is an excellent example of corporate disinvestment. General Motors phased out its original plants in that community, relocated its manufacturing sites to Mexico, and invested the profits gained from decreased labor costs into defense industry corporations.

Massive foreign investment is made possible by "permissive technology." Developments in transportation and communication have reduced what previously would have been restrictive overhead costs, thus allowing for greater distances between the location of production and the consumer without a loss of profit. Jumbo jets and computerized world telecommunications systems make overseas production possible, and new production technologies are reducing the need for a highly skilled workforce.

Bluestone and Harrison contend that deindustrialization has pitted "capital" against American communities. When corporate heads disinvest in the United States, the closing down of a plant or business sends social and economic shock waves through the community where the industry was previously located.

The devastating effects of deindustrialization on a community and its members can be illustrated by the 1987 United States Steel (USX) shutdown of its Geneva steel plant in Salt Lake City. Having provided thousands of jobs for nearly 40 years, Geneva was Utah's most important basic industry. The impact of this closing on the surrounding communities, the workers, and their families was described by the *Salt Lake Tribune:*

> After six months of no work and living on unemployment and small subsidies from the union, the 1900 workers were devastated by the announcement from USX that Geneva would be "idled until orders warrant" its resumption. . . .
>
> Ms. Smith, a nine-year Geneva veteran, was answering the phones at union headquarters Wednesday and said there was panic and even some talk of suicide after the early morning announcement.
>
> She expects alcoholism, divorce, and suicide rates to go up after Wednesday's announcement.
>
> "It's not just the workers," she said. "It's the children. I'm more worried now about that than ever" (Dowell, 1987).

It is precisely this kind of community disruption, caused by disinvestment, that Bluestone and Harrison contend forms the basis of a new struggle between American communities and big corporations. It is a struggle over whether the human and material resources of America should be used to create more profits for the rich or to provide for the needs of the majority of the population.

The Truly Disadvantaged

William Julius Wilson, Chair of the Department of Sociology at the University of Chicago and a president of the American Sociological Association, has attempted to account for the growth of an inner-city black "underclass" in terms of changing urban economics, demographics, and the loss of jobs through deindustrialization. As in his earlier work, *The Declining Significance of Race* (1978), Wilson maintains that the plight of poor blacks results more from their social-class membership rather than from their race. Although middle-class blacks have benefited from the civil rights movement and changing laws regarding discrimination, working-class blacks remain trapped in a lower-class grid that has been produced by large economic and social trends over which they have no immediate control. In his more recent book, *The Truly Disadvantaged* (1987), Wilson argues that the plight of poor blacks has not resulted from any inherent individual characteristics; nor is it essentially the product of racism.

As Wilson states:

> I have argued that these problems have been due far more to a complex web of other factors that include shifts in the American economy—which has produced extraordinary rates of Black joblessness that have exacerbated other social problems in the inner city—the historic flow of migrants, changes in the urban minority age structure, population changes in the central city, and the class transformation of the inner city (1987: 62).

Working-class and lower-class blacks have experienced high rates of unemployment and underemployment due to the exit of industry out of the central cities, and because of the change in the economy from "goods-producing to service-producing industries" (p. 39). The lack of steady, adequate paying jobs interacts with several demographic features to produce a black underclass that is concentrated in America's central cities. Northern cities are now experiencing a disproportionate concentration of poor blacks due to the pattern of rural, southern black migration to these cities. Although migration has subsided, a high birth rate continues to swell the populations of these cities. Other demographic factors that have contributed to this situation include the out-migration of middle-class blacks from the central cities and the concentration of young black men in these areas. All of these factors have contributed to the creation of an inner-city black underclass.

Poverty and Inequality as Inherent in the System

An explanation of the dynamics of capitalism can be found in Adam Smith's classic work, *The Wealth of Nations* (1776). Smith's theory states that the market value of various commodities is essentially determined by the amount of labor put into the production of those commodities. This explanation is called the "labor theory of value." Karl Marx expanded Smith's rather simplistic version of the labor theory of value, and used it as the foundation for his theory of surplus value.

In *Capital* (1965), originally published in 1867, Marx pointed out that, in a capitalist economy, commodities have two kinds of value: use value and exchange value.

The use value of a commodity, for instance a new car, is largely personal and often subjective. A new car may be perceived as a practical means of transportation as well as a status symbol. In this sense, the car has use value which is determined by its ability to provide transportation and its ability to fulfill certain ego needs.

Although the price one is willing to pay for a new car will certainly be influenced by the subjective value an individual attributes to it (as well as by supply and demand), cars also have a "market" value. Arbitrary and subjective desires on the part of the consumer or manufacturer do not determine why an average new car is more expensive than an average new bicycle. One determining factor, however, is the exchange value of a commodity, which is the equivalent of the value of one commodity relative to another commodity in the marketplace. For example, one $12,000 car is worth the same amount of money as 60 bicycles that cost $200 each. The price of a commodity usually represents one index of its exchange value. But what determines the exchange values of various commodities? Marx believed that Adam Smith's simple labor theory of value was flawed. If exchange value is determined simply by the amount of labor put into a product, then commodities produced by lazy and slow workers would have greater exchange values than those produced by more efficient workers. That makes no economic sense. Marx solved this problem by refining Smith's labor theory of value. Exchange value is not determined simply by the amount of labor that is put into a commodity; it is determined by the amount of "socially necessary labor time" required to produce that commodity. Marx meant that the current average level of technology of a particular industry would be the standard against which the measure of socially necessary labor would be determined. Thus, the exchange values of various commodities would be determined by the average amount of labor required for a particular level of technology, in a certain industry, at a specific point in history.

The principles regarding exchange value apply to the "labor market" as well as the potato market, the car market, or any other market. People who work for a living sell their ability to perform different types of labor, mental or physical, on the labor market. A ditch digger is paid less than a medical doctor because it requires a greater amount of "socially necessary labor time," through training and education, to produce the skills required from a doctor than it does to produce the skills of a ditch digger. According to Marx, labor is also a commodity, and its exchange value is essentially determined like that of any other commodity.

Marx based his theory of surplus value on the modified theory of the value of labor. Furthermore, he derived his explanation of the persistence of poverty and economic inequality from his explanation of surplus value.

The following hypothetical situation will illustrate the concepts of the theory of surplus value. Imagine a contemporary pencil factory. Every day, thousands of pencils are manufactured and sold on the "pencil market." The pencil factory possesses various machines which play a role in the production of the pencils. Workers are hired to run and maintain the machines, load and unpack the raw materials, and inspect, pack, and ship the finished pencils. Each worker, through his labor, contributes something to the production and value of the pencils that are produced. Let us say that one worker, through his labor, contributes $15 worth of value to the pencils produced in one hour. This same worker earns $30 for working an eight-hour day. According to Marx, it would take this worker two hours of work to produce $30 worth of pencil value. In other words, the worker has produced a value equal to his daily wage of $30 in only two hours. But the worker doesn't get to go home after two hours of work; he must continue to work another six hours.

As the worker continues to finish out the remaining six hours, he contributes, through his work, $90 (6 × $15) of value to all of the pencils produced. It is this additional value—the $90—which Marx calls the surplus value. The surplus value is the value of the commodities produced minus what the workers are paid. Of course, some of this surplus value must be used by the owner of the pencil factory to pay for overhead such as raw materials, heat, power, replacement of parts, reinvestment, and expansion. The net profit—what remains after paying for labor, overhead, and reinvestment—also comes from surplus value. Net profit is then used to pay dividends to investors or to simply line the pockets of the factory owners. The origin of profit, therefore, becomes the issue.

As everyone's parents have said, "Money doesn't grow on trees," and if you bury $100 in a tin can in the backyard, when you dig it up a year later, you will find it hasn't grown into $200. The question now becomes: Where does the money come from that pays for dividends on investments or interest payments? According to Marx, it comes from the exploitation of the surplus values produced by workers. This then is one source of economic stratification, i.e., the differences between incomes and wealth among classes. However, the theory of surplus value goes further in its explanation.

As most businessmen would agree, the bottom line in business is to increase profits. If you are the owner of the pencil factory, given the assumptions of the theory of surplus value so far, how could you increase your personal profits? You could introduce new machines that produce more pencils in less time. Initially, this might raise your profit margin, because now, let us say, each worker is producing $30 worth of pencils an hour instead of $15 worth of pencils an hour, and you are still only paying each worker $30 a day. Unless you have a monopoly on pencil production, however, this would produce only a temporary short-term gain. This is so because if the amount of "socially necessary labor time" required for the production of the pencils determines their exchange value, then the pencils have actually decreased in exchange value and should, ultimately, sell for less. Another possibility is a "speed up." You can simply force your workers to work faster to produce more pencils. At the same time, you sell the pencils for the old price and continue to pay the workers the same wage. Or you could implement forced overtime which requires your employees to work shifts of

10, 11, or 12 hours a day, instead of the usual 8 hours. You may have to pay them overtime, but the relative amount of profit would still increase. Besides, it is less expensive to pay overtime than to hire a whole new shift of workers. The new shift would have to be trained and would probably demand health insurance and other benefits.

You could tell your workers that in order for the company to stay in business, everyone must make a sacrifice and take a pay cut and/or a cut in benefits. Perhaps an even better strategy would be to close down the pencil factory and reopen it in Mexico, China, or Hong Kong, where, instead of paying your workers $30 a day, you could pay them $3 or $5 a day.

Regardless of the inaccuracies or flaws one might find in Marx's theory of surplus value, we can begin to see how it is a theory that thoroughly blames the system. It is not necessarily the personal greed of a particular businessman or shareholder that makes the system work this way; it is the very structure and competitive requirements of the capitalist system that demand the expropriation of surplus value.

Marx is best known (and often misunderstood) for his ideas regarding social class, class conflict, and the materialist conception of history. Less well known is his socioeconomic theory of surplus value, which underpins his better known theories.

Whether the theory of surplus value is good social science or merely biased ideology, it is, nonetheless, a comprehensive blaming the system theory of inequality. Whatever the shortcomings or problems of transition in socialist societies which advance the theory of surplus value as truth, Marx's theories continue to have an impact on the real political world. Whether we consider them valid or not, these theories have influenced millions of people and guided worldwide political and revolutionary movements. The discussions of sweatshop America and deindustrialization appear to provide some empirical support for the theory of surplus value.

Not in Their IQs

In a 1979 landmark ruling, the Superior Court of California banned the use of IQ tests as criteria for the placement of students in classes for the mentally retarded (Knickerbocker, 1979). IQ tests (specifically the Stanford-Binet and Wechsler) had been used in California schools to "track" students into special education programs. Ruling that such tests discriminate against non-white children, U.S. District Court Judge Robert Peckham stated that the tests "were developed for a white population without taking into account the cultural differences of minority groups" (Knickerbocker, 1979).

Judge Peckham found that the cultural bias of the IQ tests lead to "grossly disproportionate enrollments of black children in so-called 'educable mentally retarded' classes. . . . [S]uch classes provide only a limited dead-end education for children."

In addition to the cultural bias, expert witnesses provided evidence that IQ tests contain an urban and middle-class bias.

Even Arthur Jensen, in the light of new evidence, admits that IQ is subject to environmental influences. In a 1977 article published in the journal *Developmental Psychology*, Jensen reported the results of his study on the IQs of 1479 children. These children, both black and white, lived in a poor southeastern Georgia town. According to Jensen, an individual's IQ should remain constant throughout his or her lifetime. He was surprised, therefore, to discover that the black children, on average, showed a decrease of one point per year on their IQ scores between the ages of five and eighteen years. Jensen decided, "You have to conclude that something is happening to those kids while they are growing up." Indeed, the "something" that happened was the continuous deterioration of their social environment.

After several years of empirical investigation, researchers Samuel Bowles and Herbert Gintis concluded:

> Our findings, based for the most part on widely available pub-
> lished data, document the fact that IQ is not an important cause of
> economic success; nor is the inheritance of IQ the reason why rich
> kids grow up to be rich and poor kids tend to stay poor. The
> intense debate on the heritability of IQ is thus largely irrelevant to
> an understanding of poverty, wealth, and inequality of oppor-
> tunity in the United States (1974).

Bowles and Gintis found that when children with different
social class backgrounds but equal IQs are compared later in life,
they show little or no social mobility. In other words, the argument that higher IQs lead to higher education and thus to higher social class standing is not empirically true. The best predictor
of an adult's social class is not his or her IQ but rather the social
class into which he or she was born.

What Is Intelligence?

Those who advocate the use of IQ tests conceive of intelligence as a fixed, one-dimensional entity that can be quan-
titatively measured. Individuals can then be ranked according to
how much or how little of it they possess. Since psychology has
no single, comprehensive definition of intelligence, this conception appears somewhat limited. Critics of IQ tests, however,
conceive of intelligence as a process rather than a thing. They
view intelligence as the ability to utilize adaptive means to survive in one's environment.

Stephen Jay Gould summarized a major criticism of the IQ
advocates' position in what he calls "the hereditarian fallacy."
The fallacy involves the equating of "heritable" with "inevitable" (1987: 156). Although biological traits are genetically trans-
mitted, the potentials and limitations of these traits are not restricted to biology. Environmental intervention can either
enhance or impair biological traits. Millions of Americans, for
example, wear eyeglasses which enable them to function per-

fectly, even though they may have been born with "genes" that weakened their eyesight.

Functional Poverty

Sociologist Herbert J. Gans regards the functionalist claim that poverty and social stratification are "functional" for the whole of society as overstated. Gans (1971) argues that poverty persists because it has certain positive functions for particular segments of American society, but does not benefit the nation as a whole. He states that poverty

> makes possible the existence or expansion of respectable professions and occupations, for example, penology, criminology, social work, and public health. . . . [T]he poor have provided jobs for professional and para-professional "poverty warriors," and for journalists and social scientists . . . who have supplied the information demanded by the revival of public interest in poverty (1971: 78).

Below is a select list of the main functions that, in Gans' opinion, poverty and inequality serve for the middle and upper classes:

1. It ensures that society's dirty work gets done.
2. The poor subsidize the middle and upper classes by working for low wages and by paying a disproportionate amount of taxes.
3. Poverty creates many professional jobs in social work, counseling, law enforcement, and the like.
4. The poor buy goods and services which would otherwise be rejected: for example, day-old bread, used cars, and the services of old, retired, or incompetent "professionals."
5. The poor provide examples of failure which serve "to uphold the legitimacy of conventional norms."
6. The stereotypical "uninhibited sexual, alcoholic, and

narcotic behavior" of the poor offers "vicarious participation" in these forms of deviant behavior for the middle class.

7. Poverty has cultural functions because the middle class sometimes adopts "extinct folk cultures" as fads; examples include country music, the blues, and blue jeans.

8. The existence of poor people serves as a "measuring rod" for other classes to gauge their movement up and down the stratification ladder.

9. The economic exploitation of the poor facilitates movement up the social ladder for those members of society who are just above them.

10. Some members of the upper and middle classes who have no need to work keep themselves busy with involvement in charity affairs.

11. The poor, being politically powerless, can be forced to absorb the costs of change and growth in American society.

Although some of these "functions" of poverty may seem facetious, Gans' argument is not without merit. Is there any doubt that some segments of the middle and upper classes profit from the misery of the poor? As discussed previously in Chapters 3, 4, and 5, from the tax system to the welfare system, poor people pay—both economically and socially—for their condition, while other segments of society benefit because of it.

Gans strongly implies that these "functions" of poverty actually motivate those members of society who benefit from them to find ways of ensuring that poverty persists.

Conclusion

In *The Sociological Imagination* (1959), C. Wright Mills wrote:

> When, in a city of 100,000, only one man is unemployed, that is his personal trouble, and for its relief we properly look to the character of the man, his skills, and his immediate opportunities.

> But when in a nation of 50 million employees, 15 million men are unemployed, that is an issue, and we may not hope to find its solution within the range of opportunities open to any one individual. The very structure of opportunities has collapsed. Both the correct statement of the problems and the range of possible solutions require us to consider the economic and political institutions of the society, and not merely the personal situation and character of a scatter of individuals (p. 9).

In the last decade of the twentieth century, when 32.5 million Americans are living below the official poverty line, and millions more are hovering just above it and at least 1 to 2 million Americans are homeless, it would seem that blaming the victim theories constitute at best incomplete, and at worst simply false, misleading explanations for these conditions. Although they seem to threaten the smug security and illusions of the middle and upper classes, blaming the system explanations offer greater insight into the reality of American society. If we truly care about the future, then we must take a critical look at what is going on in the United States and make some difficult reevaluations of our priorities.

8

The Production of Poverty
What Produces Persistent Poverty?

Why does the United States experience persistent poverty? Certainly there are many causes, and they interact with each other. They are not, however, to be found primarily in the characteristics of the individual victims of poverty and homelessness, nor in the behaviors and attitudes that manifest the consequences of their condition. Rather, they can be traced to the large social and economic transformations that are occurring in this country.

Why is it that even though the last years of the 1980s have been described as a period of "economic recovery" and a decade in which official unemployment rates declined, poverty and homelessness actually increased? The answer lies beneath the surface of official statistics and superficial impressions that lead us to assume all is well.

American poverty is not a new phenomenon. Gross inequality in wealth and income have been a feature of U.S. society since before the American Revolution. The difference between contemporary poverty and that of the past is the extent of the extremes in both poverty and wealth. Although persistent

173

poverty has always permeated American society, specific factors that are, in many ways, uniquely modern have produced this current polarization.

The Changing Global Economy

Some social observers maintain that although the United States may have recently won the cold war, it is losing economic ground in both global and domestic competition. Writing for *Harper's*, Walter Mead contends that

> while the post-World War II order was designed by the United States and served our interests, the new order is being created by others, and it threatens to lock the United States into long-term economic decline (Mead, 1990).

Since the late 1960s, American industries have lost large shares of various markets, mostly to Asian countries, including Japan, South Korea, Hong Kong, Taiwan, and Singapore (Ong, 1989: 4). The consumer electronics and auto industries have experienced most of these losses. Furthermore, Asian competition accounts for over one-half of the U.S. trade deficit.

Two of the factors that have put American industry at a competitive disadvantage are higher labor costs and obsolete technology (Ong, 1989). Consequently, there has been large-scale disinvestment in U.S. industries, resulting in plant closings, layoffs, unemployment and underemployment, low wages, increased poverty, and severe disruptions of communities in which a single industry provided their economic base.

Deindustrialization

As discussed in Chapter 7, corporate executives are disinvesting in America. Since 1970, 50 million Americans have been displaced from their jobs. Economists have labeled this displacement the *Deindustrialization of America* (Bluestone & Harrison, 1982). Across the nation, factories and plants have been closed down. Cheap labor costs have motivated some CEOs to move their industries to other countries, such as Mexico, China, Hong Kong, and the Philippines, where people work for 3 dollars a day instead of 3 dollars an hour. Consequently, the American worker is confronted with the elimination of decent-paying blue-collar jobs.

It is estimated that in the first half of the 1980s, up to one million workers a year were dislocated due to plant closings. President Reagan initially vetoed a bill designed to give workers 60 days' notice before a plant was closed. A 1988 study revealed that almost 40 percent of the workers who were laid off due to plant closings during that year were not given advance notice (Bolle, 1990: 1). Subsequently, the Worker Adjustment and Retraining Notification Act (WARN) was reintroduced into Congress, passed on August 4, 1988, and went into effect on February 4, 1989.

Over the past decade, deindustrialization has hit the manufacturing industries hardest. Nearly two-thirds of the 6 million workers who were dislocated during the first half of the 1980s had been employed in blue-collar manufacturing jobs. A 1986 U.S. General Accounting Office survey found that nearly 60 percent of the plants that closed cited "high labor costs" as the reason for closing. And a Department of Labor study of the reemployment of dislocated workers found that, five years after losing their jobs, 33 percent of those studied were either still unemployed or no longer in the labor market. Among those who did find other jobs, 40 percent were earning at least 20 percent less than their previous wage.

The consequences of deindustrialization are not restricted to the workers who directly suffer economic displacement when the companies they work for undergo disinvestment. There is also the "ripple effect" of economic displacement. During the early 1980s, 20,000 steelworkers in northwest Indiana lost their jobs. A study was conducted to determine the impact of the layoffs on a two-county area of that state. Researchers found that in the nonsteel sector of the local economy an additional 10,000 jobs had been lost (Nyden, 1984).

The Congressional Research Service (CRS) summarized three principal reasons for deindustrialization in the United States, as it relates to changing world economic conditions. According to the CRS, deindustrialization results from:

1. the advanced technology of communications and transportation which has allowed capital to move more rapidly between industries, between regions of the country, and over the entire globe.
2. the increased centralization of ownership and managerial control of capital in the hands of huge multinational corporations which make it possible for these corporate giants to take advantage of new technologies.
3. a major change in world conditions affecting plant relocations has greatly increased international competition which has led to global excess capacity in many industries. This has caused rates of return to decline. Under great pressure to reduce costs and restore rates of return, some corporate managers have done so by moving operations abroad or elsewhere in the United States to take advantage of lower wage rates (and lower tax rates in some instances) (Bolle, 1986: 1).

Evidence indicating that deindustrialization has contributed both directly and indirectly to the production of the black underclass (that segment of the poverty population which receives much negative press) was presented in Chapter 7 during the discussion of Wilson's book, *The Truly Disadvantaged*. A discussion of the specific role of deindustrialization in the production of poverty and the black underclass in Los Angeles follows.

Unemployment/Underemployment

As we have noted, the deindustrialization of American companies has created unprecedented unemployment and underemployment in the United States. The disproportionate number of minority group members among the homeless, for example, explains how unemployment has significantly contributed to the homeless crisis. Although the overall national unemployment rate has temporarily decreased, among all nonwhite groups it is more than double the national rate. Among some minority groups, unemployment rates match recession and, in some cases, even depression-level rates.

At least 60 percent of all new jobs created during the last decade are low-paying, part-time, service jobs. More than 5 million Americans involuntarily work part-time, when they would rather have full-time jobs—one reason why many of the poor and homeless, about 25 percent, are called the working poor and the working homeless. Only one out of three unemployed workers receives unemployment insurance, the lowest proportion since the program was first implemented in the 1930s (Furiga, 1989).

Based on the findings of a 1988 Senate Budget Committee study, Senator Lawton Chiles (D., Fla.) concluded, "The sad truth is that jobs paying below the poverty level are growing faster than any other kind. And jobs that provide a middle-class standard of living are a shrinking part of our job landscape." The Senate study documented that wages in the United States are "becoming polarized in a downward direction." Of the 8 million jobs created between 1979 and the mid-1980s, 58 percent were "low wage" jobs. A low-paying wage was defined by the study as $11,611 or less for a family of four (Grose, 1988).

A related study by the Joint Economic Committee of Congress revealed that the increase in low-paying jobs is leading to a dwindling middle class. Between 1979 and the mid-1980s, the number of jobs that paid $14,000 a year or more declined by 1.8 million. Congressman David Obey of the Joint Economic Committee stated,

> We find [the increase in low-paying jobs] deeply disturbing. Although more Americans are working, there is less opportunity for a good job or even a reasonably good job (Grose, 1988).

It may be difficult for some of us to imagine what it would be like to work as hard as possible, yet still be unable to provide adequate food or shelter for ourselves and our families. This "difficult image" translates into a harsh reality. Working for the low minimum wage, or less, constitutes underemployment; and for the head of a household who works full-time, the amount of income received from such a job will not exceed the poverty level. In fact, it will not even equal it.

Aside from the economic consequences of unemployment and underemployment, there are substantial human costs. Department of Labor studies demonstrate that the effects of extended, involuntary unemployment (which affects over a million workers who remain unemployed for 27 weeks or more) include "increased family abuse, depression, alcohol and drug abuse, and violent behavior" (USGAO, 1989, September).

The Low-Income Housing Crisis

The lack of decent, low-income (less than $250 a month) housing is the common denominator facing all potentially homeless people. The shortage in the number of these housing units, among other factors, has contributed to the inability of the system to meet the needs of an increasing number of America's impoverished citizens. The number of low-income renters exceeds the number of available low-income housing units by approximately 4 million. Furthermore, budgets for federal government programs, which in the past assisted poor people with their housing, have been among the most severely cut of all government programs during the past 9 years, precisely when they were most needed.

According to a Congressional review of the causes of homelessness:

> the scarcity of low-income housing appears to be the main cause of homelessness. Poor people simply cannot afford . . . [the] majority

TABLE 8.1. Public Housing Units

Year	Units Authorized
1977	31,764
1978	56,245
1979	54,914
1980	36,677
1981	35,921
1982	27,611
1983	27,041
1984	24,058
1985	19,093
1986	14,867
1987	10,415
1988	9,146

Source. Based on William Tucker (1990). The source of America's housing problem. *Policy Analysis* No. 127, p. 4. Washington, D.C.: Cato Institute. Original source: Department of Housing and Urban Development.

of available housing in the United States (U.S. House, Committee on Government Operations, 1985).

During the last decade, the number of new public housing units that were authorized declined significantly (see Table 8.1).

Inadequate Social Welfare

Almost all social welfare programs suffered budget cuts during the decade of the 1980s. As documented in Chapter 4, the resulting deficiencies have contributed to the inability of many of these programs to meet the needs of recipients.

Cutbacks in social welfare programs have increased the impact of deindustrialization and underemployment. In 1990, the federal government will have spent less than one percent of its budget on training and job programs, a 70 percent reduction since 1981. In addition, 25 percent, or a quarter of a million young people, have been cut from the Summer Youth Employment Program. Since 1981, government spending for social programs, as a percentage of GNP, has shrunk from 4.2 percent to 3.7 percent (Harris and Wilkins, 1988).

The political decisions of the Reagan and Bush administrations to cut back spending on welfare programs have seriously affected increasing numbers of Americans who have fallen victim to poverty or near-poverty. Nonetheless, these political acts are not the fundamental source of the current poverty and homeless crisis. The primary factors can be traced to long-term transformations in the global economy and the resulting influence on the structure of the U.S. economy.

Big Government Corruption and Fraud

The new direction given to HUD by Jack Kemp has been overshadowed by revelations of fraud and corruption within that agency during the Reagan Administration. According to *Time* magazine, one of the cornerstones of Reagan's presidential campaigns was an attack on government waste, fraud, and abuse. As previously noted several top government officials pocketed millions of dollars in consulting fees through their association with HUD-subsidized housing contracts. By the end of 1989, it was determined that the HUD scandal involved the misuse of at least $9 billion.

Additional evidence, released in mid-1990, revealed that "one-third of the projects in a $1.6 billion elderly housing program are in or near financial ruin" (AP, 1990, April). Republican favoritism and poor management were reported as reasons for the defaulting of contractors on government-insured loans which were to be used to build or renovate housing for the elderly poor.

Undoubtedly, the corruption at HUD contributed to the growing poverty and homeless crisis. More important, however, the HUD scandal is symptomatic of the indifferent attitude of the former Republican administration regarding the issue of poverty.

Increased Family Instability

For many families, the burden of economic insecurity often results in increased family instability (Ropers & Marks, 1983). The national divorce rate is nearly one-half that of the marriage rate, and domestic violence occurs in one out of every six American households. According to a General Accounting Office study, marital disruption "directly involves the lives of 3 million adults and children" (USGAO, 1989, September 14). And, as indicated previously, almost one-half of impoverished families are headed by females.

Enormous federal budget cuts in domestic programs have compounded these factors by limiting or eliminating resources that could assist troubled families and enable them to survive periods of economic distress. These factors have also contributed to the upsurge in poverty and homelessness, not the personalities, attributes, individual characteristics, or heredity of the victims of these economic and social trends.

The Polarization of the Social Stratification System

All of these factors discussed above have combined to produce an American society that is characterized by gross inequality. Ronald Reagan was fond of saying, "In the sixties we waged a war on poverty, and poverty won." He was correct. In 1990, more Americans lived below the official poverty line, and millions more hovered just above it, than did in the 1960s, when the war on poverty was waged. In 1969, 24.1 million Americans lived below the poverty level; by 1989 that number had increased to 32.5 million. Since 1975, there has been a 52 percent increase in the number of full-time workers living in poverty. This is neither economic nor social progress.

Between 1978 and 1981, the minimum wage was raised four times. In the late 1980s, Congress considered giving itself a 50 percent pay increase; the minimum wage, however, was not raised during that decade. In April, 1990, after about a ten-year period, the minimum wage was raised to $3.80 an hour and will be increased to $4.25 an hour in April 1991. Critics have pointed out, however, that these increases "won't lift millions of low-wage workers above the poverty line" (AP, 1990, April 1). The minimum wage is payed to 3 million Americans, over 60 percent of whom are adults.

Although many Americans consider themselves members of the middle class, economic and social forces are producing a "bipolar" society that is characterized by a shrinking middle class. During the past 20 years the percentage of the U.S. population that fits the definition of middle class has declined relative to the median income of the population. Since 1980, average weekly earnings have increased from $235 to $305. However, when adjusted for inflation, a drop in *real wages* has occurred—down to $227. American society presents a tragic tale of two nations: one in which millions live the good life, and another in which even more millions live in despair and misery. America is a nation polarized more by economic class than it is by race, religion, or ethnicity.

Racism and Sexism

Discrimination based on race and gender prevails in American society. Not all Americans are treated equally in the labor, housing, and education markets, in particular. It is not coincidental that working-class minority group members and women comprise a disproportionate number of the poverty population. Unfortunately, prejudice and discrimination contribute significantly to the persistence of American poverty. Published by the National Urban League, *The State of Black America 1990* summarized the League's views regarding racism thus:

> The vicious murder of an African-American teenager in the Bensonhurst section of Brooklyn, New York in August (1989) was but one of many incidents in a long pattern of racist violence against black people and other minorities.
>
> It is no accident that open and often violent racism has re-emerged in the 1980s, for we live in a climate in which discrimination persists in spite of the laws. Just a week after the Brooklyn murder, for example, the Federal Reserve Bank of Boston released a study that documented pervasive denial of mortgage loans on properties in African-American neighborhoods (1990: 3).

If we include black men who are "discouraged and no longer looking for work," then the unemployment rate for black male adults is close to 45 percent. The Census Bureau, in 1980, could not locate 10 to 29 percent of black males between the ages of 20 and 40. If this segment of the population were counted among the unemployed, then the black unemployment rate would reach well over 50 percent. Such a level of unemployment is "more than double the figure for all workers at the height of the Great Depression" (Wilkerson & Gresham, 1989). The unemployment and underemployment of black males has a greater influence on instability within some black families than do any pathologies which may be inherent in black biology.

By the beginning of the twenty-first century, projections indicate that, although employed in similar jobs, women will be paid only 74 percent of the wages earned by their male counterparts. Currently, women are being paid only about 60 percent as much as men. The majority of women (80 percent) are employed in just 20 percent of the 427 major job categories identified by the U.S. Department of Labor (Robertson, 1989: 232); these are mainly "pink-collar" jobs such as nursing, teaching, and clerical positions.

The City of Los Angeles: A Case Study in the Production of Poverty and Related Social Problems

A research group at the UCLA School of Architecture and Urban Planning conducted a comprehensive study into the causes and conditions of poverty in Los Angeles. This research offers an excellent case study regarding the production of poverty (Ong, 1989).

The growing discrepancy between poverty and wealth in Los Angeles epitomizes the economic and social transformations that are occurring throughout the nation. With a population of about 8.6 million, the Los Angeles metropolitan area is one of the largest urban areas in the United States. Almost 30 percent of the Los Angeles labor force is engaged in manufacturing, a percentage that places Los Angeles higher than the national average. Furthermore, the manufacturing labor forces of other major cities, like New York City and Chicago, have diminished, while Los Angeles' has increased (see Table 8.2). Los Angeles' service-sector work force has also grown and now represents 56 percent of all jobs.

Despite economic growth and an increased number of jobs, Los Angeles has not avoided a gross disparity between income

TABLE 8.2. Workers in Manufacturing (thousands)

	1969	1987
New York	921	461
Chicago	983	551
Los Angeles	881	907

Source. Based on: Paul Ong (1989). *The Widening Divide: Income Inequality and Poverty in Los Angeles,* p. 13. UCLA Graduate School of Architecture and Urban Planning.

TABLE 8.3. **Poverty Rate in Los
Angeles and the Nation**

	1969	1987
Los Angeles	11%	15.6%
National	12.1%	13.5%

Source. Based on: Paul Ong (1989). *The Widening Divide: Income Inequality and Poverty in Los Angeles,* p. 15. UCLA Graduate School of Architecture and Urban Planning.

and wealth. In the late 1960s, 11 percent of the area's population lived in poverty, which ranked lower than the national average of 12.1 percent. By the late 1980s, however, the Los Angeles poverty population had increased to 15.6 percent, exceeding the national average of 13.5 percent (see Table 8.3).

Increased poverty in Los Angeles has resulted partially from the "deindustrialization in the high-wage sector and reindustrialization in the low-wage sector" (Ong, 1989: 16). For example, deindustrialization in black areas of Los Angeles has created high rates of unemployment, a primary cause of poverty:

> In the late seventies and early eighties alone, Los Angeles lost over 50,000 industrial jobs to plant closures in the auto, tire, steel, and nondefense aircraft industries. These industries traditionally offered high-paid, blue-collar employment to large numbers of minorities. Many of these plants were located either within ghettos or nearby. South Central L.A. which forms the core of the Black community, itself experienced a loss of 321 firms since 1971 (Ong, 1989: 203).

High statistical correlations exist between unemployment and poverty. The correlation between unemployed black males and poverty is .65 and .81 for black females (p. 202).

Ironically, poverty in Los Angeles' Hispanic barrios is associated not with deindustrialization but with low-wage *rein-dustrialization*. In recent years, a growing number of labor intensive, low-paying jobs in the apparel and furniture industries, located in and around the barrios, have been replacing good paying blue-collar industrial jobs.

The burden of low income, however, disproportionately affects blacks, Hispanics, women, and children. Black and Hispanic men in Los Angeles earn, on average, 30 percent and 20 percent less, respectively, than white men with comparable education and skills. Women, particularly minority women, earn about 33 percent less than the men (Ong, 1989: 19). The unfair treatment of women and black and Hispanic men in the labor market reflects, according to the UCLA study, "both overt and institutionalized discrimination." The UCLA study concludes that poverty in Los Angeles,

> represents the extreme outcome of income inequality: the lack of an income needed to achieve a minimum standard of living. Poverty is the result of the cumulative failures of our society to prepare people for meaningful work, of . . . wage discrimination, of an inadequate safety net, and of changing household structures. Despite this multitude of causes and mediating factors, there is, nonetheless, a direct and significant link between the economy and impoverishment. Given the rise in inequality in the labor market, it is not surprising that the poverty level has also risen. Poverty is a problem of both low wages and joblessness (Ong, 1989: 19).

The position of blacks and Hispanics in the labor market contributes to the explanation of the causes of many social problems that plague Los Angeles' black ghettos and Hispanic barrios—problems that also trouble white, middle-class Americans. Because decent paying, steady employment is unavailable in the ghettos and barrios, and racism and discrimination prevent many nonwhite citizens from getting and keeping good jobs outside of the poverty neighborhoods, black and Hispanic youth often feel alienated by the prospect of working at menial jobs. One consequence of this sense of alienation has been the growth of youth gangs in the ghettos and barrios. These gangs offer a system of respect and status for their members, and often provide them with illegitimate opportunities, such as dealing drugs, to make large sums of money. Another consequence of the concentration of the large black and Hispanic poverty populations in Los Angeles has been the creation of one of the largest nonwhite homeless populations in the nation.

An examination of the origins of contemporary poverty in Los Angeles provides an insightful analysis of how systemic economic and social forces, which are well beyond the control of the individuals who are inadvertently victimized by these large scale-transformations, result in the production of poverty.

Summary

Although poverty has been a persistent feature of American society for more than two centuries, the present increase in the polarization of the U.S. economic and social stratification systems is rooted in contemporary global and national economic transformations and political policies.

Increased poverty and homelessness are neither random, haphazard events, nor the consequences of ill-fate or personal pathology. Rather, they are the logical results of the structure and dynamics of the so-called "free enterprise system." American retail stores may be well stocked with consumer goods (most of which have been produced overseas); nevertheless, a substantial segment of the population does not have the means to purchase many of these products. It will be interesting to observe the reactions of the Eastern European nations when their people discover that the trade-off for reintroducing "a market system" is high unemployment, high rents, and increased poverty and homelessness. How will they deal with accelerated rates of divorce, street crime, drug and alcohol abuse, and other social problems that are associated with gross inequality?

9

The Politics of Poverty

Life, Liberty, and the Pursuit of Happiness

Life, liberty, and the pursuit of happiness are inconceivable without the opportunity to earn a decent living, secure life's basic necessities, and contribute to society. As we enter the final decade leading to the twenty-first century, America has changed direction somewhat with the election of George Bush to the presidency. The president has proposed a reevaluation of the condition of our less fortunate citizens who are the victims of poverty and homelessness. He would have us follow his leadership in promoting a "kinder and gentler" America. Let us remember his message to the nation as he put it in his inaugural address:

> America is never wholly herself unless she is engaged in high moral principle. We as a people have such a purpose today. It is to make kinder the face of the nation and gentler the face of the world.
>
> My friends, we have work to do. There are the homeless, lost, and roaming—there are the children who have nothing, no love, no normalcy—there are those who cannot free themselves of enslavement to whatever addiction—drugs, welfare, the demoralization that rules the slums. There is crime to be conquered, the rough

crime of the streets. There are young women to be helped who are
about to become mothers of children they can't care for and might
not love. They need our care, our guidance, and our education. . . .

We will make the hard choices, looking at what we have, perhaps allocating it differently, making our decisions based on honest
need and prudent safety.

And then we will do the wisest thing of all: We will turn to the
only resource we have that in times of need always grows: the
goodness and the courage of the American people.

And I am speaking of a new engagement in the lives of others—a new activism, hands-on and involved, that gets the job
done. We must bring in the generations, harnessing the unused
talent of the elderly and the unfocused energy of the young. For
not only leadership is passed from generation to generation, but so
is stewardship. . . .

And so, there is much to do: and tomorrow the work begins.
And I do not mistrust the future: I do not fear what is ahead. For
our problems are large, but our heart is larger. Our challenges are
great, but our will is greater. And if our flaws are endless, God's
love is truly boundless (Bush, 1989).

By appointing Jack Kemp to head the Department of Housing and Urban Development (HUD) the president displayed an
attempt, in his conservative way, toward concrete action in the
battle against poverty and homelessness. Kemp told Congress
during his confirmation hearing that the "appalling problem" of
homelessness would be his highest priority (AP, 1989, January
28). Public consciousness concerning the homeless and the
much larger issues of persistent poverty and growing inequality
has been raised by Kemp's public statements regarding these
aspects of American society. When he was sworn in, Kemp
stated,

> Mr. Lincoln said America cannot exist half slave, half free in
> the nineteenth century. . . . Today, the next century, we can't have
> this country half or three-quarters prosperous and some folks left
> behind. . . . I don't believe in the perpetuity of poverty so I'm
> thrilled and honored to have the opportunity to help implement
> George Bush's agenda for the '90s here at HUD, an agenda of

> compassion and opportunity, of hope and the promise of a better
> and brighter future for America (UPI, Kemp sworn in, vows to
> attack poverty, 1989).

Leading advocates for the poor and homeless welcomed this change of direction from the previous administration. In December 1988, Robert M. Hayes, a lawyer for the National Coalition for the Homeless, wrote a letter to Kemp in which he commented, "We are cheered by your pledge to fight vigorously to end homelessness" (Kemp appointed HUD chief, 1989). In a later statement, Hayes said, "It's a very encouraging sign. . . . Hopefully pragmatism is overtaking political isolation in Washington" (Bowman, 1989).

As the new head of HUD, Kemp attempted to distance himself from President Reagan's much criticized statement that homeless people are homeless by choice. Mary Brunette, a Kemp aide, said, "He [Kemp] feels that nobody would be on the streets if there were alternatives for their needs" (Bowman, 1989). When referring to the House Ways and Means Committee's recent passage of a bill which will reduce the capital gains tax, Kemp stated, "I believe the committee's priorities have been tragically misplaced by not giving poverty top billing on this nation's political agenda" (Kemp, 1989). And according to the *New York Times,*

> Housing and urban experts agree that an infusion of spirit and
> purpose into the troubled agency [HUD] has been the greatest
> achievement of Mr. Kemp's first year as Secretary. . . . To some
> degree, Mr. Kemp remains an anomaly, a conservative Republican
> who talks urgently about housing for the homeless and empower-
> ing the poor. Calling himself "a bleeding-heart conservative," Mr.
> Kemp has insisted that at least 75 percent of the agency's money be
> spent on the poor (Tolchin, 1990).

Nevertheless, some social critics are predicting that President Bush's vision of a kinder, gentler America may be subverted by a severe economic crisis within the next few years, which will produce a "leaner, meaner society." Researchers at the Center for Policy Research at George Washington University in Washington D.C. have warned that "the United States may soon face an economic disruption so severe that government spending would be cut to the bone" (AP, Economic crisis could drive us into "meaner" society, 1989). Whatever lies in store for the nation, we must attempt to better understand some of the major social problems that confront us, solve them, and secure stability and prosperity for everyone.

Despite all the enthusiastic rhetoric about a kinder and gentler America, after his first year in office President Bush was viewed by the American public as not doing enough to end poverty and homelessness. A *New York Times*/CBS poll conducted in January 1990 posed the question, "Do you think the Bush Administration has done all it should to help the homeless, or do you think it has not shown enough concern?" The majority (71 percent) of those polled believed Bush "hasn't shown enough concern." Ten percent of the respondents had no opinion, and 19 percent believed the administration had "done all it should" (Weighing concern for the homeless, 1990).

Some social science historians believe that, in the early 1960s, President Kennedy was motivated to lay the foundation for the War on Poverty, which was later implemented by President Johnson, by Michael Harrington's book, *The Other America* (1962). In *The New American Poverty* (1984), Harrington argued that "while the promises of the Johnson administration may not have been met, there was a generosity of spirit that today, under Ronald Reagan, has been replaced by cynicism and meanness" (p. 15). Because the issue of poverty simply does not interest those who set government policies and priorities, the poor continue to suffer.

Despite all the hoopla and Republican propaganda surrounding the "trickle-down theory" of economics, which promoted an image of economic recovery and unparalleled prosperity, by the late 1980s middle- and working-class Americans were wondering when the prosperity would start to trickle down. Conducted near the end of 1988, a *Time* magazine poll found that 47 percent of middle-class Americans and 60 percent of low-income groups felt they were "worse off" financially due to the Reagan policies of the 1980s. *Time* summarized the reasons for this discontent thus:

> One reason is fear that gargantuan budget and trade deficits may yet cause prosperity to fizzle. But there is also a feeling that something is wrong with the boom, that general prosperity is not bringing as much of the good life as the rosy numbers indicated. Though the wealthy are doing noticeably better, most middle-class Americans feel squeezed. They are struggling harder—and often depending on two incomes when one sufficed for their parents—to pay for housing, tuition and other expenses that have gone up much faster than inflation (Are you better off? 1988: 28).

Bush's Budget Proposals: Kinder and Gentler Talk, but the Same Old Reagan Action

In his inaugural speech, President Bush also stated, "The commitment is there, the money is there to create a better America." Despite the kinder and gentler rhetoric, however, it seems that neither the commitment nor the money is forthcoming to solve our most pressing social problems. Essentially, Bush's proposed FY 1991 budget (see Table 9.1) is a continued, although restructured form of the Reagan era type of federal budgeting that favors those who are well to do, and does nothing to make life less difficult for the poor and near poor. While drastic cuts in low-income programs continue, the tax rate for the poorest 20 percent of the population has increased by 16 percent. Meanwhile, the tax rate for the wealthiest 20 percent of the population has been reduced by 5.5 percent (Miller, 1990: 12).

Although in some cases the actual dollar amount for low-income programs appears to have increased by about 80 percent, in actuality this amount has been "frozen" relative to inflation.

TABLE 9.1. Cuts in Federal Low-Income Programs, FY 1981–FY 1991 (Based on Proposed Budget Authority, FY 1991)

Selected Low-Income Programs	% change FY1981–FY1991 (after inflation)	% change FY1990–FY1991 (after inflation)
Housing		
Housing for the elderly and handicapped	−76.1	−42.6
Rural Housing Insurance Fund	−82.3	−48.2
Additional rural housing programs[a]	−94.8	−34.0
Subsidized housing	−83.2	−8.7
Health		
Community health centers	−1.8	−0.3
Maternal and child health	−14.7	−0.8
Migrant health	−24.9	−5.0
Immunization grants	+232.2	−5.9
Education		
Indian education	−25.5	+2.4

Employment		
Older Americans' employment	-16.7	-7.6
Training and employment services	-69.2	+2.0
Other		
Community development block grants	-49.9	-9.2
Community services block grants	-94.6	-89.6
Legal services	-33.5	-3.8
Low-income energy assistance	-61.8	-27.5
Low-income weatherization	-100.0	-100.0
VISTA	-20.5	+30.6
Total cuts in low-income discretionary programs (including programs not listed here)	-55.5	-3.5

[a]Includes domestic farm-labor housing, very low-income housing repair grants, and rural housing preservation grants. *Source.* Center for Budget and Policy Priorities; based on a chart appearing in *Dollars & Sense,* May 1990, p. 13.

This has not been the case for many military-related programs. For example, the Bush Administration has made a proposal to increase spending on the Star Wars program by 23 percent in an effort to cover inflation increases.

Politics of Housing

William Tucker, a writer for the conservative CATO Institute, summarized the three main arguments commonly directed toward those policies of the Reagan Administration, and essentially continued in the Bush Administration, which are considered to have contributed to the homeless crisis:

1. Federal housing assistance was reduced unmercifully during the 1980s. In 1981 the Department of Housing and Urban Development had budget authorizations of $32.2 billion; by 1989 they had been slashed to a mere $6.9 billion—a reduction of 78 percent.
2. The federal government has abandoned its 50-year-old commitment to build public housing. In 1979 Congress authorized nearly 55,000 new units of public housing. In 1984 the number of units authorized was zero, and it has averaged less than 7400 since then. That drastic reduction in public housing construction during the Reagan years caused homelessness to increase.
3. What little money remained in federal housing programs' budgets was misappropriated—either entrusted to embezzlers or squandered on political favoritism. Between $2 billion and $4 billion was stolen from HUD by private contractors, and HUD lent well-connected developers millions of dollars' worth of Section 8 moderate-rehabilitation program funds. Although intended for the poor, many of the rehabilitated homes ended up being occupied by members of the middle class (Tucker, 1990).

By contrast, the Bush Administration continues to support military expenditures, some of which are the most costly Defense Department programs executed during the country's history. An example of one such program is the inflated cost of the

B-2 bomber. In a February 1990 report, the United States General Accounting Office concluded:

> In June 1989 the B-2 program was estimated to cost $70.2 billion, a $12 billion increase from the baseline estimate. The June 1989 estimate depends on achieving $6.2 billion in savings through a cost reduction initiatives program and multiyear procurement strategy. The amount of savings and the feasibility of achieving them are uncertain. If the projected savings are not realized, additional funding will be required, and the B-2 program's schedule may be extended. The current acquisition plan requires funding of $5.3 billion in fiscal year 1991 and $7.5 to $8 billion annually for fiscal years 1992 through 1995 to achieve the estimated program cost of $70.2 billion (USGAO, 1990, February).

Critics claim that all this spending on the B-2 is a waste of money, because by the time the plane is fully operational its technology will be obsolete. Furthermore, during the next decade, NASA is planning to spend $500 billion on space missions for exploration of the moon and Mars, and an additional $20 billion on a space station. On the other hand, since 1980, federal outlays for rent subsidies and home-building programs have been cut from $40 million to $10 million (Church, 1990, May 21).

Two Political Approaches to Understanding Poverty

Two basic paradigms (schools of thought) form the foundations for most political responses—and nonresponses—to the problem of poverty. The first which, for the purpose of discussion, we will call Political Poverty Paradigm One, is related to the assumptions of the blaming the victim perspective. The second, which we will call Political Poverty Paradigm Two, is related to the assumptions of the blaming the system perspective (see Table 9.2). Each paradigm has various assumptions and premises concerning poverty that can be grouped into three major concerns: (1) conceptions of American society, (2) intervention strategy, and (3) political orientation.

TABLE 9.2. Poverty Paradigms

Poverty Paradigm One	Poverty Paradigm Two
Conceptions of American Society	
A. Institutions are sound. Poverty due to: 1. temporary malfunction 2. individual pathology	A. Poverty built into structure of social system
B. Democratic pluralism	B. Environment shapes attitudes and behavior
C. Science can solve problems	C. Social change can solve social problems
Intervention Strategy	
A. Provide services (mopping up): rehabilitate, restore, equip	A. Publicity
B. Make self-sustaining and norm-abiding	B. Litigation
C. Problems arise in service delivery strategy	C. Social Movements
	D. Confrontation
	E. Class conflict
	F. Problems arise in structural change strategy
Political Orientation	
Conservative–liberal	Liberal–radical

Political Poverty Paradigm One

Paradigm One assumes that U.S. institutions, especially economic institutions, are essentially sound. The increases in poverty and homelessness manifest merely temporary malfunctions in some of these economic and social institutions. They are considered to be the inevitable fall-out of the transformation from an industrial–production society to a postindustrial, service-oriented society.

Other factors that may possibly contribute to the creation of poverty in an economically sound society are the pathological or defective characteristics of certain individuals and groups. According to Paradigm One, these personality traits explain the inability of some people to succeed financially in a strong economic environment. Many of the previously discussed blaming the victim theories provide excellent examples of this theory.

Viewed in the context of Paradigm One, democratic pluralism controls the American political scene. No single interest group is able to hold a monopoly of power or influence. Neither big business, big labor, the rich, nor the middle class can dominate political life. Every political interest group is counterbalanced by the pressures of those groups that adhere to opposing ideological philosophies. The temporary malfunctions, or problematic individuals and groups, can be dealt with by plugging up bureaucratic loopholes and attempting to correct system-delivery problems—for instance, clearing up the HUD scandals created during the Reagan Administration, welfare reform here, tax revision there, or by simply leaving the free enterprise system alone and allowing it to work out its own bugs over the long run.

Rhetorically at least, the Reagan and Bush administrations have approached the politics of poverty by leaving the system alone. This policy supposedly encourages private sector organizations such as charities and churches to help the "deserving" poor pull themselves up by their bootstraps so that they can take advantage of the opportunities of the marketplace.

Regarding it as one of the improved opportunities in the labor market, the Bush Administration finally agreed to an insignificant hike in the minimum wage. According to Senator Edward Kennedy (D.-Mass.), however, the increase of the minimum wage to $4.25 is a "disgrace." He believes it should be increased to "a level that is fair to millions of workers who are being unfairly exploited now" (AP, 1990, April). Kennedy blamed the small increase in the minimum wage on the Bush Administration. The initial proposal, which called for an increase from $3.35 an hour to $4.55 an hour in 1989, was vetoed.

Kennedy said the hike from $3.35 to $4.25 was "the best we could do against an antiworker administration that refuses to do justice for America's working poor." Despite President Bush's views on the minimum wage, a 1990 poll indicated a majority of Americans think the minimum wage should be at least $5.00 (Ball, 1990, April 1).

Political Poverty Paradigm Two

Many of the findings and assumptions of Paradigm Two are based on blaming the system theories and research studies. Poverty is viewed as persistent because it is considered an integral component in the economic and social organizations of the United States. Additionally, bureaucratic systems that are currently in operation, and which are supposed to be helping the victims of poverty and homelessness, often aggravate the conditions and problems of the poor.

Many empirical studies exist which demonstrate that a minority of the poor have problems with health, alcoholism, drug abuse, emotional stability, subcultural attitudes, and behaviors that deviate from "middle-class" norms. In essence, Paradigm Two views these problems as the effect, not the cause, of poverty. Taking a strong environmental stance, Paradigm Two maintains that healthy and productive living conditions produce healthy and productive individuals. You can't pull yourself up by your bootstraps if you are barefoot!

Consequently, the solutions to the problem, or at least the responsibility for mitigating the damage inflicted by social and economic poverty, is primarily placed on social, economic, and political institutions. This approach removes the focus from the presumed pathology of certain groups of individuals. Such changes, from the perspective of Paradigm Two, can be accomplished through "intervention strategies" that concentrate on altering some of our external political, social, and economic conditions. An appropriate example of social intervention is the political activism of the homeless and their advocates. Prior to the early 1980s, very little, if anything, had been published about the plight of that segment of the poor which has come to be called the "homeless."

Today, the mass media is giving more coverage than it has in previous years to issues regarding the poor and homeless, as well as to the growing gap between those at the top and those at the bottom of the country's stratification system. No doubt, the overwhelming visibility of the growing numbers of poor Americans is responsible for this increased attention. It is no longer quite so easy to look the other way and try to forget the problem exists.

If there is one name that will be recalled in the history books as a forerunner in the struggle to end poverty, hunger, and homelessness in the latter part of the twentieth century, it will probably be Mitch Snyder. I have no doubt that Mitch did not remember shaking hands with me during a conference in Washington, D.C., in December 1986, but I remember the encounter vividly. Personally, he struck me as someone who was, if not possessed, then at least preoccupied with his cause. I also had the good fortune to participate on a panel with one of his collaborators, Mary Ellen Hombs, who, with him, coauthored one of the first contemporary books on homelessness, *Homelessness in America: A Forced March to Nowhere* (1982). Many people involved in this issue believe that their book and their leadership in the Community for Creative Non-Violence (CCNV) provided the initial stimulus for awakening the nation to the upsurge in American poverty.

Hombs and Snyder commented on the purpose of their book:

> We see this book as part of a process to propagate and deepen awareness, an awareness which, when carried to its inevitable conclusion, will result in the elimination of homelessness. Our ultimate enemy is evil born of ignorance, itself a product of distance

from suffering's reality and source. . . . True power, it has been said, flows out of true knowledge. It is where and with whom we stand that largely determines what we see and, therefore, what we know (1982: viii).

Snyder's political poverty strategy, however, surpassed the publicity that had been gained through his writings. In 1984, during a dramatic 51-day fast, he almost died. He risked his life in an effort to confront the Reagan Administration with the need for renovating a rat- and vermin-infested 800-bed homeless shelter located in Washington, D.C. When asked why he was fasting, Snyder replied,

It's the equivalent of running into a burning building to save those you love. We love those people at the shelter. . . . What I seek by fasting is a change of heart and policy on the part of the Reagan Administration toward our nation's homeless (Fasting wins concessions, 1984).

The Reagan Administration finally approved renovation of the shelter just hours before a planned CBS "60 Minutes" broadcast of the story was to be aired nationally, and just two days before the 1984 presidential election.

Unfortunately, Snyder, committed suicide on July 6, 1990. Apparently, a combination of personal troubles and dismay over the lack of any substantial progress to aid the homeless led to his tragic death. The Reverend Jesse Jackson responded to Snyder's death by stating,

He learned to face death rather fearlessly and ultimately died on his own terms, on his own turf. Now, as we embrace the legacy of this servant, two things remain very clear: the homeless must not surrender, not give up, and the government must not abandon those who are homeless (Katz, 1990).

The development of national publicity regarding homelessness and Snyder's dramatic confrontations with the political bureaucracy are excellent examples of "intervention strategies" used by the proponents of Paradigm Two in their efforts to implement social and political change.

The early 1980s witnessed the emergence of other new advocacy organizations for the poor, for example, the National Coalition for the Homeless based in New York City and Washington, D.C. The Coalition is primarily involved in litigation and political lobbying on behalf of the homeless poor. I worked with the Coalition's current president, Gary Blasi, during the early and mid-1980s, when we conducted research that was used in various law suits against both the city and county of Los Angeles. Many minor concessions were wrestled away from government bureaucracies on behalf of the poor. Several examples of the consequences of advocacy litigation have been presented previously in this book (see especially Chapter 5).

Over the past decade, publicity, litigation, and confrontation have been among the major motivating forces that have spurred several incipient social movements by and for the poor. Poor and homeless individuals have organized themselves into coalitions and advocacy organizations across the nation. The combined efforts of over 200 such groups culminated in one of the largest national marches for "housing now," which was conducted on October 7, 1989. The Associated Press described the demonstration as one of the "largest demonstrations for decent and fair housing since the civil rights crusade of the 1960s" (Byrd, 1989: 1).

An estimated crowd of 250,000 people heard the Reverend Joseph Lowey, head of the Southern Christian Leadership Conference, refer repeatedly to

> President Bush's promise of a "kinder and gentler" nation. He declared, it is not kindness to have women and children comprise most of the homeless. Winter is coming and the soul of our nation is in peril. It is not kind and gentle to spend $200 billion on the savings and loan bailout. . . . If this is the home of the brave, why the hell are so many of our brave homeless? (Byrd, 1989: 2).

Sometimes social movements evolve into large-scale civil or class conflict which can leave the fabric of a society in shreds. There are many recent historical examples, such as Iran, Nicaragua, Poland, and Panama. At this time, the social movements of the American poor simply lack the consciousness, organization, and leadership that is required to effectively challenge the continuation of prevailing economic and social arrangements.

The United States is a severely divided society: racially, financially, and in terms of social class. Advocates for the poor have had limited success convincing many that this country has a very real and serious poverty problem. To quote Mitch Snyder,

> There are a number of ways of viewing America. . . . Where you stand determines what you see. . . . If the President of the Untied States . . . could reduce the distance and see people eat out of garbage cans or see people in supermarkets without enough money, he would roll up his sleeves and get to work because he would realize that there is injustice on the street (Molotsky and Weaver, 1986: A16).

Nevertheless, even Snyder thought a little progress had been made. Referring to President Bush, Snyder remarked, "The importance of what happened is that the President has recognized that the problem is serious enough to demand a response" (Maitland, 1989, November 26).

10

Justice?

As the Reagan era came to an end, *Newsweek* ran a cover story titled "The 80s are over: Greed goes out of style" (1988, January 4). Giving us a glimpse of what the Reagan presidency stood for, *Newsweek* commented:

> It had been 20 years since we'd had a leader who was so openly comfortable with wealth and the wealthy. The public seemed fascinated by the air of unembarrassed extravagance that floated around the Reagans: Mrs. Reagan eventually spent $25,000 on her Inaugural wardrobe. A planned redecoration of the White House family quarters was to cost $800,000. The price tag for new White House china would be $209,508. What a relief the Reagans were! The new First Family's imperial lifestyle seemed to open a tap in the national consciousness, and all the longings for luxury that had been repressed in the parsimonious Carter years came flowing out (1988: 41).

President Bush has a somewhat different personal style, but, under the surface, it's business as usual in America.

The United States operates under a formal democratic political system, but we have little economic or social justice (meaning fairness of opportunity and of social and economic rewards). Certainly the liberty of having free elections does not, and may-

205

be should not, guarantee justice. Democracy is an appealing theory, but without justice it is not effective in practice.

When crooked Wall Street investors use inside trader information, accrue millions of dollars in personal wealth, and receive only a slap on the wrist if caught and convicted, this is not justice. When working people find themselves homeless due to disinvestment in low-income housing and a lack of decent paying jobs, this is not justice. When millions of American citizens become victims of large economic and social forces and transformations that are beyond their immediate control, society cannot justify abandoning these people to the arbitrary whims of a "free market."

Most books on social problems, especially those about poverty, attempt to conclude with some blueprint or ideological vision of how poverty might be mitigated or even eliminated. Twenty-five years ago, when I was a young idealistic "radical" student, it appeared that fundamental social and economic transformations were just on the verge of becoming realities. Indeed, the struggles of the mid-1960s and early 1970s did influence many positive social, political, and economic changes that remain with us today. Now, of course, I am older and perhaps a little wiser, and I have not given up many of my basic ideals regarding social justice. Although it may have been more comfortable to retreat behind the doors of my classroom and office, I chose to remain actively involved in various struggles, which I hope will contribute to bringing about the changes that will be required if we are to create a more humane existence for all citizens. But the persistence and increase of injustice in American society causes me to begin to question the pace of change and how deeply changes can be made.

Almost a century ago, Robert Hunter wrote in *Poverty* (1904):

> During the entire last century many of the best minds were engaged in the study of social and economic questions. At the beginning of this new century we are still asking "riddles about the

starving." After many years of most elaborate investigations, printed in thousands of volumes issued by federal and state governments, we are almost as far from any definite knowledge concerning the extent of poverty as we have ever been. The United States spends more money than any other nation in the world upon statistical investigations, and yet we know less about the poverty of the people than almost any other great nation of the Western world (p. 12).

Apparently, not much has changed since Hunter wrote those words.

Perhaps, this book may simply add to the mountains of volumes already written on American poverty, and make no difference at all. But nothing is permanent. Certainly, the absolute poverty of millions of homeless Americans is not inevitable and it is certainly not cost effective for our society. Maybe a spark here and a spark there will help to ignite moral and political outrage that could lead to positive changes. Persistent poverty, however, will not cease merely because more books and articles are published on the topic. The fair allocation and redistribution of income and wealth ultimately results from political decisions and actions.

I have no intention of proposing a list of utopian demands or of proposing elaborate designs for the termination of poverty in the United States. Nevertheless, I am willing to suggest some considerations regarding the modification of American priorities.

Like the majority of American students, during my elementary and high school education I was instructed that social and economic improvement was possible for everyone in America. Though well intended, that myth continues to grow more and more distant from reality. Robert Hunter estimated that 20 percent of the entire population lived in economic distress during the year 1897. Today, in the 1990s, almost one-third of the U.S. population lives in poverty or near poverty. So much for progress in the given system!

A *New York Times* article titled "Working-class families losing middle-class dreams" (Chira, 1989) quoted the following from Gilbert Matthews, who earns $35,000 a year as a subway motorman: "When our parents had us, they had the American dream. They said my kids will have more than me. The American dream is gone." Mr. Matthews is having difficulty making ends meet for his wife and four children. As Paul Tepper pointed out: "Martin Luther King noted 'if we don't use her [America's] vast resources of wealth to end poverty and make it possible for all God's children to have the basic necessities of life, she, too, will go to hell" (Tepper, 1990).

Let those who think they occupy the high moral ground recognize and act on the moral imperatives which poverty and homelessness demand. For those seeking a "New Age," let it be one that transcends narrow self-interest. Empowering the poor to help themselves by creating a just society must be made a top priority. It is time to remember these words:

> For I was hungered, and ye gave me meat; I was thirsty, and ye gave me drink; I was a stranger, and ye took me in; Naked and ye clothed me; I was sick and ye visited me; I was in prison, and ye came unto me. . . . Verily I say unto you, inasmuch as ye have done it unto one of the least of these my brethren, ye have done it unto me (Matt. 26: 35, 40).

The War on Poverty that was declared in the mid-1960s is lost. But some battles have been won and some progress has been made. Journalist Hyman Bookbinder summarized some of the gains of that lost War on Poverty, stating: "The initial effort sparked other programs that have significantly helped the poor. Medicare and Medicaid, food stamps, low-income housing, manpower training, minimum-wage improvements, aid to education, beneficial tax-law changes" (1989).

And even though some of these gains have been eroded by Republican presidents, and poverty still persists, until there are fundamental political and social changes in America, poverty programs do make sustaining life itself possible for more of the poor than if these programs did not exist at all. The solution to persistent poverty is not an either/or dilemma. It is necessary to fight for reforms and, at the same time, fight for fundamental political and social change.

Invisible Inequality

The nineteenth-century writer and social critic Anatole France wrote, "The law, in its majestic equality, forbids the rich as well as the poor to sleep under bridges, to beg in the streets, and to steal bread."

As an abstraction, the concept of equality means little. Equality relates specifically to the life conditions, opportunities, and potentials of real people who live in particular social settings.

Thomas Edsall (1988) has written about "the return of inequality" to the American consciousness. Although American ideals and dreams often include hopes of diminishing economic and social inequalities, social consciousness usually lags far behind changing social reality. However, personal preoccupation with keeping one's head above troubled economic waters and not losing ground is very different from fully understanding the extent to which the gap between the haves and have nots has grown. According to Edsall, invisible inequality characterizes the majority's view of that gap. Just since 1974, the ratio of income between the top and bottom fifths of the population has increased from a difference of 1:7 to 1:9. In other words, the income of those people in the top one-fifth of the population has increased from seven times the amount of the income received by the bottom one-fifth of the population to nine times the amount received by those at the bottom. The expanding chasm between the superrich and all other classes is transforming every dimension of American society. Individually, many people may or may not consider themselves better off than they were previously. Collectively, however, strong evidence shows that, in an absolute sense, the majority of the population has lost ground to those at the top.

If every family was guaranteed a minimum annual income of $40,000, adjusted for family size and inflation, would poverty and inequality vanish? No. There is no such simple solution to such a complex problem. Certainly relative inequality will continue if people with annual incomes in the millions continue to maintain their lifestyles. Relative poverty (which means that some families continue to receive one-thousandth, one-tenth, one-fifth, or whatever fraction, of the income that other families receive) will also persist. Even if the income levels of those at the bottom are raised, relative poverty will not be eliminated. Therefore, if inequality is defined in terms relative to a specific income level, then the poor will always be with us.

Although related, poverty and inequality are different. Inequality refers to differences between people, and differences come in many varieties. For example, personal differences in hair color, preferred hobbies, food tastes, and exercise abound. It is probably desirable that they do. Inequalities in wealth and income are another matter. They can and—some people think—should be reduced, or even abolished. A society could greatly reduce differences in wealth and income and still retain and encourage the myriad personal differences that keep life interesting and rich.

New Choices?

The predominant threats to American society may now be primarily domestic. We are clearly in the post-cold war era. It takes time to change old patterns of thinking and behaving, but a change in national strategy is now necessary. We are, however, trapped in a paradox. If, as conservatives say, the United States has "won" the cold war, then the transition to a less offensive posture means additional factory closures and higher unemployment rates, especially among "defense" workers. According to a Congressional Budget Office report:

> Pentagon spending cuts would be toughest on New England, the South Atlantic states, and West Coast where most defense spending is concentrated. Disruptions are apt to be most severe in smaller communities near military bases that would be closed, or near defense plants whose contracts would be terminated (Maloy, 1990: 1).

The political choices the president has made regarding budget-spending priorities will establish trends well into the twentieth century. Democratic Party Chair Ronald Brown believes that Bush's plan to bail out the savings and loan defaults is nothing less then open, class warfare of the rich against the poor. Brown has stated,

> The S&L crisis—and especially President Bush's continuing, total bungling of the cleanup—is right at the center of the debate over the future of our country. . . . [It is] a debate between Democrats and Republicans. [It is] a debate between the upper crust and the rest of us. . . . It is a debate between those who preach policies of timidity and hiding—underestimating problems, procrastinating, idly hoping someone else, anyone else, will take care of them and those who say that we need bold aggressive economic leadership. . . . The Democratic Party's position is clear—we oppose paying for the S&L mess by unfair tax increases on working Americans (AP, 1990, July 1).

What the savings and loan bailout boils down to is about a $1 trillion debt, which will cost each American taxpayer over $1000 through increased taxes over the coming years. This transfer of money will go mainly to upper-middle- and upper-class individuals who lost savings and investments because of misguided and/or crooked banking policies.

One such example of a crooked savings and loan executive is Don Dixon. Dixon's wheeling and dealing in Texas left taxpayers with a $1.3 billion bailout tab. Dixon has been indicted on 38 criminal charges (Gallagher, 1990).

It is inconceivable that differences in status, e.g., the difference between a teacher and a student in terms of experience, training, and knowledge, could, or ever should, be eliminated. Nor will individual differences in personality, talent, interests, respect, deference, or motivation cease to exist. Inequality relative to individual differences, occupational rank, and value placed on achievements has been a universal experience, and undoubtedly will continue to exist even in the most egalitarian societies of our political visions. Nevertheless, the relative inequality of equal access to opportunity for medical care, housing, education, income, secure and meaningful employment, and "quality of life" is subject to political and economic variation. Inequality, in this sense, refers to unequal access to opportunity rather than to differences in status.

Although relative poverty may always be with us, there is no need for the plague of absolute poverty. Currently, millions of Americans are homeless, one-fourth of our pregnant women are without prenatal care, one-third of our citizens are without medical insurance, and 20 million people suffer from hunger.

At this time, it is difficult to predict what kind of economic and social organization can provide the best quality of life for all of its members. For instance, due to government deregulation of the economy, Poland is experiencing a dramatic rise in unemployment, and the purchasing power of many families has dropped by 40 percent (Borrell, 1990). As *Time* magazine put it:

> Just after noon each day, Henryka Ptasinska, 33, collects meals for herself and her six children from the soup kitchen at 10 Inwalidow Square in the leafy Warsaw suburb of Zoliborz. She is one of 250 regulars at the serving hatch in the white-tiled kitchen, opened to alleviate some of the pain produced by Poland's forced march from a centrally planned communist system to a free-market society. Her lunchtime routine shows that the success of that transformation still hangs in the balance (Borrell, 1990).

The failures and transformations of communist countries do not indicate how successfully our own system meets the needs of our people. Remember, one-third of the U.S. population lives in or near poverty, and poverty has been a constant feature of our nation since its founding.

The kinder and gentler President Bush has been accused of

> protecting the traditional power of rich people who control American culture and charity. What Bush is trying to create, with some success, is perceptions of public poverty. That, he and many other conservatives reckon, creates or adds to private wealth—particularly for those whose wallets bulge with revenues from capital gains and trust funds. The "investing class" is Bush's core constituency (Reeves, 1990).

Persistent poverty in the United States, despite all the media attention to personal greed, is ultimately one of the mechanisms of a "free market," where millions of people at the top of the stratification enjoy extreme prosperity and many more millions just get by. Meanwhile, many more millions find themselves the victims of an economy that has failed them. Somehow a balance must be struck. Today, there are Americans who must beg for handouts, not because they are fundamentally defective, but because they live in a system of inadequate alternatives and opportunities.

Unfortunately, American poverty of the 1990s all too often means an absolute inability to obtain rudimentary necessities. In this sense, persistent poverty has betrayed the American dream. It's time to wake up, America. The nation desperately needs to channel the creative and innovative nature of her people into creating an improved reality out of the ruins of that lost dream.

Postscript

In the early days of the 1990s, believers in capitalism as a system are gloating. The system's propagandists express their glee in the triumph of capitalism over socialism and communism in Eastern Europe. Domestically, these same "spin doctors" extol that the United States, in an era of "getting the government off our backs," is experiencing one of the most sustained periods of prosperity in the nation's history. In fact, they would argue, the only poor in this country of any real consequence are an urban "underclass" which just happens to consist of black people and are too "pathological" to enter or take advantage of the "American dream."

Richard Ropers' *Persistent Poverty* exposes that propaganda for what it really is and makes a major contribution to our understanding of the dynamics of poverty in the United States. Ropers shows that while "the few" are experiencing greater and greater prosperity, "the many" are becoming increasingly impoverished. Ropers' analysis will serve as an important weapon to counter the conservative argument that welfare and other so-called social programs cause poverty, in general, and the growth of the underclass, in particular. Furthermore, what his analysis clearly shows is that as an economic system capitalism extracts its wealth from workers at the expense of the quality of their livelihood and often their very lives.

In this Postscript I will add a commentary on some of Professor Ropers' points, essentially for emphasis and to show some of the major trends in the economy and the impact of those trends on the general population. This discussion will center on how the working class is being pushed down and out of the labor market. A more concentrated, directly related discussion will center on what is being touted as a new phenomenon: the so-called underclass.

The Changing Economy

In his book *The Truly Disadvantaged*, William Wilson observes "that there is a heterogeneous grouping of inner-city families whose behavior contrasts sharply with that of mainstream America" (p. 7). He considers this to be "one of the most important transformations in recent United States history" (p. 7). Although he attributes this transformation to the people, the major shift has been primarily in the economy and how it uses its labor. In a study that sought to ascertain "What is happening to American jobs?" Barry Bluestone provides some interesting data. He found that of the 12 million new jobs created between 1973 and 1979, 1 of 5 were in the low wage sector, paying $7000 or less per year. Since 1979, however, over 60 percent of the new jobs were in this low wage sector. Presently, about 90 percent of the new jobs pay $7000 or less per year. While we do not dismiss the "economic violence" that accompanies this occupational sector, the problem is not restricted to the low wage sector. For those in the high wage sector (i.e., wages at least twice the median income, or $28,000 or more per year), there has been a net loss of 400,000 jobs. What these trends represent is a general crisis in capitalism as a system. The problems are not restricted to young people, blacks or other people of color, women, or female-headed households. In fact, white males have experienced the largest relative decline in high wage jobs and the largest relative increase in low wage jobs.

Similarly, Eileen Applebaum finds that computer technology has resulted in productivity gains and at the same time reductions in unit labor requirements. United States corporations have been diligent in their cutting of wage costs through the rigid use of technology and routinizing of jobs, less skilled workers, temporary workers, and concessions from labor in their collective bargaining agreements. In the 1970s and 1980s part-time employment grew faster than full-time employment. Job growth in traditional services is fueled by the expansion of part-time employment. Part-time positions have increased by 2.5 million since 1979. Of that number, only 600,000 employees actually sought part-time work; nearly two million of these individuals are persons holding part-time jobs involuntarily. Employment growth in the part-time service sector is predicated on low wages and few benefits. In fact, this sector is one of the ways in which unemployment is hidden.

These data seem to show that what we are witnessing is a general crisis of capitalism. Labor is expendable in the face of owners' insatiable thirst for profits. The data suggest strongly that the problem is not in the values of the people as much as in this heightened exploitation of the workers for the benefit of the entrepreneurial class.

Economic Violence: In the Plant

Not unlike the sweatshops Ropers describes, the auto industry provides a vivid example of the new labor market and the impact of this transformation on the quality of life for workers in the industry. During the 1980s the auto industry "Big Three"—General Motors, Ford, and Chrysler—heightened outsourcing as a tactic to begin reducing labor costs and increase profits. By cutting portions of their production, these firms were able to cut wages, benefits, and safety costs. At the same time, their out-source suppliers took on some of the more dangerous jobs with-out an obligation to union contracts which provide the protec-tions of benefits, safety standards, and higher than poverty wages. Under these circumstances, the *Detroit Free Press* reports that injury rates are better than twice great for suppliers (2.5 injuries per 100 workers) than the Big Three (1.2 per 100). For the smaller plants among outsource employers, the injury rate tend-ed to exceed 3.0 per 100 workers. In other words, the loss of limbs and even life was greater in these smaller enterprises. Not only were base wages much less in the outsource plants, but these lower wages were reflected in the workmen's compensa-tion wages for injured workers. Compensation for Big Three injured workers exceeded $600 a week while the same compen-sation for the suppliers' workers ranged from just over $300 a week to slightly more than $400 a week.

In summing up the increasing danger in the auto industry between 1986 and 1989, the *Free Press* found:

1. While less than half the industry's workers are employed in the smaller supplier plants, the workers in these plants suffer about two-thirds of the industry's serious injuries, including amputations.
2. For stamping operations, outside suppliers tended to have injury rates about three times that of the Big Three. However, for some suppliers such injury rates were nine times as high as Ford's.
3. A similar injury rate occurred in outsource trim shops in which the rate was more than 10 times that of the Big Three.

One observer in the business stated:

> It's been a great time for the creative entrepreneur, a time of some incredible success stories. A lot of very smart people saw the shift coming and were able to capitalize on it. . . . But it has also been a

time when bad actors could prosper. There's no question that there
are some slave shops out there—that what they are referred to as
in this business—places where people are exploited, exposed to
unacceptable hazards so somebody can make a quick buck. . . .
[T]here are hundreds of them, and they don't care if people get
hurt in their shops. To them, it's just the cost of doing business
(*Detroit Free Press,* July 7, 1990, p. 6A).

Apart from the injury issue, what we are witnessing is a
more general impoverishment of the working class. Many of the
jobs which often paid $12 to $17 per hour in the Big Three are
now paying slightly more than the comparable minimum wage
at the local fast food shop. This new sector of the working class
fits very well into a group which Ropers describes as the "working poor."

Economic Violence: The Throwaways

These trends argue that contrary to Wilson's notion that the
problem of the inner-city poor is a result of their values, it is a
more general trend of workers being pushed down and out of
the labor market. As suggested above, poverty is an integral
aspect of an exploitative economic system. Ropers amply demonstrates that we must understand the phenomenon in context,
not in isolation. Wealth and poverty are positions of accumulation, or the lack thereof, within the economic system. Marx
argued that livelihoods came out of either ownership of the
means of production or the selling of one's labor in that productive process. In such a system should there be no need for one's
labor, then one cannot earn a wage to provide for one's self or
family. Consequently, for those persons not owning an enterprise or the means of production, they must be able to sell their
labor or face a desperate existence. One of the major problems
faced by poor blacks has been their high rates of unemployment
and underemployment. While many right-wing and racist ide-

ologues argue that the reason for these high rates of unemployment is that blacks are lazy, Jesse Jackson often makes the point that at one time all blacks had a job—in slavery. During slavery there was a need for black labor. But more important, the logic of Jackson's argument is that the issue is not simply a job, but the quality of the job. The high rates of unemployment among blacks seems to make a strong point that their labor is no longer needed.

Historically, blacks in the United States provided the labor for a southern plantation economy. The demand for this labor began in slavery and continued throughout the first half of the twentieth century. One might argue that the extreme poverty of blacks is a result of their having been victims of two technological revolutions, one in agriculture and the other in manufacturing through the more recent computer and robotics changes. Mandle makes a strong case showing how technology made human labor superfluous up through the first half of this century. Table P.1 indicates that whereas 90 man-hours were required in the production of cotton in 1920, only 54 man-hours were required in 1960. More dramatic, however, is the yield over that period and the man-hours required. The table shows a

TABLE P.1. **Man-Hours Required in the Production of Cotton,
1920–1960**

Category	1920	1940	1950	1960
Man-hours per acre	90	98	74	54
Before harvest	55	46	33	23
Harvest	35	52	41	31
Yields of lint				
per acre (lb.)	160	245	283	454
Man-hours per bale	269	191	126	57

Source. Historical Statistics of the United States, *Colonial Times to 1970*, Part I, Series K93–97 (Washington, D.C.: Government Printing Office, 1975).

threefold increase in pounds per acre, from 160 to 454. At the same time, the number of man-hours per bale shows a fivefold decrease, from 269 to 57. It was this 40-year period which provided one of the more dramatic shifts in the population of blacks. The high unemployment rates and underemployment for blacks are evidence of the superfluousness of their labor.

Constructing an Ominous Reality

Rather than a recognition of how the system has exploited, degraded, and now tends to discard black labor, the problem has been conceptualized and framed by conservatives and reactionaries such as Glen Loury (1984), Charles Murray (1984), and Lawrence Mead (1986), which tends to blame the victims for their own condition. Unfortunately, the very terms or concepts employed by William Wilson in his *The Truly Disadvantaged* (1987) emanate from the lexicon of the right wing: "reverse discrimination"; "preferential treatment"; "social pathology"; and, more important, the conceptualization of this sector as an "underclass." The major problem with these terms is that they grossly distort reality. Even more, these distortions carry the cloak of being grounded in science. The general practice in American society, however, is to discriminate against people of color in favor of whites in the area of employment and other spheres in our society. While affirmative action policies attempt to counter the practice, preferential treatment is still almost universally a privilege accorded to whites.

The term "social pathology" is a mystification with rather ominous overtones. The term, one may assume, is to connote a condition of disease, or deviation from normal. The "pathological" reference is to the behavior of that "large subpopulation of low-income families and individuals whose behavior contrasts sharply with [that] of the general population," rather than an economic system that no longer needs their labor and who are thereby impoverished. Instead, this population is portrayed as incorrigible and unfit for decent society. Just as important, this mystification also clouds the inherently dialectical relationship between wealth and poverty. Or, as can be gleaned from above, poverty is created from the hoarding or accumulation of wealth by the few from the many.

Like "social pathology," the conceptualization of an "underclass" is a very dangerous idea. Wilson argues the appropriateness as follows:

> Regardless of which term is used, one cannot deny that there is a heterogeneous grouping of inner-city families and individuals whose behavior contrasts sharply with that of mainstream America. The real challenge is not only to explain why this is so, but also to explain why the behavior patterns in the inner-city today differ so markedly from those of only three or four decades ago. To obscure these differences by eschewing the term *underclass*, or some other term that could be helpful in describing the changes in ghetto behavior, norms, and aspirations, in favor of more neutral designations such as *lower class* or *working class* is to fail to address one of the most important transformations in recent United States history (p. 7).

As argued above, the "pathology" is in capitalism as an economic system not, primarily, in its products.

Consequently, the use of the underclass concept looms ominously. The danger of the concept is that it places the problem "in the people," the black inner-city "underclass." As Jencks (1985) points out, the purpose of the concept is to isolate an "undeserving" poor. What does a society that supposedly "guarantees success" to anyone willing to work for it do with slovenly criminals who contribute nothing but more teenagers having babies? First of all, the society makes sure that everyone comes to accept that this population "contrast(s) sharply" from normal human beings. After there is general agreement about this sharp difference between normal people and "them," it is easy to accept the fact that *they* are the problem, or "the millstone" as characterized by the *Chicago Tribune*. That is to say, whatever goes wrong with society, its inability to put them all in jail could result in concentration camps and possibly extermination as viable alternatives. It is not as though such practices are outside the realm of so-called civilized society. In sum, the problem becomes not the loss of the legacy of their foreparents' stolen labor but their lack of education and skills.

As a counter to the Wilson thesis, Ropers makes a major contribution in *Persistent Poverty* by providing the breadth of analysis to show that the problem is not a black problem, that it is not a new problem, and that it represents a crisis in capitalism as a whole. To isolate this population as though it were somehow totally unique is to mystify rather than illuminate. Further, by focusing on this black impoverished population and making it distinctive from other impoverished populations obscures the role of the economy shaping not only their condition but the condition of others similarly situated. But most important, to argue that this population is totally unique sets the stage for a totally unique solution, possibly, in this time of rising racism in the United States and around the world, a final solution.

Conclusion: What Is to Be Done

Unfortunately, there are no pragmatic solutions to problems of poverty. Presently, the prevailing ideology of the nation is to blame the victims and progressive social policy of the past as the reason for the condition of the poor. As Wilson (1987) observes, in his attempt to a guide a social policy to ameliorate the problems of the inner-city poor, "It will require a radicalism that neither the Democratic nor Republican parties have as yet been realistic enough to propose" (p. 137).

The problem is that the "free enterprise system" has no solution to unemployment. This brutal truth is being discovered in Hungary, Czechoslovakia, East Germany, and other Eastern European countries as they adopt free market economies. Of course, what was also true is that their socialist economies were not serving the needs of their people.

The problem is that both capitalism and socialism are based on a wage system. The distribution of goods and services is based upon a wage. However, in this stage of hi-tech production the need for labor is being drastically reduced. Consequently, we are witnessing drastic reductions in the manufacturing labor force. Such production methods will undermine labor in socialist countries as well since their distribution is based upon "from each according to his ability and to each according to his work." Consequently, given the reduced need for labor, if the problem of poverty is to be solved, the distribution of goods and services must, in the future, be based on something other than the wage.

ROBERT G. NEWBY

Department of Sociology
Central Michigan University
Mt. Pleasant, Michigan

References

Detroit Free Press, July 7–9, 1990.

Jencks, C. (1985). "How poor are the poor?" *New York Review of Books,* 32, 8:41–49.

Loury, G. (1984). "On the Need for Moral Leadership in the Black Community." Paper presented at the University of Chicago.

Mead, L. (1986). *Beyond Entitlement: The Social Obligations of Citizenship,* New York: Free Press.

Murray, C. (1984). *Losing Ground: American Social Policy, 1950–1980,* New York: Basic Books.

Wilson, W. (1987). *The Truly Disadvantaged,* Chicago: University of Chicago Press.

References

A conservative war on poverty. (1989, February 27). *U.S. News and World Report*, pp. 20–23.

A second opinion from Jensen. (1977, August 8). *Time*.

Allen, Glen. (1989, July 3). The pain of poverty: welfare carries a stigma of shame. *Maclean's, 102*, pp. 38–39.

AP. (1989, January 28). Kemp's main mission: Help the homeless. Salt Lake City, Utah: *Salt Lake Tribune*, p. A3.

AP, Washington. (1989, March 2). Poor families with kids on rise. Iron County, Utah, *Daily Spectrum*, p. 12.

AP. (1989, April 22). Report: 17% of rural Americans live below poverty line. Iron County, Utah: *Daily Spectrum*, p. 2.

AP. (1989, July 19). Economic crisis could drive us into meaner society. Iron County, Utah, *Daily Spectrum*, p. B5.

AP, Washington. (1989, July 30). U.S. blacks lag in status.

AP. (1989, August 18). Study: Elevated IQ scores linked to background, family environment. Iron County, Utah: *Daily Spectrum*, p. 11.

AP. (1989, October 3). Children locked in poverty. Iron County, Utah: *Daily Spectrum*, p. 13.

AP, Washington. (1990, March 12–13). Plan to count homeless sparks criticism. Salt Lake City, Utah, *Deseret News*.

AP, Washington. (1990, March 21). Census workers target Utah's homeless. Iron County, Utah, *Daily Spectrum*, p. 1.

225

AP, Washington. (1990, April 1). Millions will remain poor despite increase in the minimum wage. Salt Lake City, Utah, *Deseret News*, p. 18A.

AP, Washington. (1990, April 29). HUD projects in financial ruin.

AP. (1990, July 1). Demos open class war on GOP foe. Iron County, Utah, *Daily Spectrum*, p. A6.

Appelbaum, Richard. (1986, December 13). *Counting the Homeless*. Paper presented at the Conference on Homelessness, George Washington University, Washington, D.C.

Appelbaum, Richard. (1988). Preface in R. Ropers. (1988). *The Invisible Homeless: A New Urban Ecology*, pp. 19–26. New York: Human Sciences Press.

Are you better off? (1988, October 10). *Time*, pp. 28–30.

Bahr, H. (1973). *Skid Row: An Introduction to Disaffiliation*. New York: Oxford University Press.

Ball, Karen. (1990, April 1). Minimum wage rises today—1st time in nearly 10 years. Salt Lake City, Utah, *Salt Lake Tribune*, p. A1.

Banfield, Edward. (1970). *The Unheavenly City*. Boston, Little, Brown.

Bannister v. *Los Angeles County Board of Supervisors*. (1985). Case No. C535833, Superior Court of California.

Barbanel, Josh. (1989, April 12). How despair is engulfing a generation in New York. *New York Times*, p. E-6.

Bardsley, J. R. (1989, June 11). Homeless are a problem, insist Utahns. Salt Lake City, Utah, *Salt Lake Tribune*, p. 2.

Bassuk, Ellen L. (1984). The homelessness problem. *Scientific American*, *251* (1): 40–45.

Bassuk, Ellen L., Rubin, L., & Lauriat, A. (1986). Characteristics of sheltered homeless families. *American Journal of Public Health*, *76* (9): 1097–1101.

Batra, Ravi. (1987). *The Great Depression of 1990*. New York: Simon & Schuster.

Batra, Ravi. (1988). *Surviving the Great Depression of 1990*. New York: Dell Books.

Blair v. *Los Angeles County Board of Supervisors* (1985). Case No. C568184, Superior Court of California.

Blasi, Gary. (1984). Testimony of Gary Blasi before the Intergovernmental Relations and Human Resources Subcommittee of the Committee on Government Relations. *In The Federal Response to the Homeless*

Crisis, pp. 1114–1292. Washington, D.C.: U.S. Government Printing Office.

Blasi, Gary. (1990, February 8). Telephone conversation with the author.

Bluestone, B. & Harrison, B. (1982). *The Deindustrialization of America: Plant Closings, Community Abandonment, and the Dismantling of Basic Industry.* New York: Basic Books.

Blum, Jeffrey M. (1978). *Pseudoscience and Mental Ability.* New York: Monthly Review Press.

Bogue, D. (1963). *Skid Row in American Cities.* Chicago: University of Chicago Press.

Bolle, Mary Jane. (1986). *Plant Closings and Business Relocations.* Washington, D.C.: Congressional Research Service, Economics Division.

Bolle, Mary Jane. (1990). *Plant Closing Legislation: Worker Adjustment and Retraining Notification Act (WARN).* Washington, D.C.: Congressional Research Service, Economics Division.

Bookbinder, Hyman. (1989, September 8). Renewing the war on poverty a cost-effective investment. Tempe (Ariz.). *Daily News Tribune*, p. A11.

Borrell, John. (1990, June 11). Poland: Living with shock therapy. *Time*, p. 31.

Bowles, S. & Gintis, H. (1974). IQ in the United States class structure. In Gartner, A., Greer, C., & Riessman, F. (Eds.) (1974). *The New Assault on Equality: IQ and Social Stratification*, pp. 7–84. New York: Harper & Row.

Bowman, R. (1989, February 17). Kemp and HUD. *USA Today*, p. 3A.

Boxer, Barbara. (1989, October 23). Bush's veto punishes the poor. *USA Today*, p. 12A.

Brown, J. (1987). Hunger in the U.S. *Scientific American*, 256 (2): 37–41.

Burck, Charles G. (1988, October). Toward two societies? *Fortune*, 118 (8): 48–49.

Burke, V. (1986). *Welfare Reform.* Washington, D.C.: Congressional Research Service, The Library of Congress.

Burke, V. (1989, October 24). *Cash and Noncash Benefits for Persons with Limited Income: Eligibility Rules, Precipient and Expenditure Data, FY 1986–88.* Washington, D.C.: Congressional Research Service, The Library of Congress.

Burnham, Stanley. (1985). *Black Intelligence in White Society.* Atlanta, GA: Social Science Press.

Bush, G. (1989, January 21). Inaugural Address. Washington, D.C.: *Congressional Quarterly 47* (3): 142–143.

Byrd, Lee. (1989, October 8). Thousands march for fair housing. Salt Lake City, Utah. *Salt Lake Tribune,* p. 1.

Chapman, Stephen. (1989, March 28). Homeless mentally ill need treatment. *Las Vegas Review-Journal,* p. 7b.

Chira, Susan. (1989, October 3). Working-class families losing middle-class dreams. Metropolitan News. *New York Times,* p. B1.

Christian, Patrick. (1990, April 25). Once-homeless man says he deserves to be counted too. (Provo, UT) *Daily Herald,* p. 2B.

Church, George. (1988, October 10). Are you better off? *Time,* pp. 28–30.

Church, George. (1990, May 21). Ignore my lips. *Time,* pp. 18–19.

City of Los Angeles vs. *County of Los Angeles.* (1990). Case No. C 655 274, Superior Court of The State of California.

Cleveland, Bob. (1990, December). Income Statistics Branch, U.S. Census Bureau, telephone conversation with the author.

Corwin, Miles. (1989, April 23). Man's idea to aid homeless lands him in the doghouse. *The Los Angeles Times,* Pt. 1, p. 1.

Currie, E. & Skolnick, J. (1988). *America's Problems: Social Issues and Public Policy,* 2nd ed. Scott, Foresman.

Daly, Margaret. (1988, October). Homeless families in America. *Better Homes and Gardens,* pp. 21–24.

Davis, Kingsley & Moore, Wilbert. (1945, April). Some principles of stratification. *American Sociological Review, 10,* 242–249.

Donald Trump, a man who has come to embody the acquisitive 80's (1989, January 16). *Time.*

Dowell, T. R. (1987, February 5). Steelworkers feeling abandoned. Salt Lake City, Utah: *The Salt Lake Tribune,* p. 1.

Edsall, Thomas B. (1988, June). The return of inequality. *The Atlantic, 261* (6): 86–94.

Eitzen, D. Stanley. (1982). *In Conflict and Order: Understanding Society,* 2nd ed. Boston: Allyn and Bacon.

Farley, John. (1990). *Sociology.* Englewood Cliffs, NJ: Prentice-Hall.

Farr, R. (1982). *Skid Row Project.* (Mimeographed). Los Angeles, CA: Los Angeles County Department of Mental Health, Program Development Bureau.

Farr, R. (1986). A mental health treatment program for the homeless mentally ill in the Los Angeles skid row area. In Billy Jones (Ed.). *Treating the Homeless: Urban Psychiatry's Challenge*, pp. 66–92. Washington, D.C.: American Psychiatric Press.

Farr, R., Koegel, P., & Burnam, A. (1986). *A study of homelessness and mental illness in the skid row area of Los Angeles*. Los Angeles, CA: Los Angeles County Department of Mental Health.

Fast, Paul. (1990, February 7). Telephone conversation with the author.

Fasting wins concessions on shelter for homeless. (1984, November 5). *New York Times*.

Feagin, Joe. (1973). *Subordinating the poor: Welfare and American beliefs*. Englewood Cliffs, NJ: Prentice-Hall.

Furiga, P. (1989, August 16). Less than 1 in 3 receive unemployment benefits. Iron County, Utah: *Daily Spectrum*, p. 1.

Gabe, Thomas. (1989). *Progress Against Poverty in the United States (1957–1987)*. Washington, D.C.: Congressional Research Service, The Library of Congress.

Galbraith, J. (1958). *The Affluent Society*. Boston: Houghton Mifflin.

Gallup, George, Jr. (1989, March 26). Did '86 tax reform shift burden unfairly? Salt Lake City, Utah: *Salt Lake Tribune*, p. A15.

Gallagher, John E. (1990, June 25). Good ole bad boy. *Time*, p. 42.

Gans, Herbert, J. (1971, July/August). The uses of poverty: the poor pay all. *Social Policy*, pp. 78–81.

Gans, Herbert, J. (1974). *More Equality*. New York: Random House.

Gould, Steven J. (1981). *The Mismeasure of Man*. New York: Norton.

Gould, Steven J. (1987). Jensen's last stand. In *An Urchin in the Storm*, pp. 124–144. New York: Norton.

Green, Bob. (1989, April 17). Homeless boy sought escape in death. Las Vegas, Nevada: *Las Vegas Review-Journal*.

Green, Stephen. (1989, March 25). Homeless suffer while treasury funds sit idle. Washington, D.C.: Copley News Service. Iron County, Utah: *Daily Spectrum*, p. 5.

Greenwald, John. (1989, February 27). Gimme shelter. *Time*, p. 50.

Grose, Thomas. (1988, September 26). Low-paying jobs are "dominant trend." Iron County Utah: *Daily Spectrum*.

Guest, Ted. (1990, May 7). Did Miliken get off too lightly? *Time*, p. 22.

Gwynne, S. C. (1990, April 23). Eruptions in the Heartland. *Time*, pp. 26–27.

Harrington, Michael. (1962). *The Other America*. New York: Macmillan.

Harrington, Michael. (1984). *The New American Poverty*. New York: Holt, Rinehart and Winston.

Harris, F., & Wilkins, R. (Eds.). (1988). *Quiet Riots: Race and Poverty in the United States*. New York: Pantheon.

Hawkings, David. (1989, April 15). Poverty worse in rural than urban areas. Iron County, Utah: *Daily Spectrum*, p. 3.

Hawkings, David. (1990, April 17). Study says gap between rich, poor widening. Iron County, Utah: *Daily Spectrum*, p. 1.

Hernandez, Marita. (1985, February 16). "Informal" economy changing L.A. into "Third World City," study says. *Los Angeles Times*. Part II. p. 4.

Herrnstein, Richard. (1971, September). IQ. *Atlantic*.

Heskin, A. (1984). Availability of overnight housing at/under $10.00 per night in the Los Angeles County market. Unpublished paper, Los Angeles: UCLA School of Architecture and Urban Planning.

Holmes, S. J. (1936). *Human Genetics and Its Social Import*. New York: McGraw-Hill.

Hombs, Mary Ellen & Snyder, Mitch. (1982). *Homelessness in America: A Forced March to Nowhere*. Washington, D.C.: The Community for Creative Non-Violence.

Homeless by choice? Some choice. (1984, February 7). *New York Times*, Pt. 4, p. 8.

Hunter, Robert. (1904). *Poverty*. New York: Macmillan.

Huntley, S. & Witkin, G. (1983, May 23). America's Indians: Beggars in our own land. *U.S. News & World Report*, pp. 70–72.

Institute of Medicine. (1988). *Homelessness, Health, and Human Needs*. Washington, D.C.: National Academy Press.

It's who you knew at HUD. (1989, May 22). *Time*, p. 39.

Jacob, J. (1990). Black America, 1989 an overview. In *The State of Black America 1990*, pp. 1–24. Washington, D.C.: National Urban League.

Jensen, A. (1976). Interview. In Richard Evans (1976). *The Making of Psychology*, pp. 54–67. New York: Knopf.

Jensen, A. (1981). *Straight Talk about Mental Tests*. New York: Free Press.

Katz, Lee M. (1990, July 6–8). Symbol of hope for homeless dies. *USA Today*, p. 1.

Kemp appointed HUD chief. (1989). *Safety Network* (8), 2: 1.

Kemp, J. (1989, September 24). Creating enterprise zones will let investors help the poor. Salt Lake City, Utah: *Salt Lake Tribune*.

Knickerbocker, B. (1979, October 26). IQ tests for special pupils banned. *Rocky Mountain News*, p. 40C.

Koning, H. (1989, December 19). On Eastern Europe. New York, N.Y.: *The Village Voice*, p. 18.

Lacayo, Richard. (1990, January 16). A capital offense. *Time*, p. 27.

Lamb, H. R. (Ed.). (1984). *The Homeless Mentally Ill: A Task Force Report of the American Psychiatric Association.* Washington, D.C.: American Psychiatric Association.

Landi, A. (1989, April). When having everything isn't enough. *Psychology Today*, 23:27–30.

Lawler, James. (1978). *IQ, Heritability and Racism.* New York: International Publishers.

Lee, B. (1980). The disappearance of skid row: Some ecological evidence. *Urban Affairs Quarterly, 16* (1): 81–107.

Lewis, Oscar. (1959). *Five Families: The Children of Sanchez.* New York: Random House.

Lewis, Oscar. (1965). *La Vida: A Puerto Rican Family in the Culture of Poverty—San Juan and New York.* New York: Random House.

Lewontin, R. C., Rose, S. & Kamin, L. (1984). *Not in Our Genes: Biology, Ideology, and Human Nature.* New York: Pantheon Books.

Liazos, Alexander. (1989). *Sociology: A Liberating Perspective,* 2nd ed. Boston: Allyn & Bacon.

Loecher, Barbara. (1990, January 14). In affluent towns the working poor are filling shelters. *New York Times*, B1.

Long, Robert. (Ed.). (1989). *The Welfare Debate.* New York: H. W. Wilson Co.

Los Angeles County Department of Public Social Services. (1983). *General Relief Recipient Characteristics Study.* Los Angeles: Author.

Lowry, Katherine. (1987, November 1). The Designer Babies are Growing Up. *Los Angeles Times Magazine*, p. 7.

Maitland, Leslie. (1989, November 26). Plan for homeless is called modest. *New York Times*, National Section, p. 35.

Maloy, Richard. (1990, June 13). End of the Cold War likely to bring factory closures, unemployed defense workers. Iron County, Utah: *Daily Spectrum*, p. 2A.

McCormick, L. Hamilton. (1921). *Characterology: The Principles, Rules, and Methods of Scientific Character Reading and Analysis.* Chicago: Rand McNally.

Marx, Karl. (1965). *Capital*, Vol. 1, Moscow: Progress Publishers.

Mead, Walter Russell. (1990, March). On the road to ruin: Winning the cold war, losing the economic peace. *Harper's Magazine*, pp. 59–64.

Miller, John. (1990, May). Reaganomics redux: Bush budget puts new words to familiar tune. *Dollars & Sense*, pp. 12–15.

Miller, R. (1982). *The Demolition of Skid Row*. Lexington, MA: Lexington Books.

Mills, C. Wright. (1959). *The Sociological Imagination*. London: Oxford University Press.

Molotsky, I. & Warren, W., Jr. (1986, February 5). Washington talk: Briefing. *The New York Times*, p. A16.

Mosca, Susan. (1989, October). Economic progress of blacks has stalled. American Psychological Association, *Monitor*, p. 18.

Moynihan, Daniel Patrick. (1965). The Negro Family. In Lee Rainwater and W. L. Yancey (Eds.) (1967). *The Moynihan Report and the Politics of Controversy*. Cambridge, MA: M.I.T. Press.

Murray, Charles. (1984). *Losing Ground: American Social Policy, 1950–1980*. New York: Basic Books.

Nader, Ralph. (1990, March 5). Corporate welfare state is on a roll. *Los Angeles Times*.

National Academy of Science. (1988). Washington, D.C.: *Homelessness, Health and Human Needs*.

National Coalition for the Homeless. (1989, December). *American Nightmare: A Decade of Homelessness in the United States*. Washington, D.C.: Author.

National Urban League. (1990). *The State of Black America: 1990*. New York, New York.

Nyden, P. (1984, September). Unemployment: Its social costs. *Progressive Forensics*, pp. 8–10.

O'Hare, William. (1987, September). *America's Welfare Population: Who Gets What?* Washington, D.C.: Population Reference Bureau, Inc.

O'Hare, William. (1988). *The Rise of Poverty in Rural America*. Washington, D.C.: Population Reference Bureau, Inc.

Ong, Paul, et al. (1989). *The Widening Divide: Income Inequality and Poverty in Los Angeles*. UCLA School of Architecture and Urban Planning.

Painter, Kim. (1989, October 20). Needy children fall through Medicaid gaps. *USA Today*, p. 1.

Painton, Priscilla. (1990, April 16). Shrugging off the homeless. *Time*.

Palmer, D. (1986, February 22). Psychiatrist says treatment needed by many homeless. Salt Lake City, Utah: *Deseret News*.

Paris v. Los Angeles County Board of Supervisors (1984). Case No. C523361, Superior Court of California.

Pear, Robert. (1985, November 16). Homeless in capital resisting move. *New York Times*, p. 32.

Pearce, Diana. (1984). Farewell to alms: Women's fare under welfare. In Terry Reuther (1990). *Sociology: Empowerment in a Troubled Age*, pp. 121–130. Boston, MA: Copley Publishing Group.

Physician Task Force on Hunger in America. (1985). *Hunger in America: The Growing Epidemic*. Middletown, CT: Wesleyan University Press.

Piven, Frances Fox & Cloward, Richard. (1971). *Regulating the Poor*. New York: Vintage Books.

Piven, Frances Fox & Cloward, Richard. (1982). *The New Class War*. New York: Pantheon Books.

Predator's fall, marking the end of money-mad era (1990, February 26). *Time*, p. 47.

Rainwater, Lee & Yancey, W. L. (Eds.). (1967). *The Moynihan Report and the Politics of Controversy*. Cambridge, MA: M.I.T. Press.

Redway, J. & Hinman, R. (1898). *Natural School Geography, Part 2*. New York: American Book Co.

Reeves, Richard. (1990, May 21). Bush policies protect the nation's rich. *Las Vegas Review-Journal*.

Reich, Robert B. (1989, May 1). As the world turns: U.S. income inequality keeps on rising. *The New Republic*, pp. 23, 26–28.

Rensch v. Los Angeles County Board of Supervisors (1986). Case No. C595155, Superior Court of California.

Robbins, William. (1985, February 10). Despair wrenched farmer's lives as debts mount and land is lost. *New York Times*, p. 1.

Robertson, Ian. (1989). *Society: A Brief Introduction*. New York: Worth Publishers.

Robertson, M., Ropers, R., & Boyer, R. (1985a). Emergency Shelter for the homeless in Los Angeles County. In Intergovernment Relations and Human Resources Subcommittee of the Committee on Government Operations, *The Federal Response to the Homeless Crisis*, pp. 904–983). Washington, D.C.: Government Printing Office.

Robertson, M., Ropers, R., & Boyer, R. (1985b). The Homeless in Los Angeles County: An Empirical Evaluation. In *The Federal Response to the Homeless Crisis*, pp. 984–1108. Washington, D.C.: Government Printing Office.

Roosevelt, F. D. (1937, January). Second Inaugural Address. In R. Will & H. Vatter (1965). *Poverty in Affluence*, pp. 13–15. New York: Harcourt, Brace & World.

Ropers, R. (1975). *Poverty.* Unpublished paper. Western Michigan University.

Ropers, R. (1985a). The contribution of economic and political policies and trends to the rise of the new urban homeless. In *The Federal Response to the Homeless Crisis*, pp. 833–856. Washington, D.C.: Government Printing Office.

Ropers, R. (1985b, December). The Rise of the New Urban Homeless. *Public Affairs Report, 26* (5 and 6). Berkeley: University of California, Institute of Governmental Studies.

Ropers, R. (1986, November). *Blacks and Other Minorities among the Homeless.* (Working Paper Series). Chicago: Urban League.

Ropers, R. (1988). *The Invisible Homeless: A New Urban Ecology.* New York: Human Sciences Press.

Ropers, R. (1989, May 5). *The Homeless Crisis.* Speech delivered at the Lowell Bennion Community Center, University of Utah, Salt Lake City.

Ropers, R. (1989, November 30). *Toward a Kinder and Gentler America: Ending Poverty and Homelessness and Fulfilling the American Dream.* ISBN 0-935615-07-5, Faculty Honor Lecture, Southern Utah University.

Ropers, R. & Boyer, R. (1987a). Perceived Health Status among the Homeless. *Journal of Social Science and Medicine, 24* (8): 669–678.

Ropers, R. & Boyer, R. (1987b). Homelessness as a Health Risk. *Alcohol, Health and Research World, 11*, pp. 38–41. Rockville, MD: U.S. Department of Health and Human Services.

Ropers, R., & Gordon, O. (1988, April 15). *The Sociology of the Rural Homeless.* Paper presented at the Western Social Science Conference, Denver, Colorado.

Ropers, R., & Marks, T. (1983). *Unemployment Resource Handbook.* Los

Angeles: Didi Hirsch Community Mental Health Center/Los Angeles Psychiatric Services.

Ropers, R., & Robertson, M. (1985). The Inner-City Homeless of Los Angeles: An Empirical Assessment. In *The Federal Response to the Homeless Crisis*, pp. 858–903. Washington, D.C.: Government Printing Office.

Ross v. Los Angeles County Board of Supervisors. (1984). Case No. C501603, Superior Court of California.

Rossi, Peter, & Wright, James. (1986, December 13). *The Determinants of Homelessness*. Paper presented at The Conference on Homelessness, George Washington University, Washington, D.C.

Rossi, Peter. (1989a). *Without Shelter: Homelessness in the 1980s*. New York: Priority Press Publications.

Rossi, Peter. (1989b). *Down and Out in America: The Origins of Homelessness*. Chicago: University of Chicago Press.

Ryan, William. (1971). *Blaming the Victim*. New York: Pantheon Books.

Safety Network. (1990, September). *Growing Gap between the Rich and Poor*. Washington, D.C.: Coalition for the Homeless.

Sanchez, Sheila. (1990, April 5). Utah leads region in child labor violations, agency says. Salt Lake City, Utah: *Deseret News*, p. B4.

Seifman, David. (1980, February 29). Nobel scientists are trying to father a "Master Race." *New York Post*, pp. 1, 13.

Seifman, David. (1980, February 29). The shocking thoughts of Professor Shockley. *New York Post*, p. 13.

Sheak, Robert. (1988). Poverty estimates: Political implications and other issues. *Sociological Spectrum, 8*, 3:277–294.

Shelter Partnership. (1989, October). Increasing homelessness in Los Angeles. Los Angeles, California.

Shelter Partnership. (1990, January). Study reports increase in homelessness, cutbacks in shelter programs, pp. 1, 9. Los Angeles, California.

Stein, Andrew. (1986, June 8). Children of poverty: Crisis in New York. *New York Times Magazine*, pp. 39, 65, 68–69, 88.

Sterilizations urged to cut welfare cycle. (1980, February 28). *Rocky Mountain News*.

Stewart, Jill. (1990, May 4). Estimate of homeless in L.A. County up sharply. *Los Angeles Times*, Metro. p. B1.

Suffer the little children. (1990, March 26). *Time*, p. 18.

Taeuber, Cynthia. U.S. Census Bureau (1990, June 21). Telephone conversation with the author.

Taking it all back, plus interest: The U.S. wants billions from the king of junk bonds. (1989, April 10). *Time*, p. 42.

Tepper, Paul. (1990, May 2). *The Number of Homeless People in Los Angeles County: July, 1988 to June, 1989*. Los Angeles, CA: Shelter Partnership.

Terman, Lewis, M. (1916). *The Measurement of Intelligence*. New York: Houghton Mifflin.

The hidden poor. (1988, January 11). *U.S. News & World Report*, pp. 18–24.

The homeless: A growing priority. (1990, January 28). *The New York Times*, p. 22.

The return of skid row: Why alcoholics and addicts are filling the streets again. (1990, January 15). *U.S. News & World Report*, pp. 27–29.

The return of Arthur Jensen. (1979, September 24). *Time*, p. 49.

Tolchin, Martin. (1990, February 5). With Kemp at helm, HUD gains new spirit, but some doubts linger. *The New York Times*, National Section, p. B7.

Toner, Robin. (1989, January, 22). Americans favor aid for homeless. *New York Times*, Front Section, pp. 1, 21.

Torrey, Edwin Fuller. (1988, March). Homelessness and mental illness. *USA Today*. (116) No. 2514, pp. 26–27.

Torrey, Edwin Fuller. (1988). *Nowhere to Go: The Tragic Odyssey of the Homeless Mentally Ill*. New York: Harper & Row.

Total income of America's richest 1 percent nearly matches bottom 40 percent. (1990, September). *Safety Network, 9* (9), p. 10.

Tucker, William. (1990). *The Excluded Americans: Homelessness and Housing Policies*. Washington, D.C.: Regnery Gateway.

UPI. (1980, January 24). Psychologist hits IQ tests "middle-class urban bias." *Rocky Mountain News*, p. 76.

UPI, Washington, D.C. (1987, November 12). Prolonged illness may cause poverty among elderly in U.S. Iron County, Utah: *Daily Spectrum*.

UPI. (1989, February 14). Kemp sworn in, vows to attack poverty. Salt Lake City, Utah: *Salt Lake Tribune*, p. A5.

UPI, Washington. (1989, February 19). Homeless kids are often deprived of education too. Iron County, Utah: *Deseret News*, p. A16.

UPI, Washington. (1989, October 5). Homelessness increasing in all regions. Iron County, Utah: *Daily Spectrum.*

UPI. Washington, D.C. (1989, October 13). Number of homeless rises 18% in 15 months to about 2 million. Iron County, Utah: *Daily Spectrum.*

UPI. (1990, April 16). 25% of Children under age 6 live below poverty line. Salt Lake City, Utah: *Deseret News*, p. 2.

U.S. Bureau of the Census, Current Population Reports, Series P-60, No. 166, *Money Income and Poverty Status in the United States: 1988 (Advance Data from the March 1989 Current Population Survey)*, Washington, D.C.: U.S. Government Printing Office, 1989.

U.S. Bureau of the Census, *Statistical Abstract of the United States: 1990*, 110th ed. Washington, D.C., 1990.

U.S. Congress. Joint Economic Committee. (1986, July). *The Concentration of Wealth in the United States: Trends in the Distribution of Wealth among American Families.* Washington, D.C.

U.S. Department of Commerce, Bureau of the Census. (1987, July). *Money Income and Poverty Status of Families and Persons in the United States: 1986.* Current Population Reports, Series P-60, No. 157.

U.S. Department of Commerce, Bureau of the Census. (1989). *We, the First Americans.* Washington, D.C.

U.S. Department of Commerce, Bureau of the Census. (1989, April). *Characteristics of Persons Receiving Benefits From Major Assistance Programs.* Household Economic Studies, Series P-70, No. 14.

U.S. General Accounting Office. (1988, August). *Sweatshops in the U.S.* GAO/HRD-130BR, Washington, D.C.

U.S. General Accounting Office. (1989, January). *Welfare Hotels: Uses, Costs, and Alternatives.* GAO/HRD-8926BR, Washington, D.C.

U.S. General Accounting Office. (1989, March 15). Testimony of John M. Ols, Jr., Director, Housing and Community Development Issues. Before the Subcommittees on Government Activities and Transportation, and on Employment and Housing, House of Representatives. Washington, D.C.

U.S. General Accounting Office. (1989, June). *Children and Youths: About 68,000 Homeless and 186,000 in Shared Housing at Any Given Time.* GAO/PEMD-89-14, Washington, D.C.

U.S. General Accounting Office. (1989, June). *Sweatshops in New York City*. GAO/HRD-89-101BR, Washington, D.C.

U.S. General Accounting Office. (1989, August). *Housing Conference: National Housing Policy Issues*. Washington, D.C.

U.S. General Accounting Office. (1989, September). *Mental Health: Prevention of Mental Disorders and Research on Stress-Related Disorders*. Washington, D.C.: U.S. Government Printing Office.

U.S. General Accounting Office. (1990, February). *Strategic Bombers: B-2 Program Status and Current Issues*. Washington, D.C.: U.S. Government Printing Office.

U.S. General Accounting Office. (1990, March 16). *Testimony: Child Labor Violations and Sweatshops in the U.S.* Washington, D.C.: U.S. Government Printing Office.

U.S. House of Representatives, Subcommittee on Oversight and Subcommittee on Public Assistance and Unemployment Compensation. (1983, October 17). *Background Material on Poverty.* Washington, D.C.: U.S. Government Printing Office.

U.S. House of Representatives. (1985). *The Federal Response to the Homeless Crisis.* Hearings before a Subcommittee of the Committee on Government Operations. Washington, D.C.: U.S. Government Printing Office.

U.S. Senate. Select Committee on Indian Affairs. (1989, March 3). *Report of the Alaska Federation of Natives on the Status of Alaska Natives: A Call for Action.* Washington, D.C.: U.S. Government Printing Office.

United Way of Los Angeles. (1989). *Environment Scan 1990.* Los Angeles: Author.

Vander Zanden, James W. (1990). *Sociology: The Core,* 2nd ed. New York: McGraw-Hill.

Weighing concern for the homeless. (1990, January 28). *New York Times,* p. 1.

Welch, William, M. (1989, April 28). Probe says ex-Reagan officials profited off housing for poor. Salt Lake City, Utah: *Salt Lake Tribune,* p. 4A.

Whitman, D., et al. (1988, January 11). America's hidden poor. *U.S. News & World Report,* pp. 18–24.

Wilkerson, Margaret & Gresham, Jewell. (1989, July 24–31). The racialization of poverty. *The Nation, 249,* p. 126.

Wilson, William J. (1980). *The Declining Significance of Race: Blacks and Changing American Institutions,* 2nd ed. Chicago: University of Chicago Press.

Wilson, William J. (1987). *The Truly Disadvantaged.* Chicago: University of Chicago Press.

Wright, James, & Weber, Eleanor. (contribution from Peter Rossi). (1987). *Homelessness and Health.* Washington, D.C.: McGraw-Hill.

Zaldivar, R. (1990, February 17). Study shows tax imbalance may spell trouble for capital gains. Salt Lake City, Utah: *Salt Lake Tribune,* p. 2.

Index

Abortion, welfare poor and, 93
Adams, Paul, 83
Agriculture, rural poor and, 51–52
Aid to Families with Dependent Children (AFDC), 97, 100
Alcoholism. *See* Substance abuse
American Indians. *See* Native Americans
Appelbaum, Richard P., 74–75, 85
Applebaum, Eileen, 217
Automobile industry, 217–219

Bahr, H., 24
Ball, Karen, 200
Banfield, Edward, 14, 126, 127–130
Bank failures, concentration of wealth, 67–68
Barbanel, Josh, 96
Bassuk, Ellen L., 77, 148–149, 150
Batra, Ravi, 62–63, 64–68
Binet, Alfred, 119–120, 121
Biology
  race differences and, 15
  reductionism and, 117–118

Blaming the victim perspective, 115–153
  characterology, 120–121
  craniology, 119–120
  culture of poverty and, 130, 140–141
  described, 14–15
  family structure and, 141–144
  functional inequality, 144–146
  genetic intelligence and, 118
  homelessness and, 74–76
  luck and, 148
  mental illness and, 146–152
  mystification and, 221–222
  overview of, 115–116
  political results of, 198–200
  poverty causes and, 18
  reductionism, 117–118
  social Darwinism, 116–117
  urban environments and, 127–130
Blasi, Gary, 102, 105, 108, 110, 203
Bluestone, Barry, 16, 159–160, 175, 216
Blum, Jeffrey, 120

241

Boesky, Ivan, 55
Bogue, D., 24
Bolle, Mary Jane, 175
Bookbinder, Hyman, 208
Borrell, John, 212
Bowles, Samuel, 17, 167–168
Boyer, R., 104
Brinkley, David, 2
Broca, P., 119
Brooke, Edward, 84
Brown, J., 26
Brown, Ronald, 211
Brunette, Mary, 191
B-2 bomber, 197
Buckley, William F., Jr., 30
Burck, Charles G., 29, 32, 56
Burke, V., 95, 98
Burnam, A., 151
Burnham, Stanley, 125
Burt, Cyril, 124
Bush, George, 62, 82, 88, 180, 189,
     193, 199, 204, 205, 211, 213

CATO Institute, 84
Cavazo, Lauro, 153
Chaffee, Robert, 101
Chapman, Stephen, 146
Characterology, described, 120–121
Child labor laws, violations of, 156–
     157, 158–159
Children
   poverty and, 11, 24, 43, 44–46
   social welfare recipients, 99–100
Chiles, Lawton, 177
Chira, Susan, 208
Christian, Patrick, 73
Church, George, 197
Class structure. See Social stratifica-
     tion; Socioeconomic status
Cloward, Richard, 17, 113
"Comic Relief" telethon, 1

Conspicuous consumption concept,
     60–61
Consumer Price Index, 36
Corruption and fraud, poverty
     causes, 180–181
Craniology, described, 119–120
Crime
   corruption and fraud, 180–181
   symptom of, 6
   white-collar crime, 55–56, 93–94,
     206
Culture
   characterology and, 121
   intelligence testing and, 167
   poverty and, 130, 140–141
   socioeconomic status and, 33

Daly, Margaret, 148
Darwin, Charles, 116
Davis, Kingsley, 14, 144–146
Debt, concentration of wealth, 67
Defense spending, 196–197
Deindustrialization
   economic factors, 159–161
   poverty causes, 174–176
   underclass and, 161–162
Democracy and democratization
   justice and, 205–206
   sources of, 9
Democratic party. See also Politics;
     Republican party
   savings and loan bailout and, 211
   solutions to poverty, 223
Deserving/undeserving poor, work-
     ing poor, 51–52
Discrimination, 182–183. See also Race
Disinvestment policy, described, 16–
     17
Distribution of wealth
   concentration of income, 57–59

Distribution of wealth (*cont.*)
concentration of wealth, 59–61
concentration of wealth, consequences of, 64–68
income and, 29–30
inequity in, 5, 10, 12, 56–57
savings and loan bailout, 211
social stratification and, 27–28
taxation and, 62–64
wage system and, 224
Dixon, Don, 211
Drug abuse. *See* Substance abuse

Earth Day, 8
Eastern Europe
democratization and, 9
free market economy and, 223–224
Economic factors
blaming the victim perspective
and, 148
capitalism and, 162–166
concentration of wealth, consequences of, 64–68
deindustrialization, 159–161, 174–
176
disinvestment policy, 16–17
distribution of wealth, 5
Eastern Europe, 223–224
federal budgets and, 193–196
global economic changes, 174
politics and, 191–193
poverty and, viii
taxation and, 62–64
violence and, 217–221
Edsall, Thomas, 209
Education
federal government and, 124
social mobility, 27
socioeconomic status and, 17
Eitzen, D. Stanley, 124

Elderly
poverty and, 11, 43, 47–48
social welfare recipients, 100
Employment. *See also* Unemployment; Wages
homelessness and, 79
inequality in, 216–217
job creation, 2
rural poor and, 53
sweatshop conditions, 155–159
wage cuts and, 217–219
women and, 47
working poor, 51–52
Environmentalism, public awareness
and, 8
Equality, employment and, 216–217

Faith, Bill, 80
Family structure, blaming the victim
perspective, 141–144
Farley, Frank, 55
Farmers. *See* Agriculture
Farr, Rodger, 77, 151–152
Fast, Paul, 108
Federal government. *See also* Politics
budgets and, 193–196
deindustrialization and, 175
education and, 124
financial aid to wealthy and, 63–
64
homelessness, McKinney Act of
1987, 82–83
housing policy, 196–197
poverty definition and, 36–41
poverty population estimates by,
39
social welfare system and, 95, 179–
180
tax policy and, 62–64
Flynn, Kevin, 107
Food stamps, 98

Foreign labor, unemployment and, viii
Foreign trade
  concentration of wealth, 67
  global economic change, 174
France, Anatole, 209
Free enterprise system
  Eastern Europe, 223–224
  myths of, 9–10
Free enterprise zones, homelessness and, 88
Functional inequality, blaming the victim perspective, 144–146
Furiga, P., 177

Gabe, Thomas, 48
Galbraith, John Kenneth, 24
Gallagher, John E., 211
Gans, Herbert J., 17, 169
Genetics, 15
  homelessness and, 150–151
  intelligence and, 118, 122–127, 168–169
  mental illness and, 146
  sperm banks, 126–127
Gintis, Herbert, 17, 167–168
Gordon, Oakley, 86
Gould, Stephen Jay, 119, 120, 168
Graham, Robert K., 126–127
Great Depression, 5, 6, 65
Great Society program, 6
Green, Stephen, 45, 82
Gresham, Jewell, 47, 183
Grinker, William J., 46
Grose, Thomas, 177

"Hands Across America" project, 1
Harrington, Michael, 192
Harris, F., 180

Harrison, Bennett, 16, 159–160, 175
Hawkings, David, 53
Hayes, Robert M., 191
Health care, lack of, 7
Heraclitus, 9
Hernandez, Marita, 157
Herrnstein, Richard, 15, 125–126
Hinman, R., 118
Hispanics. See Minorities; Race
Holmes, S. J., 122
Hombs, Mary Ellen, 201–202
Homelessness, 2, 69–91
  census statistics for, 38, 71–77
  conditions of, 80–81
  fear and, 4–5
  free enterprise zones for, 88
  government response to, 6
  housing crisis and, 178–179
  HUD scandal and, 83–84, 180–181
  increase in, 69–71
  institutionalization of, 89–90
  justice and, 212
  McKinney Act of 1987 and, 82–83
  mental illness and, 146–148
  politics and, 190–191, 201–203
  public views of, 3, 4
  rent policies and, 84–88
  rural poor and, 78–80
  stereotyping and, 76–78
  studies of, 19
  working poor and, 51
Housing
  homelessness and, 149
  politics and, 3, 190–191, 196–197
  poverty causes, 178–179
  rent policies and, 84–88
  welfare hotels, 89
Hunger. See Nutrition
Hunter, Robert, 91, 206–207
Huntley, S., 49
Hyman, Pam, 51

Income. *See also* Wages
  concentration of, 57–59
  of Native Americans, 51
  socioeconomic status and, 29–30
  taxation and, 62–64
Indians. *See* Native Americans
Individual responsibility. *See also*
  Blaming the victim perspective
  blaming the victim perspective
    and, 148
  institutional causes compared, viii
Infant mortality rates, increases in,
  10
Inflation, poverty definition and, 38
Influence peddling, politics and, 3
Institutional causes, individual
  responsibility compared, viii
Intelligence
  defined, 168–169
  genetics and, 118
  socioeconomic status and, 17
Intelligence tests
  culture bias in, 167
  origin of, 119–120
  overview of, 121–127
Interest rates, concentration of
  wealth, 67

Jackson, Jesse, 202, 220
Jacob, John E., 20
Japanese-Americans, internment of,
  World War II, 5
Jencks, C., 222
Jensen, Arthur R., 15, 124, 167
Job creation, wages and, 2, 177, 216
Johnson, Lyndon B., 6, 192
Justice, 205–213
  homelessness and, 212
  inequality and, 209–210
  politics and, 205–206, 210–212
  poverty and, 206–209, 212–213

Kamin, L., 117
Kemp, Jack, 88, 180, 190–191
Kennedy, Edward, 199–200
Kennedy, John F., 192
King, Martin Luther, Jr., 208
Kluge, John, 31
Koch, Edward I., 46, 70
Koegel, P., 151
Kuhn, George, 70

Labor theory of value, 162
Lamb, H. R., 77
Lee, B., 24
Lewis, Oscar, 14, 130, 140–141
Lewontin, R. C., 117
Liazos, Alexander, 31
Life chances, socioeconomic status
  and, 30
Life conditions, socioeconomic status
  and, 30
Lifestyle, socioeconomic status and,
  30
Loecher, Barbara, 51
Loury, Glen, 221
Lower class, 33–34. *See also*
  Underclass
Lowey, Joseph, 203
Luck, blaming the victim and, 148

Magnet, Myron, 70
Maitland, Leslie, 204
Marks, T., 181
Marx, Karl, 16, 162–166
McCormick, L. Hamilton, 120
McKinney Act of 1987, 82–83
Mead, Lawrence, 221
Mead, Walter, 174
Media
  public awareness and, 2
  socioeconomic status and, 32, 33
Medicaid, 98

Mental illness
  blaming the victim perspective,
    146–152
  homelessness and, 77, 146–148
  poverty and, 13, 26
Meritocracy, 126
Middle class
  decline of, 2, 28, 32
  described, 31–33
  poverty's uses for, 169–170
Migration, underclass and, 162
Milken, Michael, 93–94
Miller, George, 53
Miller, John, 193
Miller, R., 24
Mills, C. Wright, 10–11, 170–171
Minimum wage laws, 182, 199–200
Minorities. See also Race
  children of, 45
  elderly populations and, 48
  homelessness and, 77, 79
  income distribution and, 58–59
  poverty and, 12, 43, 48–49
  social welfare recipients, 99
Mitchell, John, 84
Mobility. See Migration; Occupational
    mobility; Social mobility
Moore, Hilmar G., 93
Moore, Wilbert E., 14, 144–146
Moynihan, Daniel Patrick, 14, 142–
    144
Murray, Charles, 15, 100, 221

Nader, Ralph, 63–64
NASA, 197
Native Americans. See also Minor-
    ities; Race
  homelessness and, 77, 79
  poverty and, 49–51
  reservation system, 5
Newby, Robert G., 215–224

New Deal, 5–6
Nunn, Louise, 84
Nutrition, 26, 37
Nyden, P., 176

Obey, David, 177–178
Occupational mobility, socioeconomic
    status and, 34
O'Hare, William, 52
Ols, John M., Jr., 82–83
Omnibus Budget Reconciliation Act
    of 1981, 95
Ong, Paul, 174, 184
Orshansky, Mollie, 36

Painton, Priscilla, 70–71
Palmer, D., 151
Pearce, Diana, 46–47
Peckham, Robert, 167
Perot, H. Ross, 31
Personal troubles, 10–11. See also
    Blaming the victim perspective;
    Individual responsibility
Piven, Frances Fox, 17, 113
Politics, 189–204. See also Federal
    government
  blaming the victim perspective
    and, 148, 198–200
  budgets and, 193–196
  Bush Administration, 189–190
  economic factors and, 191–193
  homelessness, 73, 190–191
  homelessness, McKinney Act of
    1987, 82–83
  housing policy, 196–197
  HUD scandal and, 83–84, 180–181
  justice and, 205–206, 210–212
  minimum wage laws, 182
  poverty and, 3, 5, 18–21, 208–209
  social factor perspective and, 200–
    204

Politics (*cont.*)
   social welfare system and, 94–95, 179–180
   solutions to poverty and, 223
Poverty
   causes of, 17–18, 173–187. *See also* Poverty causes
   children and, 44–46
   consequences of, 12–13, 25–27
   definitions and measures of, 35–37
   definitions and measures of, criticized, 37–41
   elderly and, 47–48
   functions of, 169–171
   historical perspective on, 23–24
   increases in, 2
   justice and, 206–209, 212–213
   minorities and, 48–49
   Native Americans and, 49–51
   politics and, 3, 5, 18–21. *See also* Politics
   populations composing, 43, 44, 45, 46, 48–49, 51, 52
   public views of, 4, 11
   rural poor and, 52–53
   social welfare system and, 100
   women and, 46–47
   working poor and, 51–52
Poverty causes, 17–18, 173–187
   corruption and fraud, 180–181
   deindustrialization, 174–176
   discrimination, 182–183
   global economic changes, 174
   housing crisis, 178–179
   Los Angeles case example, 184–187
   overview of, 173–174
   social stratification, 181–182
   social welfare system and, 179–180
   unemployment/underemployment, 176–178

Poverty line
   adequacy of income at, 39–41
   census statistics and, 38, 40, 181–182
   official definition, 11, 35
   wages at or below, 177
Power, socioeconomic status and, 30–31
Prison population, increase in, 6
Public awareness
   environmentalism and, 8
   homelessness, 3
   limits of, 1–2
   media access and, 2
   reality and, 5
   scapegoating and, 6–7
   taxation and, 63–64
   white-collar crime, 93–94
Public factors. *See* Social factors

Race. *See also* Minorities
   biology and, 15
   blaming the victim perspective and, 14
   characterology and, 121
   discrimination and, 182–183
   family structure and, 141–144
   intelligence and, 118, 122, 124–127
   intelligence testing and, 167
   poverty and, 12, 43
   social welfare recipients, 99
   underclass and, 161–162
   unemployment and, 219–221
   urban environments and, 127–130
Rainwater, Lee, 144
Reagan, Ronald, 1, 2, 3, 7, 56, 62, 77, 82, 83, 94, 95, 175, 180, 181, 191, 196, 199, 202, 205
Reductionism
   described, 117–118
   homelessness and, 151

Redway, J., 118
Reich, Robert B., 57
Rent policies, homelessness and, 84–88
Republican party. *See also* Democratic party; Politics
  economics and, 192–193
  homelessness and, 73
  HUD scandal and, 83–84, 180–181
  poverty and, 208–209
  solutions to poverty, 223
Reservation system, Native Americans, 5
Robertson, Ian, 183
Roosevelt, Franklin D., 6, 23
Ropers, Richard, 51, 70, 77, 82, 86, 104, 148, 151, 181, 215, 223
Rose, S., 117
Rossi, Peter, 73–76
Rostenkowski, Dan, 62
Roybal, Edward, 48
Rural poor
  homelessness and, 78–80
  poverty and, 52–53
Ryan, William, 14, 115

Sanchez, Sheila, 159
Savings and loan bailout, 211
Scapegoating, public awareness and, 6–7. *See also* Blaming the victim perspective
Schizophrenia, homelessness and, 147, 150–151
Seifman, David, 127
Self-esteem, poverty and, 25
Sheak, Robert, 37, 38
Shockley, William B., 15, 126–127
Siegel, Martin, 55
Smith, Adam, 162
Snyder, Mitch, 201–202, 204

Social Darwinism
  critique of, 118
  described, 116–117
  persistence of, 3
  Ronald Reagan and, 2
Social factors, 155–171
  capitalism and, 162–166
  capital versus community, 159–161
  defined, 10–11
  functional poverty, 169–171
  intelligence definition and, 168–169
  intelligence testing bias, 167
  overview of, 15–17
  political results of perspective of, 200–204
  sweatshop conditions, 155–159
  underclass and, 161–162
Social mobility
  intelligence and, 167–168
  social stratification and, 27–28
  socioeconomic status and, 34
Social pathology concept, 221–222
Social stratification
  concentration of income, 57–59
  concentration of wealth, 59–61
  described, 27–28
  functional inequality and, 144–146
  intelligence and, 124
  poverty causes, 181–182
  taxation and, 193
  underclass and, 161–162
Social welfare system, 93–113
  benefits of, 95–96, 97, 98, 101, 102, 103
  expenditures on, 94–95, 97, 98
  homelessness and, 89–90
  Los Angeles case study, 101–111
  population demographics of recipients, 99–100
  poverty causes, 179–180
  poverty cycle and, 100

Social welfare system (*cont.*)
program overview, 96–99
reductions in, viii, 194–195, 197
workfare program, 4, 94
Socioeconomic status
class structure and, 28–34
determinants of, 17
income and, 29–30
individual effects of, 13
intelligence and, 167–168
life conditions and, 30
lower class, 33–34
Marx and, 166
middle class, 31–33
power and, 30–31
social mobility and, 34
social stratification, 27–28
upper class, 31
wealth and, 30
Solomon, Fredric, 80
Southern Christian Leadership
Conference, 203
Soviet Union, democratization
and, 9
Space program, 197
Stanford-Binet Intelligence Scale,
121
Stein, Andrew, 46
Stereotyping
homelessness and, 76–78, 152
poverty and, 11
Sterilization, welfare poor, 93
Stock market, distribution of wealth
and, 5
Stratification. *See* Social stratification
Substance abuse
homelessness and, 78, 152
unemployment and, 178
Supplemental Security Income (SSI),
97–98
Surplus value concept, 16, 164–166

Sweatshop conditions, social factors,
155–159
Swift, Jonathan, 20–21

Taeuber, Cynthia, 73
Taxation
Bush Administration, 193
distribution of income and wealth,
62–64
poverty definition and, 38
savings and loan bailout and, 211
Tepper, Paul, 72, 110, 111, 208
Terman, Lewis M., 121, 122
Tomb, David, 150
Toner, Robin, 69, 77
Torrey, Edwin Fuller, 77, 147, 150
Trade deficits. *See* Foreign trade
Trump, Donald, 10, 56, 60, 61
Tucker, William, 75–76, 84–88, 179,
196

Underclass. *See also* Lower class
mystification and, 222
social stratification, 161–162
Undeserving/deserving poor, working poor, 51–52
Unemployment. *See also* Employment
deindustrialization and, 159–161,
174–177
homelessness and, 79
minorities and, 12
poverty causes, 176–178
race and, 219–221
self-esteem and, 25
underclass and, 161
unemployable people, viii
U.S. Census Bureau, 36, 37, 38, 72–
77
U.S. Department of Agriculture, 36,
37–38

U.S. Department of Commerce, 50
U.S. Department of Housing and
Urban Development (HUD)
homeless populations and, 71–72
McKinney Act of 1987, 82–83
scandal in, 3, 83–84, 180–181
U.S. government. See Federal
government; Politics
U.S. Office of Management and
Budget, 36
U.S. Social Security Administration,
36
Upper class
concentration of wealth, 66
described, 31
distribution of income and wealth,
62–64
poverty's uses for, 169–170
Urban environments, blaming the
victim perspective and, 127–130

Vander Zanden, James, 50
Veblen, Thorstein, 60
Violence
concentration of wealth and, 68
economics and, 217–221

Wages. See also Income
cuts in, 217–219
economic systems and, 224
foreign competition and, 175
job creation and, 2, 177, 216
lower classes, 33–34
minimum wage laws, 182, 199–
200
minorities and, 12
poverty level and, viii, 177–178
socioeconomic status and, 29–30,
33

Wages (cont.)
sweatshop conditions, 156, 158
working poor, 51–52
Walton, Sam Moore, 28, 31
War on Poverty program, 6, 192, 208
Washington, D.C., poverty in, 10
Watt, James, 84
Wealth. See also Distribution of
wealth
concentration of, 59–61
concentration of, consequences,
64–68
defined, 60
socioeconomic status and, 30
white-collar crime and, 30
Welch, William M., 83, 84
Welfare hotels, 89
Welfare system. See Social welfare
system
White-collar crime
justice and, 206
motivation for, 55–56
public reactions to, 93–94
Whitman, D., 51
Wilkerson, Margaret, 47, 183
Wilkins, R., 180
Wilson, William Julius, 16–17, 161–
162, 176, 216, 221–222, 223
Witkin, G., 49
Wolff, Goetz, 157–158
Women
discrimination against, 182–183
employment and, 47
homelessness and, 79
poverty and, 11, 43, 46–47
social welfare recipients, 99
Workfare programs
limitations of, 4
politics and, 94
Working class, described, 32–33
Working poor, poverty and, 51–52

Working women. *See* employment, women; Women
World War II, Japanese-Americans interned during, 5
Wright, James D., 74, 76

Yancey, W. L., 144
Yerkes, Robert, 121

Zaldivar, R., 62
Zaleznik, Abraham, 55